The Trump White House

ALSO BY RONALD KESSLER

The First Family Detail
The Secrets of the FBI
In the President's Secret Service
The Terrorist Watch
Laura Bush
A Matter of Character
The CIA at War
The Bureau
The Season
Inside Congress
The Sins of the Father
Inside the White House
The FBI
Inside the CIA
Escape from the CIA
The Spy in the Russian Club
Moscow Station
Spy vs. Spy
The Richest Man in the World
The Life Insurance Game

The Trump White House

CHANGING THE RULES OF THE GAME

Ronald Kessler

CROWN
FORUM
NEW YORK

All rights reserved.
Published in the United States by Crown Forum,
an imprint of the Crown Publishing Group,
a division of Penguin Random House LLC, New York.
crownforum.com

CROWN FORUM with colophon is a registered trademark
of Penguin Random House LLC.

Library of Congress Cataloging-in-Publication data
is available upon request.

ISBN 978-0-525-57571-9
Ebook ISBN 978-0-525-57572-6

PRINTED IN THE UNITED STATES OF AMERICA

Insert photos courtesy of Getty Images; last three images
courtesy of the author

Jacket design by Dan Donohue
Jacket photograph: Evan Vucci/Pool/Getty Images

10 9 8 7 6 5 4 3 2 1

First Edition

For Pam, Rachel, and Greg Kessler

CONTENTS

CONTENTS

The Trump White House

PROLOGUE

Having laid claim to the most powerful perch on the planet, Donald Trump and his White House aides gathered in the Oval Office after the inauguration. They were euphoric as the forty-fifth president of the United States directed government agencies to freeze government regulations, took steps to weaken Obamacare, and proclaimed a National Day of Patriotic Devotion. But already, tension was beginning to develop.

Trump had named Chief of Staff Reince Priebus and Chief Strategist Stephen Bannon as coequals. In the coming weeks, it would turn out that not only Bannon but economic adviser Gary Cohn; Trump's daughter and adviser Ivanka Trump; her husband, Senior Adviser Jared Kushner; counselor Kellyanne Conway; Communications Director Hope Hicks; Senior Adviser Stephen Miller; and eventually National Security Adviser

H. R. McMaster would report directly to the president, entirely bypassing the new chief of staff.

Priebus was already feeling some initial unease after Trump, during the transition, met with Cohn, a Democrat who voted for Hillary Clinton, in his office at Trump Tower and appointed him on the spot to head the National Economic Council. Normally, a president would consult with his chief of staff and make sure he was comfortable with such an appointment. But there was nothing normal about Donald Trump.

As his presidency developed, the White House evolved into a *Game of Thrones*: Who would rise to the top? Who would crash and burn?

Apparently feeling resentment that she had not been named chief of staff, Kellyanne Conway, who had the title of campaign manager during the bruising campaign but actually did little more than appear on television, unleashed vicious, completely untrue attacks on Priebus and other staffers that wound up in press reports as anonymous quotes from a White House aide. Rarely was Conway even included in Oval Office meetings. From the beginning, Ivanka and Jared, along with Trump's sons, Don Trump Jr. and Eric Trump, opposed hiring her, and they continued to try to get Trump to fire her.

Meanwhile, while they later developed a cooperative relationship, Priebus and Bannon were initially in competition with each other, jockeying to influence Trump with their sometimes disparate positions.

A hard-right mover and shaker, Bannon viewed Ivanka and Jared as New York liberals whose lack of judgment made them uniquely unqualified to advise a president. Trump himself seemed to agree. At one point, he flatly told Jared and Ivanka that they never should have left New York and made it clear to them that he would not mind if they gave up their White House roles.

"Look at Jared, he looks like a little boy, like a child," Trump remarked to aides as he watched Kushner on TV speaking to the press.

Jared and Ivanka, in turn, waged a daily battle through their advice to Trump and whispers to the press against the conservatives on the payroll: Priebus, Bannon, Conway, Miller, and Press Secretary Sean Spicer. The couple seemed to have envisioned the White House as a land of milk and honey, where they would exercise power over other aides by virtue of their relationship to the president. When they had to butt heads with other White House power centers, they became disappointed and tried to rid the staff of rivals and replace them with the likes of Anthony Scaramucci.

For all the turmoil and internal feuding, Trump's aides agreed on one thing: Melania Trump, who often weighed in with her opinion at strategy sessions, had impeccable judgment.

"Melania's a good influence at keeping things focused on the main thing and not being in the weeds over a lot of small stuff," Priebus says. "She has good political sense and comes down the right way on what the focus and agenda needs to be."

Melania is "the classiest thing in the White House by two orders of magnitude," Bannon says.

The internal strife led to a continuing stream of often false swipes in the media aimed at each of Trump's White House staff members. And members of the media, who mocked Trump among themselves as a fool and dangerous, were only too glad to run with the latest story denigrating the president and his choices of White House aides.

On that first day, Zeke Miller of *Time* was already incorrectly reporting that Trump had removed a bust of Martin Luther King Jr. from the Oval Office. Trump only added to the negative coverage by making outlandish claims, either directly or through Spicer, who began his tenure looking uncomfortable trying to push Trump's narrative that the turnout for the inauguration was the largest in history. Trump made the lives of staffers even more miserable by unleashing screaming tirades on aides over often minor shortcomings or misperceived mistakes.

But beyond the outrageous comments and the tweeting, beyond the infighting and dissension, there was another story that the media largely ignored: sweeping presidential action that indeed was making America great again. Never before has an American president had so much impact on the country and the world in so short a time as Donald Trump.

In a matter of months after Trump took office, consumer confidence hit an all-time high, job growth spurted, CEOs said the removal of regulations was spurring them to expand and hire more workers, unemployment plummeted to the lowest level in seventeen years, the stock market zoomed to repeated record highs, manufacturing activity reached a thirteen-year high, companies began reversing plans to ship production overseas, illegal border crossings from Mexico plunged by 76 percent, border arrests dropped 25 percent, and an outstanding conservative appeals court judge took his seat on the Supreme Court.

At the same time, ISIS was nearly defeated, Arab countries banded together to stop financing terrorists and promoting radical Islamic ideology, both China and Russia took the unprecedented action of voting at the United Nations to impose sanctions on the threat that was North Korea, and Trump's decision to send missiles into Syria because of its use of chemical weapons and his strident warnings to North Korean leader Kim

Jong-un made it clear to adversaries that they take on the United States at their peril.

Yet no president has stirred so much controversy, dominating media coverage daily and conversation both pro and con.

The question remained: Who is Donald Trump?

1

THE TWO FACES OF
DONALD TRUMP

For twenty-six years, Norma Foerderer was Donald Trump's top aide. When she joined the Trump Organization in 1981, he had only seven other employees. During her career with him, Foerderer oversaw almost every aspect of the mogul's business, including public relations, hiring and firing, and negotiating book deals and contracts. No one knew so well both the personal and business side of Donald Trump.

In the only in-depth interview she ever gave, Foerderer, who has since died, told me there are two Donald Trumps: One is the Trump that appears to the public, making often outrageous comments on television to get attention; the other is the real Trump only insiders know.

"I mean Donald can be totally outrageous, but outrageous in a wonderful way that gets him coverage," Foerderer told me. "That persona sells his licensed products and his condominiums. You know Donald's never been shy, and justifiably so, in talking about how wonderful his buildings or his golf clubs are."

The private Trump, on the other hand, is "the dearest, most thoughtful, most loyal, most caring man," Foerderer said. That caring side inspires loyalty and is one of the secrets to his success.

Confirming Foerderer's point, Trump wrote in *The Art of the Deal* that "if you are a little different or a little outrageous, or if you do things that are bold or controversial, the press is going to write about you." Trump followed his own advice in spades.

Illustrating the difference between the public and private Trump, the Hispanic Chamber of Commerce, which represents 3.2 million business owners, announced during the campaign that its members would be boycotting all Trump's properties following his statements on illegal immigrants and his vow to build a wall across the entire Mexican border. But Trump subsequently met privately with Javier Palomarez, the chamber's CEO.

"There were no bombastic statements of any sorts," Palomarez said admiringly on CNN as he left the meeting. "It's kind of interesting, the dichotomy between the private Donald Trump and the public Donald Trump. He listened a lot more than he spoke."

Yet even back when he was running his business, Trump played employees off against each other and could erupt in unmitigated anger at them. For nearly three decades, Anthony P. "Tony" Senecal was Trump's personal butler at Mar-a-Lago, Trump's home and club in Palm Beach, Florida. When Trump hired Bernd Lembcke to be the managing director of his newly opened club, he introduced Senecal to him.

"He's mine," Trump told Lembcke. "Nobody touches him but me."

From that day on, Trump would give Senecal instructions

that Lembcke, given his job title, should have been carrying out, including plans for renovation and suggestions on employees who should be fired. According to Senecal, Lembcke steadfastly ignored him, never carrying on a conversation with him. "It was like he would see me, and he would see the wall," Senecal says.

As with everything else in his empire, Trump exaggerated Senecal's importance. Senecal is a former mayor of Martinsburg, West Virginia. He came to national attention when the *Washington Post* accompanied a front-page feature story about changes in West Virginia with a photo of Senecal sitting with his cat Morris on the shoeshine stand of his tobacco shop.

"When I first started, I wasn't the servant type," Senecal told me. "It was touch-and-go, until Mr. Trump found out I was a former mayor. That made me a cut above. Then," Tony said wryly, "I became the mayor of the wealthiest and largest town in West Virginia." In fact, Martinsburg is neither.

One Saturday, alerted that there was a visitor, Senecal opened the door at the main entrance to Mar-a-Lago to find Martha Stewart standing there. She had bicycled over to the club, and she asked if she could take a tour. Happy to oblige, Senecal asked her to return the next day at three p.m. when it would be convenient for Senecal, whom Trump eventually named the Mar-a-Lago historian.

When Trump came by later that day, Senecal told him about Martha Stewart and the tour he had set up for Sunday.

"Fine, just treat her right," Trump said.

But hours later, Senecal went to see if Trump needed anything. He encountered his boss outside the master bedroom in what is known as the Pine Hall, a glittering antechamber with a crystal chandelier and murals that had once graced the walls of homes in France.

Without warning, Trump lit into the butler, screaming at him and calling him a "dumb ass" for scheduling the tour at three p.m. when workers would be shifting furniture around. Trump yelled that Senecal instead should have scheduled the tour for lunchtime, when well-heeled club members would be on hand to impress and be impressed by Martha Stewart. A perfectionist, Trump could not stand it when things were not done his way.

As her husband was tearing into Senecal, Melania entered the Pine Hall.

"I don't think you should talk to Tony in that tone," Melania said to Trump in her usual soft voice.

Stewart had not left a phone number nor said where she was staying. But Senecal used what he calls the "Palm Beach butler network" to find her and reschedule the tour for around noon the next day.

Trump never said another word about it. But the next morning when he and Senecal were in the mansion's living room, Trump, without explanation, handed him two thousand dollars in twenties.

"It was his way of apologizing," Senecal says.

Despite the occasional blistering tirades, Senecal says he loved working for Trump, who would act as if nothing had happened after delivering an attack. To be sure, giving his butler cash in twenties was strange, but, "Everything about Mr. Trump is strange," Senecal says.

Trump was often generous with praise for employees at all levels when they were doing a good job. He would make it a point to compliment them in front of their bosses.

"He keeps a wad of hundred-dollar bills in his pants pocket and will distribute them widely to groundskeepers, plumbers, or other low-level employees when he likes the job they are doing," Senecal says.

There are three things none of Trump's employees should do, Senecal says: "You don't steal from him, you don't lie to him, and you don't embarrass him."

Senecal says Melania's quiet comment and her husband's later remorse are typical of her influence. Almost always, Melania delivers her advice in private, but occasionally, Senecal would pick up on their exchanges.

"Melania rules the roost," Senecal says.

Some years ago, when Senecal's home air-conditioning system gave out, Trump had it replaced. When Senecal paid his own way to attend Trump's father's funeral in New York in June 1999, Trump was so touched he ordered his pilot to fly the butler back to Palm Beach, a passenger of one. The cost for jet fuel and maintenance for the flight to Florida and the return was forty thousand dollars.

When Senecal needed surgery to implant a stent, Trump called him and asked, "So when do you go under the knife?"

"Tomorrow," said Senecal.

"Well, if you don't make it, don't worry about it. You've had a good life," Trump said. And then he said, "Listen, I don't want you going back to your place. You come and recuperate at Mar-a-Lago."

Trump will hand out hundred-dollar bills to janitors or McDonald's cashiers and write checks for tens of thousands of dollars to people he has learned are in distress. But one of the White House media staff's frustrations was that Trump did not want the public to see this side of him and know what he is like behind the scenes, Spicer says.

"He'll walk into a room with a bunch of workers, and gather

them up and hand them out each a hundred-dollar bill," an aide says. "There's no camera there. Those are the moments people just don't see, like when he's telling us about how an emotional event has impacted him, and he doesn't want anyone to see it. He likes to display the tough, rough exterior."

In the same way, Ronald Reagan quietly wrote personal checks to people who had written him with hard-luck stories.

"Reagan was famous for firing up Air Force jets on behalf of children who needed transport for kidney operations," says Frank J. Kelly, who drafted Reagan's presidential messages. "These are things you never knew about. He never bragged about it. I hand-carried checks for four thousand or five thousand dollars to people who had written him. He would say, 'Don't tell people. I was poor myself.'"

Like Reagan, Trump never forgot what it is like to be down and out. That was in the 1990s when his companies were $3.4 billion in the hole, and he was personally liable for $830 million of that debt, giving him a negative net worth.

One day, Trump was walking along Fifth Avenue near Trump Tower with his then-wife Marla Maples.

"I pointed across the street to a man holding a cup and with a seeing eye dog," Trump wrote in *The Art of the Comeback*.

"Do you know who that is?" Trump asked Marla.

"Yes, Donald. He's a beggar. Isn't it too bad? He looks so sad!" she replied.

"You're right. He's a beggar, but he's worth about $900 million more than me," Trump said to her.

When Trump came up with the idea of branding his condos and office buildings back in the 1980s, everyone in the real estate business thought he was nuts: Traditionally, obscure companies that no one had ever heard of sold and leased real estate.

But the Trump brand came to stand for quality, prestige, and success. In the same way, Trump brands his presidency, marketing himself by making provocative comments to get attention. That brand consists of the tough-guy image Trump wants to project, never admitting a mistake or showing his softer side, keeping his emotions in check, always counterpunching when he is attacked.

Whether in real estate or politics, Trump sees himself as the Lone Ranger, always fighting for what he believes in against the establishment. To Trump, admitting mistakes or showing an emotional side is a sign of weakness. As president, Trump wanted staff photographer Shealah Craighead to photograph him mainly at official functions and from a distance, gazing out a window, never betraying emotion. His typical facial expression is to set his mouth in a moue, somewhere between a pucker and a pout. It says, *I'm a handsome guy; I'm going to WIN.*

Trump's tough-guy image goes back to his childhood growing up in Queens, New York, where he could erupt in anger, pummeling another boy or smashing a baseball bat when he struck out. In school, he misbehaved so often that the initials DT became his friends' shorthand for detention.

Trump has said that his primary focus in elementary school was "creating mischief, because for some reason, I liked to stir things up, and I liked to test people"—not out of maliciousness but rather aggressiveness.

"Who could forget him?" said Ann Trees, who taught at Kew-Forest School, where Trump was a student through seventh grade. "He was headstrong and determined. He would sit with his arms folded with this look on his face—I use the word *surly*—almost daring you to say one thing or another that wouldn't settle with him," according to the *Washington Post* book *Trump Revealed* by Michael Kranish and Marc Fisher.

His older sister, Maryanne Trump Barry, described Trump as extremely rebellious.

"He tested the rules and the teachers to their limits," said Barry, now a senior circuit judge of the United States Court of Appeals for the Third Circuit. A camp counselor said Trump had an "ornery" disposition. He said he would "fight back all the time."

"He had a reputation for saying anything that came into his head," said Donald Kass, who was a schoolmate. When Trump misidentified Rocca, the pro wrestler, Kass recalled, "We would laugh at him and tell him he was wrong, and he'd say he was right. The next time, he would make the same mistake, and it would be the same thing all over again."

Trump wanted to be first at everything and wanted everyone to know he was first. His highly competitive nature came out in his love of baseball.

"I like to hear the crowd give cheers, so loud and noisy to my ears," Donald wrote as a poem in his yearbook. "When the score is five to five, I feel like I could cry. And when they get another run, I feel like I could die . . ."

To teach him discipline, Trump's father sent him to military school when he was in the eighth grade. Like Trump, Fred Trump, a builder and developer, was a perfectionist. He wore a jacket and tie even at home. While his father could be sharply critical if tasks were not performed perfectly, Trump respected him and has described him as his hero. His mother, Mary Anne

MacLeod Trump, was charming, vivacious, and shrewd. Like her son, she enjoyed socializing and being the center of attention.

Trump's self-destructive moves—from the firing of FBI director James Comey that led to the appointment of a special counsel, to failing to emphasize his condemnation of white nationalists and domestic Nazis in Charlottesville—go back to an instinctive, defensive need to hit back at critics, no matter the consequences. For all his wealth and all his power, he seems to feel cornered, much like the instincts that led him to be a bad boy as a kid.

"I've gotten a sense he always feels under attack," Spicer says. "That people are saying that he didn't earn this, that he's not this, he didn't win this, he can't do X. He's not smart enough. He didn't do whatever it is. I think that he constantly feels under attack, and he feels the need to justify his position, either on an issue or position or how he came to achieve something. He has built up a DNA of defensiveness."

Now that bad boy had become president.

2

LIFE IS A GAME

As the pressure of being president intensified, Trump would erupt in anger more often. As a rule, Trump unleashes his anger when he legitimately feels a task has not been performed correctly. It's his way of imposing accountability. But his anger is often a scattered blast out of proportion to the issue at hand and sometimes aimed at the wrong target.

"When he really gets mad, he's screaming at you," Bannon says. "But the bark is worse than the bite."

Aides compare Trump's anger with taking a two-by-four and hitting someone over the head if they spilled water on the floor. The White House staff tends to work eighteen hours a day, but if one thing goes wrong, Trump will lash out. Instead of focusing on successes, he tends to focus on the faults.

What Trump sees on TV drives much of his anger, and he is never far from a set that is turned on. According to aides,

Trump will see something negative about himself on TV and will then go crazy about it and berate whoever he thinks is at fault. Whether the report is true or not, he will focus on it and bring it up two days later. He'll continue to hammer on it because someone on TV said it was true. Aides would tell him the report was not true, but if someone said it on TV, it's true.

While Trump hates the *New York Times* for running dishonest stories and calls it a "pipe organ for the Democratic Party," he craves the respect of his hometown paper and other mainstream outlets like the *Washington Post*. Thus, he continues to give the paper interviews, disregarding the advice of his media staffers.

"He believes like this is his hometown paper," Spicer says of the *New York Times*. "He likes the respectability of being in the *Times*. Those stories in the *New York Times* mean more to him than say others."

"It was like a dorky kid in high school who makes a million dollars in Silicon Valley and then wants to go back and ask out the hot homecoming queen," an aide says. "He just wants to prove that you should have gone out with me—I made it!"

"He always thinks he can charm the media and get a good story," Bannon notes. "I keep telling him these guys are killers. They're all assassins. I know some of these people very well, and I like them. They're still assassins."

Trump phones Maggie Haberman of the *New York Times* directly, as well as Philip Rucker of the *Washington Post*, and Jonathan Swan of Axios, feeding them stories attributed to "a senior White House official," creating the impression the White House leaks even more than it already does. In other cases, the media has picked up reports on what Trump himself has said to his friends.

While generally accurate, Haberman's stories about Trump and his White House are uniformly negative.

Yet, "He wants eventually to win her over," a Trump aide says. "The president subscribes to the general theory that a little love can go a long way. Even if a story will be bad, give it a shot and maybe it will come out a little better."

"He will say he had seven *New York Times* page-one stories before he ran for president, but on one day as president, he counted seven," Bannon says.

Trump has a similar fixation with *Time* magazine, a publication he has said he grew up with. On the one hand, he seems to crave being named *Time*'s person of the year. On the other hand, he has described it as a "paper-thin" publication that will "soon be dead."

Yet at the same time, Trump did not grant interviews or was slow to do interviews with outlets like Newsmax, Daily Caller, or *Daily Mail* that give him generally positive coverage.

"It was always a frustration of mine, because I didn't understand why we weren't taking care of people who were either fair or favorable," Spicer says.

Early on, Joe Scarborough and Mika Brzezinski of MSNBC's *Morning Joe* were fans. Scarborough and Brzezinski met with Trump at Mar-a-Lago when the black-tie New Year's Eve party to ring in 2017 was about to begin, to try to arrange an interview during Trump's first week as president. I was standing a few feet away from the two cohosts, who were dressed casually, as they checked in with Trump and he led them off to meet with him.

Contrary to some press reports, they were not guests at the party. Nonetheless, some reporters attacked them for attending a Trump party. If they had attended an Obama party, the coverage would have been far different: Those same reporters would have been jealous.

While he did not give them an interview, Trump invited the MSNBC cohosts to lunch at the White House and gave them a tour of the White House residence. But Trump soured on them when they began attacking him on their show.

"I think he felt as though Joe Scarborough was very two-faced and would say things to him, to his face and on the phone and then would go out and say these crappy things about him on television," Spicer says. "I think he just got tired of it."

As the fulcrum between Trump and the media, Spicer was a constant target of the president's criticism, voiced directly to him and to others. Trump micromanaged the press secretary, critiquing his briefings. Adding to the pressure, reporters would try to trip him up with their questions.

"I think in a lot of cases, it became less about the news and more about them," Spicer says. "For many reporters, the goal is to figure out, 'How can I get a moment of fame?' There were days when I'd go see the president afterwards, and he'd say I didn't like that answer and why didn't you answer it this way?" Spicer says. "Or he would say, why did you even call on that reporter?"

Trump would complain that Spicer wasn't closing well or wasn't answering questions well. While Trump could change his mind, most of the time once he comes to a conclusion about a staffer, he sticks with it.

Early on, Trump would complain to aides about Spicer's gray suits, and the president's grumbling would end up in the press. Seeing the press reports, Trump volunteered to Spicer at one point that he had never complained about his suits. However, Spicer took to wearing darker suits.

Trump even blamed Spicer for the fact that Melissa McCarthy was hilariously portraying him as "Spicey" on *Saturday Night Live*. Trump thought that was an insult, and he didn't like that Sean laughed about it.

Often the problem was that while Spicer gave a perfectly reasonable explanation, reporters nitpicked and made an issue of it. Reporters loved to put Spicer and later Sarah Huckabee Sanders on the defensive by prefacing their questions, "Are you concerned that . . ." In fact, Spicer's press briefings brilliantly explained conservative principles and often addressed attacks with humor.

Even conservative journalists with no ax to grind would ask incredibly dumb questions of both Spicer and Trump. The *Weekly Standard*'s Daniel Halper, for example, asked Trump if the Ninth Circuit Court's decision upholding a lower court ruling that imposed an injunction on the ban on travel from certain countries "caused you to rethink your use of executive power?"

In other words, now that the administration had lost one court ruling, would Trump pack up his bags, abandon his presidency, and not exercise his power as the chief executive and commander in chief?

Another reporter at a press briefing asked, "Sean, generally speaking, within the Trump administration, how important is it for the president that everyone working for this administration is honest on their security clearance forms?"

Whenever Spicer spoke passionately in defending Trump, the press would say that he had lost his cool.

Nothing changed when Sarah Huckabee Sanders took over. Before Thanksgiving in 2017, she tweeted a photo of a chocolate pecan pie she had baked to serve at the family farm. April Ryan, American Urban Radio Networks' Washington bureau chief and a CNN political analyst, responded in a tweet by implying that Sanders lied about baking the pie herself.

"I am not trying to be funny but folks are already saying #piegate and #fakepie. Show it to us on the table with folks eating it and a pic of you cooking it," she tweeted.

Sanders's father, Mike Huckabee, weighed in, saying his daughter has been baking pecan pies for years, while Sanders graciously said she would bake more pies for reporters.

Decades ago, reporters understood that press briefings were to convey and clarify the news. Questions were asked to elicit information. Now that briefings are televised, reporters seize the opportunity to preen before the cameras and badger the briefer—conduct that years ago editors considered unprofessional. In those days, if reporters wanted to uncover their own facts, they could engage in investigative reporting. Any reporter publicly questioning without any evidence whether the White House press secretary had made up a story about baking a pie would have been fired as a disgrace to the profession.

The fact that Spicer's briefings generated high TV ratings grated on Trump even more. In contrast, while Sarah Sanders could be witty, Trump seemed to like the fact that she attracted less attention than Spicer did.

"A lot of times the president just wanted to do press conferences on his own," Priebus says. "He would just say, 'I'm going to do a press conference this week. And I don't know what day it's going to be, but I'm just going to feel when the time is right, and I'm going to tell you when.' He would just wake up in the morning and say, 'Today, I'm going to do a press conference.'"

While the staff prepared him, Trump did not want to be overly prepared.

"He had a good knack for giving us a few days of a breather from all of the crazy stories that were out there," Priebus says.

Trump's habit of making outrageous or incendiary comments is both a blessing and a curse.

"I do know he [Trump] shoots from the hip, and he says whatever flies out at the time . . ." Trump's second wife, Marla Maples, offered during the campaign. "But I also don't think that his intentions are negative for this country."

While Trump's tweets and comments in interviews sometimes seem bizarre, they position him as the number one topic of the day and thus enhance his power. As he famously said in his book *The Art of the Deal*, "good publicity is preferable to bad, but from a bottom-line perspective, bad publicity is sometimes better than no publicity at all. Controversy, in short, sells."

Thus, when Trump claims that the head of the Boy Scouts called to say his was the best speech ever delivered to the organization, or he claims that the president of Mexico picked up the telephone to let him know that his tough enforcement efforts at the border were paying off, Trump knows that his comments will be exposed as falsehoods, undercutting his credibility. But he simply doesn't care.

Some aides thought that when making a statement that will quickly be exposed as false, Trump convinces himself that it is true in order to retain some degree of intellectual integrity and still pursue his agenda.

"Look, I think that he has an amazing belief in his own ability to will what he thinks into reality," Maggie Haberman of the *New York Times* told David Remnick of the *New Yorker*. "And I think that he thinks of reality as something that is subjective.

So I think that what people characterize as 'he's out of touch' or 'he's not understanding this' or 'he seems off,' or whatever—I think he has an amazing capacity to try to draw the world as he wants it."

While his comments often get him in trouble, Trump's candor, with his signature asides, endears him to his voters. His no-nonsense approach helps him make deals. But Trump's public stream-of-consciousness complaints about his own staff undercut morale and turned off potential White House hires, especially when Trump's more caustic comments land in the press.

Like everything else about Trump, no one can be sure exactly what is going on in his complex head. But in *The Art of the Deal*, Trump said that he promotes by bravado.

"I play to people's fantasies," Trump wrote. "People may not always think big themselves, but they can still get very excited by those who do. That's why a little hyperbole never hurts. People want to believe that something is the biggest and the greatest and the most spectacular. I call it truthful hyperbole. It's an innocent form of exaggeration and a very effective form of promotion."

Aides see Trump's attitude as his way of marketing. Maybe no one will know whether or not the Boy Scouts or the president of Mexico called. Or if he is questioned about it, it will stir another controversy, garnering more publicity. If the false claims create blowback, he enjoys being the center of attention regardless. In the same way, his constantly shifting positions are a marketing ploy to see what sticks.

Trump will "sort of throw vitriolic things out there to see the reaction," an aide says. "And once in a while, he floats things, inappropriate things, out there and he gets pounded for it, but instead of backing down, he doubles down. And he sort of regrets doing it. He'll come back and say, 'Ah, man, maybe I shouldn't have done that tweet. Do you think that tweet was a good idea?'"

For example, Trump asked aides if he thought his tweet claiming that he had been wiretapped by President Obama in Trump Tower was a good idea. The claim was untrue and was quickly shown to be false. It went back to unsubstantiated media reports, including most notably a claim by former federal prosecutor Andrew McCarthy of *National Review* based on those reports, that the "Obama administration is now monitoring an opposing presidential campaign using the high-tech surveillance powers of the federal intelligence services." But remarkably, despite his bluster, Trump created an atmosphere where aides felt comfortable disagreeing with him and giving their honest opinions, telling him the tweet about Obama wiretapping him was not a good idea.

To be sure, Obama told his share of lies, such as "If you like your doctor, you'll be able to keep your doctor" and "If you like your health-care plan, you'll be able to keep your health-care plan" with Obamacare, but his untruths were not as patently obvious. The *Washington Post*'s fact checker Glenn Kessler called Trump "the most fact-challenged politician that the Fact Checker has ever encountered."

Whether you approve or not, Trump does indeed have a strategy. He is gaming the media: If the claims are believed, they burnish his image and enhance his aura as a showman.

"[F]rom a pure business point of view, the benefits of being written about have far outweighed the drawbacks," Trump said in *The Art of the Deal*. "It's really quite simple. . . . The funny thing is that even a critical story, which may be hurtful personally, can be very valuable to your business."

Back in 2006, I faxed Trump my column demonstrating that

the claim that Barack Obama was born in Kenya was a hoax. Headlined "Obama Was Born in the United States," it said, "Aside from that official verification of Obama's birth in Hawaii, back on Aug. 31, 1961, the *Honolulu Advertiser* and *Honolulu Star-Bulletin* each ran an announcement of his birth. 'Mr. and Mrs. Barack H. Obama, 6085 Kalanianaole Highway, son, Aug. 4.'"

Thus, unless Obama's parents knew when he was born that the baby Barack wanted one day to run for president of the United States and deviously placed the announcement of his birth in the Honolulu paper to provide evidence that he was born a U.S. citizen, the conspiracy theory that was gaining widespread traction on the far right was bogus. But Trump continued to push the false claim because it served his political purposes.

Finally, tacked on to the end of a campaign appearance with military veterans at his new Trump International Hotel in downtown Washington in September 2016, Trump said, "President Barack Obama was born in the United States, period." Now, he added, ". . . we all want to get back to making America strong and great again."

While Trump's outrageous comments may seem unhinged and turn off an array of voters, they inspire fear in the minds of foreign leaders and business tycoons whose help he needs and elicit cooperation from those he wants to woo. And in contrast to some of his comments, his actions—such as his carefully considered strategy for ramping up military engagement in Afghanistan—are perfectly reasonable. In private he may exaggerate but does not fabricate.

Given everyone's short attention span heightened by the twenty-four-hour news cycle, Trump's controversial claims are forgotten quickly. After Trump demonstrated a command of recovery efforts in Texas following Hurricane Harvey and its aftermath, Senator Dianne Feinstein, a California Democrat who had criticized Trump's pardon of former Arizona sheriff Joe Arpaio, shocked a San Francisco audience when she said in answer to whether he should be impeached, "The question is whether he can learn and change. If so, I believe he can be a good president."

"The real excitement is playing the game," Trump said in *The Art of the Deal*. Winning is everything.

3

DARKNESS IS GOOD

On Friday afternoon, October 7, 2016, on the twenty-fifth floor of Trump Tower, Priebus was playing the moderator to prepare Trump for the second presidential debate. New Jersey governor Chris Christie was playing Hillary. Everyone in Trump World was watching.

One by one, aides began leaving the conference room to huddle outside the glass doors to the room.

"What the hell is going on out there?" Trump asked Priebus and Christie. Hope Hicks, Trump's campaign press secretary who would be named White House communications director, entered the conference room, her head down. As tears welled up in Ivanka Trump's eyes, Hicks handed Trump a packet that contained a transcript that the *Washington Post* was about to run of Trump's lascivious comments in 2005 to Billy Bush, an anchor on NBC's show *Access Hollywood*.

Trump slid the packet across the conference table to Priebus, then-chairman of the Republican National Committee, and Christie. Priebus and the RNC had provided the ground game for the campaign.

"Oh, my gosh, this is really bad," Priebus said to Trump.

Jared Kushner came in and tried to make light of it, saying it was no big deal.

"What are you talking about?" Priebus asked. "This is bad stuff."

Trump claimed the transcript of the audio recording, which included Trump bragging about grabbing women's private parts, did not sound like his remarks. But then the *Post* sent the audio recording itself. Everyone was in despair. That evening and the next day, Republican members of Congress called Priebus and members of the Republican National Committee to urge Trump to drop out of the race.

"Well, I wasn't going to do that," Priebus tells me.

The next morning, Priebus met with Trump again.

"What are people saying?" Trump asked him.

"It's bad. This is as bad as I've ever seen," Priebus said. "People are saying you should drop out. People are saying that you're going to lose in the biggest way that anyone has ever lost before. You can either get out of the race, or you can lose in a huge landslide."

Priebus felt some aides weren't being blunt enough and honest with Trump about the gravity of the situation. Priebus wanted to make sure Trump understood what a blow this was. No one in the room challenged Priebus.

"I had people from the RNC telling me nonstop that we should just not even move forward with him as our candidate, that we should deem the candidacy vacant and figure out another way to get around it and declare the position vacant,"

Priebus says. "Call an emergency meeting of delegates, do something." Priebus considered the advice legally and ethically questionable, and he was not going to go along with it in any case.

The effect on the party became public when Paul Ryan, the Speaker of the House, uninvited Trump from an event in Wisconsin. Priebus suggested to Trump that the general sentiment that he should drop out was correct. But Priebus continued to support him and transfer money to his effort while continuing debate preparation with him the next day.

As Republican National Committee chairman, "I supported Trump a hundred percent. I was the one spending all the money on the race," Priebus says. "We were paying for some of the ads. We were paying for most of the ground staff. We spent more money and devoted more resources on this presidential race than any other in the history of the party. If I didn't believe in Trump, I would have just diverted the money to the Senate, which is what many in leadership wanted me to do."

Priebus has a Columbo-like, self-deprecating manner. While he seems nonchalant, he is actually sizing you up, quizzing you, and finding out everything you know. He's personable and open, with relaxed shoulders, soft dark brown eyes, and an easy smile, a trustworthy appearance.

When wearing a suit, Priebus often sports an oversize flag pin, very shiny, on his lapel. He has even worn it on a tuxedo. When speaking, with his thumb and forefinger, he makes a gesture that typically means "an inch" or "this much." But Priebus holds an idea he is expressing there. For instance, when he speaks of "putting a wall on the southern border," he seems to be holding the wall between his thumb and forefinger.

Priebus grew up in Green Bay, Wisconsin. He graduated from the University of Wisconsin-Whitewater and from the

University of Miami School of Law in 1998. He met his wife, Sally, at a high school youth group. Their first date was a Lincoln Day conservative dinner.

As Priebus likes to tell you, his first name *Reince* rhymes with *pints*, as in pints of his favorite beer, Miller High Life from Wisconsin.

"I've got a bizarre name, but I'm about as normal as they come," Priebus tells me. "I always tell people it's what happens when you have a Greek and a German who get married. It's a bit of a disaster."

"As a little guy, the one thing that I remember is that my grandfather in Athens loved America," Priebus says. "It didn't matter what it was about America, but he loved it."

In 2007, Priebus was elected chairman of the Wisconsin Republican Party. He then served as general counsel of the Republican National Committee under Michael Steele before becoming chairman of the RNC in January 2011. After taking over, Priebus sat down with his financial people and got grim news: The once-mighty RNC was broke. It didn't have the money to meet its payroll and other financial obligations the following week.

To cut spending, Priebus reduced staff by 40 percent. While Steele emphasized raising money from small donors, thereby increasing costs, Priebus pushed targeting big potential donors along with expanding the number of small donors and focusing on developing data on voters.

Grover Norquist, president of Americans for Tax Reform, applauded what he called the "turnaround" that Priebus engineered at the RNC.

"Priebus has righted a ship that was sinking," Brad Blakeman, a Republican strategist and Fox News contributor who is a former Bush White House aide, told me after Priebus took over the RNC. "With Priebus, it's not about him and getting on TV. It's about the party."

The second debate in St. Louis was to take place two days after the *Access Hollywood* tape came out. Appalled at hearing Trump's comments, Christie did not show up for the next day's debate preparation, when he was supposed to play the part of Hillary Clinton. Nor did Christie attend the actual debate. Priebus ended up playing both the moderator and Hillary.

As it turned out, "Trump killed it in the second debate," Priebus says. "He was focused like a laser beam on the material and the information for that second debate like I had never seen him before. The second debate was a new beginning for Donald Trump. He dealt with *Access Hollywood* head-on, he made all his pivot points on Hillary Clinton, and he looked confident. It created an entirely new narrative on Monday morning. If it wasn't for that performance in the second debate, I don't think that he'd be president."

Priebus's candor with Trump during the *Access Hollywood* episode demonstrated that, rather than being a yes-man, he would tell Trump the truth as he saw it. But while Trump called him up on the stage when he gave his victory speech and named him to the coveted position of White House chief of staff, Trump never forgave Priebus for advising him to drop out or lose. Later when complaining to aides about Priebus as weak, he would cite Priebus's advice.

Once in the White House, Priebus soon recognized that he was the chief of staff in name only.

"It was a structure set up from day one that ensured failure," Spicer says. "You can't have multiple people reporting to the president and pursuing their own agendas. You either have a chief of staff or you don't."

Trump was used to running his operation as a one-man show and was not willing to transfer any of his power to a chief of staff. On top of that, he brought in his daughter and son-in-law as commissioned officers, giving them more power than the chief of staff had by virtue of their family ties. But Priebus felt he would rather have some influence in the White House than none at all. While Trump made Bannon a coequal and the two White House aides differed on key policy questions such as maintaining troops in Afghanistan, Priebus figured they were both Republicans and could manage to operate effectively.

A powerhouse who headed Breitbart News, Bannon decided to join the campaign after reading an August 13, 2016, *New York Times* story about Trump's falling poll numbers and erratic behavior.

"Advisers who once hoped a Pygmalion-like transformation would refashion a crudely effective political showman into a plausible American president now increasingly concede that Mr. Trump may be beyond coaching," the story by Alexander Burns and Maggie Haberman said. "He has ignored their pleas and counsel as his poll numbers have dropped, boasting to friends about the size of his crowds and maintaining that he can read surveys better than the professionals."

Having pushed a hard-right agenda as the head of Breitbart News, Bannon was up for a challenge. Born in Norfolk, Virginia, Bannon was an officer in the United States Navy for seven years in the late 1970s and early 1980s and became a special assistant to the chief of Naval Operations. He never forgot his experience in the Navy of being on a mission to help rescue fifty-two U.S. Embassy hostages held in Tehran. President Carter had ordered the rescue attempt after six months of frustration over Iran's refusal to release the hostages.

It was just after midnight on March 21, 1980, when the Navy destroyer navigated by Bannon met with the supercarrier USS *Nimitz* in the Gulf of Oman. The convoy headed near the Iranian coast, where a secret mission would be launched a month later to rescue the hostages. Bannon's ship, the USS *Paul F. Foster*, trailed the *Nimitz*, which carried helicopters for retrieving the hostages. Yet before the mission launched, Bannon's ship was suddenly ordered to sail to Pearl Harbor. He learned while at sea that the rescue had failed due to the mechanical failure of three helicopters. Eight U.S. soldiers had been killed during departure when another helicopter collided with a transport plane.

In retrospect, the plan for the April 25, 1980, mission, called Operation Eagle Claw, was overly complex and amateurish. Nor did the planners envision the possibility of a sandstorm that clogged the engines of two of the helicopters. Writing in the *Air & Space Power Journal*, war gaming professor Charles Tustin Kamps observed that "the things which did cause the mission to abort were probably merciful compared to the greater catastrophe which might have taken place if the scenario had progressed further. . . ."

"I have the perfect word" for how the crew felt upon learning that the mission had failed, Andrew Green, one of Bannon's shipmates, said. "Defeated. We felt defeated."

Bannon has called the failed hostage rescue one of the defining moments of his life, providing a searing example of failed military and presidential leadership. He concluded that then-president Jimmy Carter had undercut the Navy and was responsible for blowing the rescue mission.

"I wasn't political until I got into the service and saw how badly Jimmy Carter f—ed things up. I became a Reagan admirer," Bannon told *Bloomberg Businessweek* in 2015.

If Bannon never got over that sense of betrayal, he also never forgave Wall Street for the loss of his father's savings. On October 7, 2008, in the cramped TV room of his modest home in Richmond, Virginia, his father Marty Bannon watched with alarm as plunging stock markets dragged down his shares of AT&T, the nest egg he had accumulated during a fifty-year career at the telephone company.

Steve Bannon and his four siblings would joke that their devout father, a product of the Great Depression, would sooner leave the Catholic Church than sell those shares. The stock symbolized his deep trust in the company and had doubled as life insurance for his children. As Marty Bannon switched between TV stations, financial analysts warned of economic collapse, and politicians in Washington seemed to mirror his own confusion. So he sold his AT&T shares.

Marty Bannon still regrets the decision and seethes over Washington's response to the economic crisis. He says he lost more than $100,000 because he sold the shares for less than he paid for them. The shares subsequently regained much of their value.

Steve Bannon says the scary moment crystallized his own antiestablishment outlook and helped trigger his desire to rectify what he saw as more failed national leadership.

"The only net worth my father had besides his tiny little house was that AT&T stock. And nobody is held accountable?" Steve Bannon told the *Wall Street Journal*. "All these firms get bailed out. There's no equity taken from anybody. There's no one in jail. These companies are all over-leveraged, and everyone looked the other way."

Bannon graduated from Virginia Tech, Georgetown University School of Foreign Service, and Harvard Business School. He then joined Goldman Sachs in Los Angeles for two years where he became a vice president, then left to become a deal maker and entrepreneur in Hollywood. Under the terms of his sale of his firm, he continues to receive a cut of *Seinfeld* residuals, according to Bannon.

Having immersed himself in politics at Breitbart, Bannon was reading the paper and drinking coffee at seven a.m. in Bryant Park near his New York City apartment when he was drawn to the *New York Times* story that triggered his decision to join the Trump campaign. The story was "a complete takedown of Trump and his campaign," Bannon tells me. "Total disorganization—it's over, guys."

Back in his apartment, he checked and learned Trump was down sixteen points in the polls compared with rival Hillary Clinton.

"I made some calls," Bannon says. "All the donors were bailing."

Bannon talked with Rebekah Mercer, a friend and major Republican fund-raiser and donor, along with her father, the billionaire hedge-fund manager Robert Mercer.

"Rebekah is like apoplectic because they're writing big checks now, and it's a horrible story. It's just brutal," Bannon says.

"What do you think can be done?" she asked.

Bannon had long admired Kellyanne Conway, a Republican pollster.

"What I ought to do is step in there and make Kellyanne Conway the campaign manager, put her on TV nonstop," Bannon said. "I'll run the thing. I know we can win this, or worst case, we'll lose by three points and hold the House and the Senate."

The Mercers, who had supported Senator Ted Cruz in the

primary campaign, switched to supporting Trump after he was nominated. They supported Bannon becoming Trump's campaign chairman. While Trump later chafed at the publicity Bannon received, Bannon provided a philosophy and strategy that undergirded the campaign.

"When I stepped in, there wasn't a campaign," Bannon says. "They would have Education Week, then Women's and Parents' Week, all ideas of Ivanka and Jared. There was nothing."

Instead, the campaign would portray Hillary Clinton as "the corrupt, incompetent status quo," Bannon says. He would tell Trump, "You are the agent of change, of real change. And all we have to do is give people permission to vote for you. They don't need to think you're a good guy. They don't need to think you're a great man. They don't need to think you're even their cup of tea. They just have to give themselves permission to vote for a true agent of change because the voters wanted this economic nationalism, populism, anti-establishment, lock her up, drain the swamp, and the media's the enemy approach."

In contrast to any other White House aide, Bannon cultivated a scary, bad boy persona, saying "darkness is good" and wearing a beat-up green leather Orvis combat jacket every day. Bannon looks a little rough, like he hasn't had enough sleep, and he hasn't been eating well, and he has a lot on his mind that is pissing him off. His eyes are puffy and red-rimmed, as though he just got off the red-eye. His skin is splotchy with sun damage on his forehead and he has rosacea, a common skin condition, on and around his nose. But Bannon has been blessed with generous hair, a salt-and-pepper pompadour whitening at the temples. Think Johnny Cash.

Bannon has a determined mouth, clenched lips. He rarely smiles, if you could even call it that. When speaking and wanting to convey a point, he pushes around an imaginary weight with his hands, chopping and pounding, stirring the air in the room. Whenever he mentions the media, he holds his palms out as in No Way.

Because of his weight, Bannon's habit of wearing several layers of clothing works for him. Lately, with the help of a dietician, Bannon has been taking off weight and looks a little more like the Goldman Sachs banker he once was. He typically wears a dark blazer over a black shirt with Ivy League collar over a black T-shirt. When he and Priebus were being interviewed at the Conservative Political Action Conference (CPAC), Priebus was asked, What do you like most about Bannon? Priebus eyed Bannon for an instant and replied, "I love how many collars he wears, interesting look."

Asked what "darkness is good" means, Bannon responds that he uses the expression "in the spirit of fun."

Critics claimed that Bannon was anti-Semitic, but Andrew Breitbart, who brought Bannon into the enterprise, was Jewish. Bannon made it clear he had no use for the Klan or other Far Right hate groups.

In person, Bannon was the opposite of the image he projected. He was polite, genuinely interested in countervailing arguments, and erudite. He owns ten thousand books and claims to have read them all.

"Unlike what you see on TV, Bannon was pretty reasonable when I worked with him," Priebus says. "In the White House at least he was not reckless. In fact, in the White House I would say he was risk averse."

As Bannon sees it, Trump personifies the populist revolution that has been building for many years. "We're only at the beginning of this anti-elite, anti-establishment revolt," he says.

It was Bannon who introduced Trump to the idea that he is a President Andrew Jackson figure, lending legitimacy to Trump's convention-shattering style. Trump's personality bears a striking resemblance to that of Jackson, a populist who, despite his own great wealth, championed the common man against what Jackson called "the aristocracy of the few"—the established elite of the East Coast cities.

When President Jackson was dining with friends at the White House, someone whispered to him that the Senate had rejected the nomination of Martin Van Buren as minister to England. Jackson jumped to his feet and exclaimed, "By the Eternal! I'll smash them!" And that is what he did: His favorite, Martin Van Buren, became vice president and succeeded to the presidency when "Old Hickory" left the White House.

Jackson was "combative, thin-skinned, quick-tempered," Jon Meacham wrote in *American Lion: Andrew Jackson in the White House*. Meacham said of the seventh U.S. president, "To friends, he was considerate and generous. He was a good listener, Van Buren said. To enemies, mean-spirited and spiteful. He would explode in anger, but it was believed he never really lost his temper. Rather, he launched into tirades purposely to intimidate the opposition or to end debate that dragged on too long."

While George Washington saw swagger as a moral failure, Jackson saw it as a virtue. With his charisma and willingness to challenge established conventions and exercise executive authority, Jackson created the modern presidency as a national force or, as President John F. Kennedy called it, "the vital center of action." Unlike previous presidents, Jackson did not defer to Congress in policy-making but used the power of the veto and his party leadership to assume command. Jackson was the embodiment of a populism that venerated and served "the people," promoting American nationalism.

The political class in Washington feared Jackson's great triumph. "The rich and powerful," Jackson said, "too often bend the acts of government to their selfish purposes." Jackson warned they had turned government into an "engine for the support of the few at the expense of the many."

Along with Bannon, Senior Policy Adviser Stephen Miller gave Trump articles about Jackson, and Trump hung a portrait of Jackson in the Oval Office. It was Miller who drafted Trump's inaugural address with contributions from Bannon and Trump himself.

Miller grew up in a liberal Jewish family in California. He became a committed conservative after reading *Guns, Crime, and Freedom*, a book by National Rifle Association chief executive officer Wayne LaPierre. While attending Santa Monica High School, Miller began appearing on conservative talk radio. Miller was shocked by the reaction of his high school classmates to the 9/11 attacks and the loss of almost three thousand American lives.

"During that dreadful time of national tragedy, anti-Americanism had spread all over the school like a rash," he said in a column. "The co-principal broadcasted his doubts about the morality of the air strikes against the Taliban to the entire school via the PA system. One teacher even dragged the American flag across the floor as we were sending off brave young men to risk their lives for it." In another column, Miller concluded, "Osama Bin Laden would feel very welcome at Santa Monica High School."

At Duke University, Miller came to the defense of the lacrosse players who were accused of rape by a black stripper. In several columns, he alleged that the media's overwhelming condemnation of the white lacrosse players was a result of the radical left's prejudice against whites. Eventually, charges against the lacrosse players were dropped, and North Carolina attorney general Roy Cooper announced that "we believe that these three individuals are innocent of these charges."

After graduating from college, Miller worked as a press secretary for Congresswoman Michele Bachmann and Congressman John Shadegg, both members of the Republican Party. In 2009, he started working for Alabama senator and future attorney general Jeff Sessions. In January 2016, Miller joined Trump's campaign.

In contrast to Miller, who is reserved, Bannon mirrored Trump. He was brash, opinionated, boastful, and smart. Like Trump, he viewed China with suspicion, seeing it as sucking jobs from America because of its low wages and manipulation of its currency. Like Trump, he was infuriated by U.S. immigration policies that treated illegal immigrants the same as U.S. citizens, encouraging more illegal immigrants to enter the United States and flout American laws. And like Trump, Bannon had no use for political correctness and the hate-America scourge that was overtaking colleges and the left wing of the Democratic Party.

At the same time, "I have a problem with these extremists on both sides—the Klan, the Neo-Confederates, the white nationalist group, the white supremacy groups—coming and looking for a fight," Bannon says. "Those guys should all be shut down immediately, as with Antifa and Black Lives Matter."

As a populist, Bannon's main issues coincided with Trump's views, but in other ways, he adopted the views of liberal Democrats. He was against intervening militarily overseas and continuing the war in Afghanistan. He also floated the idea of a top income-tax rate of 44 percent for Americans earning more than five million dollars a year.

But as Trump liked to point out, he was his own strategist. Trump was sitting in his office on the twenty-sixth floor of Trump Tower on November 7, 2012, the day after Mitt Romney lost what had been presumed to be a winnable race against President Obama, when he decided to trademark the winning slogan "Make America Great Again."

4

TEFLON AIDES

A real estate broker who thought they could make deals to-gether introduced Jared and Ivanka to each other in 2005. While they had much in common—they were both children of wealthy real estate developers—when it came to romance, religion was a problem. Jared's parents, Charles and Seryl Kushner, hoped that Jared, an orthodox Jew, would marry a Jewish woman.

"I know he loved Ivanka dearly," Jared's friend Nitin Saigal told the *New Yorker*. "But the religious thing was important to him."

Like her father, Ivanka was raised a Presbyterian. After he married Melania, a Catholic, Trump began going to church more often. He keeps a Bible in a nightstand next to his bed at Mar-a-Lago.

In the documentary *Born Rich*, Ivanka appears wearing a

necklace with a silver cross. She was not what Kushner's parents had in mind for their son. Jared was close to his parents, calling them every day when he attended Harvard and visiting his father on weekends in prison. Charles Kushner was serving two years after pleading guilty to felony counts of filing false tax returns, making illegal campaign donations, and retaliating against his sister—a government witness—by hiring a prostitute to entrap her husband.

Ivanka was hurt that Jared didn't take her side against his parents. The couple broke up in 2008. The split was brief. Wendi Deng, who was then married to Rupert Murdoch, invited Jared on a cruise with the media king on the family yacht. When Jared arrived on the yacht, he found that Ivanka had been invited as well.

During their courtship, Kushner had met Donald a few times in passing. When it seemed the relationship was getting serious, Jared asked Trump for a meeting. Over lunch at the Trump Grill in Trump Tower, Jared said to him, "Ivanka and I are getting serious, and we're starting to go down that path."

"You'd better be serious on this," Trump said.

Once the couple had reconciled, Ivanka converted to Judaism under the instruction of Rabbi Haskel Lookstein of the Congregation Kehilath Jeshurun, known as K.J., a Modern Orthodox synagogue on the Upper East Side of Manhattan. She took the Hebrew name Yael. Jared bought Ivanka a 5.22-carat diamond engagement ring. They were married in 2009. They keep kosher and observe the Sabbath.

Before entering the White House, Jared was chief executive officer of his father's Kushner Companies, a real estate holding and development company, and was publisher of the *New York Observer.* Ivanka was an executive vice president of the Trump

Organization. She oversaw the development of Trump International Hotel in Washington, a sparkling, luxurious addition to the city. Earlier in her life, she was a model.

Ivanka has her own fashion line of clothes, handbags, shoes, and accessories available in major U.S. department stores. Her book *Women Who Work: Rewriting the Rules for Success* was a bestseller full of advice and wisdom for both men and women.

When Trump was accused of tweeting what some erroneously claimed was a Jewish Star of David superimposed on a photo of Hillary Clinton surrounded by hundred-dollar bills with the caption, "Most corrupt candidate ever!" Kushner sprang to his defense.

"My father-in-law is not an anti-Semite," he said in an op-ed published in his newspaper. "The fact is that my father-in-law is an incredibly loving and tolerant person who has embraced my family and our Judaism since I began dating my wife. His support has been unwavering and from the heart."

Indeed, close to half of Trump's top executives in New York are Jewish, including several orthodox Jews who take off early on Fridays to observe the Sabbath.

As White House aides, both Kushner and Ivanka, who forgo government salaries, operated independently of Priebus, who found himself chief of a staff whose most senior members did not report to him. In fact, the president's own daughter and son-in-law were bad-mouthing Priebus in the press. Hyperconcerned about his image, Kushner even put Josh Raffel, a New York public relations man, on the White House payroll to promote him and Ivanka and arrange background interviews for them with reporters about their pet initiatives. While at the White House, Bannon retained his own public relations consultant, Alexandra Preate, as his "personal spokeswoman."

Bannon saw Jared and Ivanka as liberals whose views were closer to Hillary Clinton's than to Trump's. Bannon and Jared went to war, leaking critical material about each other.

"Oh, you've got to be moderate, you've got to make everyone your friend," is the way Bannon characterized advice from Javanka, as he derisively called Jared and Ivanka.

"They're nice people, but they don't know anything," Bannon told me. "If their name wasn't Trump, they would be midlevel marketing managers somewhere," he said. "They are so opposed to his program that they're there to destroy him. This White House was very divided from the beginning, but those divisions were papered over during the campaign because everyone was focused on winning. But it was always from the very beginning the Democrats versus the conservatives."

Jared had a particular dislike of Chris Christie, who, as U.S. attorney in New Jersey, had prosecuted his father. No matter what Christie proposed, Jared would block it. In the end, Jared was the chief reason Christie never got a position in the Trump cabinet.

Aside from advising her father on key decisions, Ivanka had her own pet projects, including promoting the STEM initiative to enhance science, technology, engineering, and mathematics education in the schools. She also advocated for women's issues, including pushing legislation to provide a child-care tax credit and required paid family leave. She weighed in as well on topics ranging from climate change and deportation to education and refugee policy.

In advancing her agenda, Ivanka had to put up with incidents such as occurred in Connecticut when some parents complained about her visit to Norwalk Early College Academy at Norwalk High School with IBM CEO Ginni Rometty. The two spoke about a new educational model IBM developed and that is already being adopted by communities throughout the country. It prepares students for what Rometty calls "new-collar jobs" with six-year public high schools. The schools combine a relevant traditional curriculum with practical skills taught at community colleges, along with mentoring and real-world job experience. Some of the Norwalk school parents complained to the news media that they would have pulled their kids from school that day if they had been given notice of Ivanka's visit.

"Suddenly, after my father declared his candidacy, it became that all the things that I was doing that I was praised for, the same people, the critics, viewed them through this different lens," Ivanka said at one point, as quoted by the *New York Times*. "Somehow, all the same things they applauded me for as a millennial, as a female entrepreneur, were now viewed very cynically as opportunistic."

Jared took on a range of duties that included establishing what he called the Office of American Innovation. Complete with a staff, its scope was ridiculously broad and included upgrading the federal government's $82 billion worth of information technology, spurring the creation of new jobs, changing how the country thinks about apprenticeships, and "unleashing American business."

Other aides felt Jared was way over his head as he mouthed platitudes about achieving peace in the Middle East and solving problems but had no real idea what he was doing.

"Jared is the kind of guy who likes to go to meetings and say, 'We need to solve this problem' or 'We need peace in the Middle East,'" Spicer says.

Aides felt Jared and Ivanka were simply power hungry and

were happy to throw their weight around, a malady known as White House-itus.

"Every administration has people in it who get White House-itus," says Robert Gates, a former National Security Council staffer in the White House and a former director of Central Intelligence. "The first giveaway is when a relatively junior staffer has his secretary place calls saying, 'The White House is calling,' instead of 'Joe Schmo from the National Security Council is calling.'"

During one heated discussion with Bannon, Ivanka made it clear she did not have to go through Priebus to discuss issues with her father. Bannon told her she was just a staffer. Ivanka reminded him that she is the first daughter, above staff.

Both Jared and Ivanka are all about "puppies and rainbows," says an aide. In the view of many Trump aides, the notion of neophyte Jared Kushner negotiating with Israeli prime minister Benjamin Netanyahu and Palestinian leader Mahmoud Abbas was laughable. But like Ivanka, Jared could claim real contributions.

"I do think Jared does a very good job of handling big issues overseas," Priebus says. "He has to get credit for the Saudi Arabia trip. It was really Jared's creation. He came up with the idea of visiting Riyadh first, showing that Trump is not anti-Muslim and is ready for business as a world leader."

In the end, Jared and Ivanka would push the most disastrous and most foolish decisions of Trump's presidency. Trump even admitted to aides that Jared and Ivanka had screwed up and that he understands that they are a problem. Trump repeatedly told Jared and Ivanka that they had made a mistake by joining his White House team.

"A couple of times, he told them right in front of me in the Oval, 'I told you guys you should have stayed in New York, because it's going to be vicious,'" Bannon says. "He wasn't saying that they're useless but that you're hurting yourselves by being here. But I think he was also giving a hint. If they had taken the hint and skedaddled, he'd be fine with it."

"He told them both before they came to Washington that they shouldn't come to the White House," a Trump aide says. "He said that would be a big mistake. He told them, 'You don't understand how this town is going to kill you. Don't come.'" Once they came, Trump told Jared and Ivanka "the worst thing they ever did was to come into the White House, they shouldn't have, and he warned them not to."

Trump was not just looking out for them.

"He didn't really want them to come," another aide said. "He encouraged them not to. The thing is he's a good family man, and he loves his family. So once they decided they had to come and they must come, then the president said, okay, fine, he supported it. But his instincts were don't do this. It's not worth it."

After it became clear that they would be attacked daily in the media and that they had pushed some of his biggest fiascoes, Trump told them in front of aides, "Remember I told you not to do this, and you had to do it? Now look."

Displaying her usual candor, Maggie Haberman of the *New York Times* said in the interview with David Remnick of the *New Yorker* that "if Jared Kushner were not related to the president—any other person with this fact set would have been fired, in any other White House. There is a reason why nepotism laws exist."

Yet they were the Teflon aides, their status intact by virtue of the fact they are family.

5

BLUEBERRY

At a party at the British Embassy, while chatting with Ambassador Kim Darroch and guests who were reporters, Kellyanne Conway began criticizing her coworkers. According to a Politico article, she mimicked Priebus and his efforts to stop leaks. She also questioned what legislative director Marc Short does all day.

"No leaks, guuuys," Conway allegedly mimicked Priebus as saying. Mocking him, she quoted him as saying at a staff meeting, "I'm upset because there's someone working on a story who pronounces it RAYNSE instead of REINCE."

Conway immediately enlisted Sean Spicer to try to paper over her comments, but the fact was she was a constant leaker to the press about her own colleagues. Through friends of reporters who received them, White House aides saw texts from Conway purporting to leak information about them.

Technically, a leak is accurate information given to reporters without authorization. But Conway often provides reporters with information that disparages her colleagues. According to Trump aides, Conway is the number one leaker.

In a White House interview with me, Conway, apparently forgetting that she was speaking on the record, said far worse things about Priebus than what she had said at the British Embassy, remarks so cutting and obviously untrue that out of fairness I am not including them here.

While Conway likes to claim that appearing on TV takes up only 5 percent of her time, in fact, beyond attending some conferences, no one knows what she does in the White House. Nor, despite the title, had she been campaign manager.

"We had to give her a title to put her on TV," Bannon says. "She can't make decisions, and in a campaign, you just got to make a million decisions." In fact, "The Republican National Committee was the campaign, and Trump was our candidate. Those few people working around Trump were part of that operation around Trump, but they were a Trump candidate operation. They were not a Trump campaign operation."

After Trump was in the White House, in an interview with *New York* magazine, Conway said, "When I want to talk to him [the president], I go talk to him," meaning she can waltz into the Oval Office unannounced. "Eighty-five percent of what I discuss with him will never be revealed. . . . I don't need to talk to him through the TV. I just go in and talk to him." The article noted, "In conversation, she is eager to explain that she's in important meetings, important events, and privy to important information."

But Bannon says, "Kellyanne wasn't in any policy meetings, very rarely in the Oval. Never around when decisions were made."

In the same vein, Omarosa Manigault had no real job. Her title of communications director for the Office of Public Liaison did not exist before Trump said he wanted her to join the White House staff. She rarely spoke with Trump. However, she always made it a point to show up at events covered by TV cameras and would occasionally help out.

Conway brilliantly articulates Trump's policies on TV and effectively skewers the mainstream media's coverage of the Trump administration. But Trump pounced on her flubs, such as saying there are "alternative facts" on the issue of crowd size at Trump's inauguration. She later said her comment was a mistake.

At one point in February 2017, Trump took Conway off the air, saying, according to Bannon, "She can't hit the fastball."

When asked about it, she claimed to the press that she was off the air because of family commitments.

"I don't think I have to explain myself if I'm not going on TV if I'm out with four kids for three days looking at houses and schools," the counselor to the president told Fox News's Sean Hannity. She added: "A lot of my colleagues aren't trying to figure out how to be a mother of four kids, I assure you."

Personable, witty, and chatty, Conway grew up in the southern New Jersey town of Atco. Conway's Irish father owned a small trucking company, and her Italian mother worked at a bank. They divorced when she was three.

"I grew up in a house with my mom and her mom, and two of my mother's unmarried sisters," Conway told me. "So four Italian Catholic women raised me. I grew up in a house where we never had a single political discussion, ever. We had pictures of like the Last Supper and the family dog on the wall."

Conway admits to winning the 1982 New Jersey Blueberry Princess pageant, leading her to choose the Secret Service code name Blueberry. But she says it is more relevant that in 1987, she was named the World Champion Blueberry Packer. For eight summers beginning at age twelve, she packed blueberries on a farm and was known as the fastest at the job.

Conway traces her conservative outlook to growing up in a household "where family and faith and self-reliance were premier. We were not encouraged or allowed to complain or talk about what we didn't have."

In her senior year in high school, Conway watched the nominating conventions on TV.

"I thought I'm going to have a great deal of commonality with Geraldine Ferraro," she remembers. "But I found myself much more riveted with and in agreement with what Ronald Reagan had to say and what the Republican Convention had to say. His messages were optimistic yet sensible and realistic."

In 1989, Conway graduated magna cum laude from Trinity Washington University and was inducted into Phi Beta Kappa. She studied at Oxford University, then obtained a law degree from George Washington University Law Center.

After practicing law, she began her polling career at the Wirthlin Group, a GOP polling organization that worked for Ronald Reagan. She moved on to Luntz Research Companies, then founded The Polling Company in 1995. Her clients have included Newt Gingrich, Microsoft, ABC News, American Express, the National Rifle Association, and Major League Baseball.

Ivanka, Don Jr., and Eric as well as Jared were opposed to Conway being hired in the first place. While Bannon had thought Conway would be fine pretending to be campaign manager but actually doing nothing but appearing on TV, he did not want her in the White House, either, because she could not make decisions. Ultimately, Trump hired her, but with no specified role.

Apparently the children and Jared thought that early on, she displayed disloyalty toward Trump, refusing to go on TV after his *Access Hollywood* tape came out, allegedly trying to line up paid TV deals, and privately making disparaging comments about Trump to Joe Scarborough and Mika Brzezinski of MSNBC's *Morning Joe*.

"This is a woman, by the way, who came on our show during the campaign and would shill for Trump in extensive fashion, and then she would get off the air, the camera would be turned off, the microphone would be taken off, and she would say, 'Blech, I need to take a shower,'" Brzezinski said on the show. "Because she disliked her candidate so much."

Scarborough echoed her comments, noting that Conway confided after being interviewed on air that she had only taken the job for money and that she would soon be done defending Trump.

"From day one, Jared and Ivanka wanted to give it to Kellyanne," Bannon says. "They tried to get her fired."

"They thought that she was disloyal because she was using the last week of the campaign to have a bunch of meetings to shop herself [to networks]," a Trump aide says. "And they just also didn't think she really did anything."

Yet instead of reporting to Priebus, Kellyanne reported directly to Trump, along with Bannon, Gary Cohn, Stephen Miller, Hope Hicks, Sean Spicer, and Ivanka and Jared.

Aside from Conway's disparaging comments, as part of their vendettas against one another, Trump White House staffers regularly feed misinformation to the press. As an example, Maggie Haberman and Glenn Thrush wrote in the *New York Times*, "The president's first chief of staff, Reince Priebus, a former chairman of the Republican National Committee, made only a cursory study of the structure and history of the West Wing, much to the disgust of a half-dozen Obama administration officials who offered to coach him but were, for the most part, politely rebuffed."

In fact, Priebus met twice with Denis McDonough, Obama's chief of staff, and often consulted with former chiefs of staff Andy Card and Josh Bolten from the Bush administration, James Baker from the Reagan administration, and Rahm Emanuel from the Obama administration. In addition, Priebus had a luncheon meeting in the White House with twelve former Republican and Democrat chiefs of staff going back to Jimmy Carter's administration.

Nor were widespread press reports that Trump humiliated Priebus by ordering him to swat a fly true. The story had its origin in the fact that the West Wing, built on a swamp, is beset by flies. Trump hates flies. Staffers use air-pressured salt guns called Bug-a-Salt to kill them. Priebus was attacking an especially annoying fly in the Oval Office when Trump said jokingly, "Kill it! Kill it!"

6

THE REAL TRUMP

For all his talk about improving the economy and helping the middle class, since records were first kept during the presidency of Herbert Hoover, Barack Obama was the first president to fail to achieve an annual increase in the gross domestic product of 3 percent.

During the eight years of Obama's presidency, the average annual growth in the economy was a pathetic 1.8 percent, meaning millions could not find jobs. Measured by net worth, the economic chasm between black and Hispanic families and their white counterparts widened in the final three years of Obama's presidency.

It's not hard to see why. If you watched any of the financial television channels, you saw hundreds of CEOs of companies large and small complain that because of the Obama administration's crusade to impose more regulations on American business, their costs were increasing, and they were afraid to expand and hire more workers.

At the same time, Obama's demonization of business and his swipes at entrepreneurship imposed a psychological restraint on American capitalism. During a talk in Roanoke, Virginia, Obama diminished successful people by saying no one gets there on his own. "If you've got a business, you didn't build that. Somebody else made that happen," Obama said.

Obama cited the obvious fact that everyone needs teachers, roads, and bridges. But to detract from the achievement of any successful person—whether a student graduating from college or a Thomas Alva Edison, Steve Jobs, or Bill Gates—is to attack the very essence of the free enterprise system and what makes America a magnet for immigrants from all over the world.

Behind Obama's failure on the economic front was a blind spot to understanding that people respond to incentives and disincentives. Funneling taxpayers' money through the federal government has no multiplier effect and does not give businesses incentives to expand and hire more people.

Looking at Obama's approach, I am reminded of sitting in the dining room at the National Hotel in Moscow when writing my book *Moscow Station* during the Cold War. Since they were government employees, the waiters milled around and chatted in groups, ignoring my wife Pam and me. Why should they wait on us? They were paid by the Soviet Union regardless and got no tips. Similarly, their bosses had the same lack of incentive to properly supervise them.

Instead of demonizing business, in his first year as president, Trump touted the accomplishments of American capitalism and decapitated government regulations that were strangling large and small companies. In doing so, he achieved even more than his efforts to enact a new health-care law and reduce taxes to supercharge the American economy and give businesses and the stock market a psychological boost.

The conventional wisdom is that Donald Trump only became a conservative the day he announced his candidacy for the presidency. But like most conventional wisdom about Trump, it was wrong.

Less than a year after President Obama took office, Trump told me at his New Year's Eve party at Mar-a-Lago that the new president was a "disaster" whose economic policies were going to ruin the country. Trump told me then he wasn't yet ready to be quoted knocking Obama. As a businessman, he did not want to appear to be taking sides. But six years before he took office, in a book that was largely overlooked during the campaign, Trump laid out exactly what was wrong with Obama's vision and why conservative policies are needed to turn around the country's anemic economic growth.

In Trump's *Time to Get Tough: Making America #1 Again*, the Wharton School at the University of Pennsylvania graduate presented a detailed economic critique that any fiscal conservative would applaud. The reason "this country is an economic disaster right now," he wrote, "is because Barack Obama doesn't understand how wealth is created—and how the federal government can destroy it."

Liberals "scratch their heads and wonder why businesses don't want to hire," Trump wrote. The answer: "Companies know Obama is anti-business, and his government-run health-care takeover has created a major disincentive to hire new workers."

Raising taxes, as Obama wanted to do, merely forces business owners to "lay off employees they can no longer afford," Trump noted. "It also drives up prices, encourages businessmen and women to move their businesses (and their jobs) to other countries that have far lower tax rates and regulatory costs, and sends people scrambling for tax shelters," Trump said.

The same lack of market sense led to Obamacare's skyrocketing premium increases and deductibles as high as $8,000 a year, making the insurance useless in most cases. Requiring that health insurance cover birth control and dental care for children is like requiring that auto insurance cover gasoline purchases. It drives up premiums to cover expected expenses, exactly the opposite of what insurance is for.

In addition, requiring coverage for individuals with preexisting conditions like cancer allows anyone to sign up for Obamacare coverage after they experience illness. That's like requiring that auto insurance cover an accident that occurred before coverage started. The Republican alternative would cover preexisting conditions but would spread the additional cost among all taxpayers rather than by charging health insurance subscribers and boosting premiums.

During the transition, Trump's staff drafted two hundred executive orders, most of them designed to roll back the stranglehold on the economy imposed by Obama. Then, to get them through quickly, the White House abandoned what is known as regular order, which requires executive action to go through a vetting process among cabinet officers and government agencies.

"If you look at the first few weeks, we started out like gangbusters with executive orders, trying to get as much of the Trump agenda done as we could," Priebus says. "We knew that as time went on things would slow down and start to clog because you have everyone getting involved. That's exactly what eventually happened."

Four days after his inauguration, Trump signed executive orders or memos to expedite environmental reviews and approvals for future infrastructure projects, reverse the Obama administration's halt on the Keystone XL and Dakota Access oil pipelines, and order the government to reduce regulatory burdens affecting domestic manufacturing.

Despite approval by the State Department, Obama had rejected TransCanada's application to build the Keystone pipeline filed as far back as 2008. Likewise, Obama had held up approval of the Dakota Access pipeline over protests by the Standing Rock Sioux tribe, whose reservation abuts Lake Oahe in North Dakota. The tribe claimed the pipeline, which was to run under the lake, would trample culturally historic sites and threaten their water supply. But eight pipelines already go under the lake without causing any problems, a fact rarely mentioned in press stories about the controversy.

In addition to giving the green light to oil pipelines, Trump took steps to permit drilling in most U.S. continental-shelf waters, including protected areas of the Arctic and the Atlantic. It was part of his push for U.S. "energy dominance" in the global market, diminishing U.S. dependence on oil from the Middle East.

While the Trump White House released a government report affirming that global warming is indeed real and caused in part by human activity, Trump withdrew from the Paris Climate Accord, saying its voluntary standards would have done nothing to change the climate. On the one hand, the United States would have faithfully adhered to the voluntary standards, impairing the economy and resulting in millions of lost jobs, Trump said. On the other hand, under the agreement, "China . . . can do whatever they want for thirteen years. Not us," Trump pointed out in a Rose Garden speech on June 1, 2017. "India makes its participation contingent on receiving billions and billions and billions of dollars in foreign aid from developed countries. . . . But the bottom line is that the Paris Accord is very unfair, at the highest level, to the United States."

Both Jared and Ivanka pushed Trump to change his mind, enlisting Trump friends who opposed withdrawing from the Paris agreement to lobby him. Trump held multiple meetings on the subject, including with the Principals Committee, which serves as the cabinet-level senior interagency forum for considering policy issues that affect the national security interests of the United States. Aides felt Trump knew where he wanted to be from the beginning. While Trump listened to those who lobbied him, he came back to where his gut was originally.

Obama-era regulations were not only strangling business growth, they were impinging on the rights of college students to obtain justice when accused of sexual harassment. Betsy DeVos, Trump's education secretary, announced plans to reverse the Obama administration's so-called guidance that shifted the burden of proof when college students make accusations of sexual attacks to "preponderance of the evidence." That standard had led to a number of false findings against male students. Rather than the "beyond a reasonable doubt" standard used in criminal cases or the "clear and convincing" standard many universities had previously used for sexual assault investigations, the Obama Education Department had required school administrators to use a standard that amounted to a "fifty percent plus one" threshold when determining responsibility in such cases. The Obama administration's emphasis on placing grave decisions about sexual misconduct in the hands of education bureaucrats instead of the police invited injustice.

In the ensuing weeks and months after becoming president,

Trump required that the government rescind two regulations for every new one imposed, eliminated restrictions on energy production, and froze federal government hiring. In fact, the administration wound up eliminating twenty-two regulations for every new one imposed.

Each year, the General Accountability Office (GAO) reports that cutting duplicative programs could save tens of billions of taxpayer dollars. But cutting programs nibbles around the edges of the spending problem. The real problem is bloated bureaucracy.

Those of us who have dealt with the federal government for decades have an impression that in most agencies, half the workers could be cut without impairing services. That's because, lacking a profit motive, government workers by and large have a different work ethic from those in private industry.

When they could make a phone call, federal workers call a meeting. When they could find an answer on the Internet, they form a study committee. Instead of appointing one supervisor, they appoint five.

To be sure, there are exceptions. FBI agents, CIA officers, and the military work incredible hours and risk their lives to protect us. But even within those agencies, there are unnecessary levels of supervision and support staff who could perform their work in half the time.

At one office in the Labor Department, employees on flex-time were supposed to arrive at six a.m. but generally did not show up until nine a.m., a former Labor Department employee told me. At the Department of Housing and Urban Development, a new appraiser was told he performed his appraisals too fast. Instead of taking a week, he should take four months, a supervisor told him.

Remarkably, when I have asked current and former government workers, they uniformly agree that government employment could be cut in half by attrition without losing any output. Indeed, a study by the Center for Naval Analyses found that when private contractors performed the same work as federal employees in the Defense Department, the cost was 30 percent lower. Other studies by the government have found savings of about a third when private contractors perform government work ranging from maintenance, data processing, and procurement to education and training.

Only when you are self-employed do you fully realize how much more efficient you can be when your output directly correlates with how much money you make. But instead of looking for ways to save, near the end of the fiscal year, government agencies look for ways to spend more money so their budget won't be reduced by Congress the following year.

Trump's father, Fred, taught him to be cost conscious. A workaholic, Fred would take Donald to construction sites and to his headquarters, a converted dentist's office near Coney Island. On his own projects, Fred would pick up unused nails off the floor and return them to his carpenters. He saved money by ordering lab analysis of store-bought products, buying the ingredients, and then having them mixed to make his own.

When the father of a childhood friend of Trump's bought his son a new thirty-dollar baseball mitt with intricate webbing that Rawlings had begun manufacturing, Donald could not persuade his father to buy him one. Fred bought him a cheaper mitt.

Trump passed along that concern about costs to his kids, who booked economy class plane tickets as Trump executives.

"As children, I remember we were made to mow the lawns, to cut down trees, and do all kinds of chores," Eric Trump says. "Out of all my friends, I believe I'm the only kid whose dad made us work to cut rebars. We laid bricks in construction sites and did other real work every summer for minimum wage. Our dad said that it's important in the future that when we tell people to dig a hole, you personally know how long it will take to dig that hole. He taught us the value of the dollar."

"He taught us to learn the ropes of the business early on and not to rest on our laurels," Don Trump Jr. remembers. "He told us the company will not shoulder our stay in the company just because, and that we need to continue earning the right to be in the Trump Organization through our own diligence and astuteness." In addition, Don Jr. says, "He always tells us to never give up, never get discouraged during difficult times, and to get up even when the going gets tough."

By August 2017, Trump imposed a surgically targeted government hiring freeze. Staff may be increased only where an agency like the Secret Service is slated for expansion under his budget proposal. Other agencies will be expected to downsize.

Trump constantly made it clear to employees that they would be held accountable if they did not do their jobs properly. During the campaign, Trump angrily complained at a rally about the faulty microphone at his podium. He vowed not to pay the contractor who had installed it. That attitude sent a message that Trump would not tolerate laziness and incompetence.

As president, Trump pushed a bill allowing the Department of Veterans Affairs to fire incompetent or lazy employees more easily. The measure was prompted by a scandal at the Phoenix VA medical center, where thirty-five veterans died after waiting months for care. During one week in October 2015, thirty-nine hundred appointments were canceled, and twelve patients "may have experienced harm that could have been prevented without the delay in care," according to a report by the Office of Special Counsel. On average, the VA facility had eleven hundred patients waiting more than thirty days for a medical appointment.

"What happened was a national disgrace and yet some of the employees involved in these scandals remained on the payrolls," Trump said when signing the bill. "Outdated laws kept the government from holding those who failed our veterans accountable. Today we are finally changing those laws."

Obama had promised to reform the VA. At a town hall meeting, the widow of Army veteran Barry Coates spoke up. Her husband had waited about a year for a colonoscopy at a VA hospital and died because by the time he got one, doctors found that he had Stage Four cancer and was terminally ill. She asked Obama what he was doing to fulfill his promise.

In response to her question, Obama said that "we have, in fact, fired a whole bunch of people" who ran VA facilities where there were cover-ups and other problems. In fact, according to the *Washington Post*'s Fact Checker, only three senior officials who ran facilities had been fired since Obama promised to fix the problems.

Veterans Affairs secretary David J. Shulkin had a unique perspective. A former Army psychiatrist who served as the president and chief executive officer of Beth Israel Medical Center in New York City, Shulkin was Obama's pick as the department's undersecretary for health. When Trump entered the White House, he named Shulkin VA secretary.

"I have found that mandate from him, to get this organization fixed and the support and freedom to go out and challenge old assumptions, is exactly what the VA needs right now," Shulkin said when asked about the difference between Trump and Obama. Now that Trump is president, "I think the organization feels more empowered to fix problems than they have in the past, and my hope is that we will be able to set the path so that the organization is earning back that trust that it needs," Shulkin told the *Washington Examiner.*

Trump looks at the VA as a business and "understands that you need to allow the manager of the business to have the freedom to go out and to challenge assumptions and to make decisions," Shulkin said. Trump "did not come in to make incremental change. He came in to set a fundamental different course in direction when it comes to providing services to veterans," Shulkin noted. "Acting quicker and more decisively is part of that management style."

Trump invited to the White House Brian Krzanich, CEO of Intel, who announced plans to invest seven billion dollars to build a new factory that would provide three thousand high-paying new jobs. Krzanich said that while plans had been discussed for some time for the new factory, he decided to go ahead with the project specifically because he believed Trump's policies would encourage economic growth.

As Trump pressured automakers to invest in the United States, Fiat Chrysler and General Motors announced plans to open new plants in America instead of Mexico or other countries. On Twitter, Trump badgered specific companies about moving jobs overseas. He called in the chief executive of Lockheed Martin to complain about the cost of the F-35 fighter jet. As a result, Lockheed Martin agreed to sell ninety new F-35 fighter jets to the Defense Department for $8.5 billion, a reduction in cost of more than $700 million over the last batch of aircraft delivered. Lockheed Martin credited Trump with helping to "accelerate negotiations" and "drive down the price" of what is already the most expensive weapons program in history.

By using the bully pulpit of the White House, Trump reintroduced the idea that "Made in the USA" was a proud symbol that Americans should embrace. And his speeches encouraged American companies to think twice about relocating plants to other countries.

To promote American industry and raise American wages, Trump withdrew from the Trans-Pacific Partnership but said he would negotiate new trade deals that are fairer to the United States with individual countries. He canceled restrictions on the production of oil, natural gas, and clean coal. Meanwhile, he signed a $110 billion deal to supply Saudi Arabia with top-tier military equipment and services, including missiles, bombs, armored personnel carriers, combat ships, missile defense systems, and munitions.

"That was a tremendous day," Trump said after signing the Saudi agreement. "Tremendous investments in the United States. Hundreds of billions of dollars of investments into the United States and jobs, jobs, jobs."

A year after Trump was elected, the economy came roaring back, with a red-hot stock market and historically low unemployment numbers. Just in the last two years of Obama's presidency, his administration imposed 7,000 new rules and regulations. In his first eight months in office, Trump knocked out 860 of them.

As the *Wall Street Journal* aptly noted, the "biggest change has been in U.S. economic policy, notably the Trump administration's deregulatory efforts and the boost they have given business confidence. Barack Obama's economists dismissed regulation as a minor concern, and even called it a boon to growth, but the costs of compliance were real and added to uncertainty. Businesses held back because they didn't know how or when government might strike next, which contributed to historically low levels of capital investment in this expansion."

7

MELANIA

It was at Manhattan's trendy Kit Kat Club that Donald Trump first met Melania Knauss in September 1998. He was fifty-two years old and a billionaire. She was a twenty-eight-year-old model.

Then living in a one-bedroom Manhattan apartment, Melania was no party girl but later explained, "It was Fashion Week, and it was a fashion party, and we were both invited, and that's where we met."

Trump brought a date to the party. At the time, Trump was separated from Marla Maples, whom he divorced in 1999. Having spotted Melania at the party, Trump took advantage of his date's trip to the ladies' room to chat her up. However, Melania knew of Trump's reputation, confirmed by the fact that he had come to the party with a date and was now asking for her number. Melania refused. Instead she asked Trump for his contact information.

"If I give him my number, I'm just one of the women he calls," she remembered. Melania wanted to see if he would offer a business number. "I wanted to see what his intention is. It tells you a lot from the man what kind of number he gives you. He gave me all of his numbers." They had "a great connection, we had great chemistry, but I was not starstruck," she said. "And maybe he noticed that."

Melania told her best friend, Edit Molnar, a fellow model, about the encounter. Molnar said Melania was turned off by the fact that Trump had asked her out while with another woman. Giving him her number was "absolutely out of the question."

"Melania said, 'He's here with a woman. I am absolutely not giving him my number,'" recalled Molnar. "She wouldn't even consider it."

Back at Trump Tower, Donald told his longtime aide Norma Foerderer about her.

"He said he met a beautiful, beautiful, fantastic girl at a party in New York," Foerderer told me. "He thought she was stunning, and she was a brunette, not a blonde."

Melania called him when she returned from a modeling trip, and they began dating. In the early stages of their relationship, Melania was on her way into Trump's triplex in Trump Tower for a trip they had planned that afternoon to Mar-a-Lago. Out came Kara Young, a model whom Trump had dated for almost two years before meeting Melania.

Melania walked into the apartment and broke up with Donald on the spot.

"Women were positively shameless in pursuing Donald—but

not Melania," Foerderer said. "To see these women throw themselves at him . . . no shame."

Indeed, when Hillary Clinton said in a BBC interview that Trump, based on his own statements in the *Access Hollywood* audio recording, was an "admitted sexual assaulter," she overlooked the fact that in boasting about touching women's private parts, Trump was making it clear that the women in question welcomed his advances and therefore the encounters were consensual. "And when you're a star, they let you do it," Trump said on the tape. "You can do anything."

But Melania was no groupie and meant what she said. Trump may have billions, but he was not going to push her around. She called Mar-a-Lago to have her clothes returned to her, impressing Trump and spotlighting her character.

"She called me and asked me to please pack up her things and send them back with Mr. Trump, and I said okay," Trump's former butler Tony Senecal recalls. "And then I cleared it with him. He said do what she wants. So I packed up her stuff, and they went up on the plane."

Over the course of the next week, Trump wooed her back, promising to be monogamous. "The next week, she was back," Senecal remembers. "When she called me, her suitcases were still on the plane in New York. When they came back and she came back, I just carried them back into the mansion kind of laughing."

Originally Melanija Knavs, Melania was born April 26, 1970, in Slovenia, then part of Yugoslavia. She Germanized her name to Melania Knauss. Her father, Viktor Knavs, is a onetime auto dealership manager. Her mother, Amalija Ulčnik, worked developing patterns at a factory that manufactured children's clothing. They met when Viktor was the chauffeur for a nearby town's mayor, and they married in 1966.

Amalija spent evenings after work sewing clothing for herself and her two daughters, Ines and Melania. Once she learned to draw, Melania sketched her own designs, and her mother or sister sewed them. Melania also made her own jewelry.

Melania's parents arranged for her to attend a technical high school before she went on to the University of Ljubljana to study architecture. Having begun modeling at the age of sixteen, she signed with her first modeling agency in Milan at the age of eighteen. Working in Paris and Milan, she appeared on the covers of European editions of *Vogue*—an exotic, dark-haired Slavic beauty.

In Milan, Melania met Paolo Zampolli, founder of ID Models Management, who invited her to join his agency in the United States. He told the *New York Post* in 2005 that she was a "homebody" and not a "party girl" like many young models. When Melania wasn't modeling. she spent her time reading, watching old movies on television, and designing clothes.

"It was unusual for her to go out. She never went to clubs or bars," Zampolli said. "She never dated anyone in New York before Donald. She only went to movies by herself and to the gym."

After arriving in New York City in 1996, her image appeared on a Camel cigarettes billboard in Times Square. The leggy beauty began posing in the catalogs of Lord & Taylor and Bergdorf Goodman.

Zampolli described the future Mrs. Trump as determined and very professional when it came to her career.

"This is a woman who modeled for Camel cigarettes on a huge billboard in Times Square but stayed home all the time," he said. "She was absolutely business oriented. She took her career very seriously. She came to do a job. She didn't come for any other reason. So she was doing what a model should be doing—go to the gym and go to work."

Soon, the biggest names in fashion photography were shooting her, and she was gracing the covers of *Vogue*, *Harper's Bazaar*, *British GQ*, and *New York* magazine. Her major layouts included the *Sports Illustrated* swimsuit issue, *Allure*, *Glamour*, *Vanity Fair*, and *Elle*, and she appeared in TV commercials.

Manolo Blahnik, the designer of sexy, expensive women's shoes, called her a "true beauty" and declared, "She has IT."

On January 22, 2005, a little over six years after they met, Trump and Melania were married in Palm Beach at the Episcopal Church of Bethesda-by-the-Sea. When Trump considered having their wedding televised, Melania put her foot down. The offer to broadcast the wedding had come from NBC, home of Trump's *The Apprentice*.

Melania registered for her wedding at Frette, the Upper East Side luxury linen store, where she asked for sets of cream-white, 500-count cotton bedsheets from Italy, $1,195 for a set. Trump bragged that he paid $1.5 million for her diamond ring after getting a 50 percent discount.

Melania's older sister, Ines Knauss, an artist, was Melania's maid of honor. The bride wore an embroidered couture dress from Christian Dior whose ornamentation alone required more than five hundred hours of stitching, at a cost estimated at more than $100,000. For her "something old," Melania carried rosary beads that are a family heirloom.

The press and the paparazzi were out in force, with helicopters buzzing the celebration and shooting photos of the dozens of celebrities. The 350 guests who attended the reception at Mar-a-Lago included Bill and Hillary Clinton, Rudolph W. Giuliani, Barbara Walters, and Tony Bennett. Billy Joel sang "Just the Way You Are."

As for their honeymoon, Trump said in an interview with Larry King on CNN shortly after the wedding, "Why would we leave Palm Beach? We have the most beautiful palm trees—they don't call it Palm Beach for no reason. So why are we going to leave the gorgeous, beautiful house called Mar-a-Lago and venture out onto some tropical island where things aren't clean?"

Vogue concluded that Donald was "lucky" to marry Melania and said that the designer Tom Ford had suggested that she do something about his often joked-about hair.

Her response: "I like him the way he is."

Asked by Larry King if Trump is a control freak, Melania said, "I don't think so. Maybe he makes demands in his business because he needs to. You know, he's kind of a general. He needs to have people in line. But not at home. We are very equal in the relationship, and that's very important. You know, to marry a man like Donald is—you need to know who you are, and you need to be very strong and smart and, you know, he needs to know that he could rely on me sometimes."

Sophisticated, poised, and beautiful, Melania Trump is the second first lady to have been born outside the United States. The first was Louisa Catherine Johnson Adams, the wife of the sixth president, John Quincy Adams. She was born in London. Melania has another distinction: She is the only first lady to have posed nude.

"We have incredible sex at least once a day," Melania told shock jock Howard Stern over the phone in 2000. "Sometimes even more." Asked what she was wearing, Melania said, "Not much." Trump boasted to Stern about how she looks in a very small thong. Melania shrugged it off.

The couple claims they have never argued.

"We literally have never had an argument. Forget about the word 'fight,'" Trump told Larry King. "We just are very compatible. We get along. . . . I work very hard from early in the morning till late in the evening. I don't want to go home and work at a relationship."

Work is Trump's passion, Melania said. "I don't want to change him. I don't want to say, come home and you know, be with me. I don't want to change him. I want to give him space, and I think that's very important in the relationship."

While she doesn't have to worry about money, Melania said that growing up, "You always taking care of the money." She said she is not a big spender and doesn't buy an item unless she likes it a hundred percent.

"You know, I made a lot of money myself," Melania said. "So, it's like, I know how it is to work and what money means. So, it's not that I would say, okay, now I will have the latest bag. I want that bag, and then in one month, that bag will be in the closet, and it's not even . . . in fashion. I'm not into that."

"She has the perfect proportions—five feet eleven, 125 pounds—and great boobs, which is no trivial matter," Trump boasted to Howard Stern. He said he appreciates Melania's restraint when it comes to shopping.

"She's never taken advantage of that situation, okay, as many women would have, frankly," Trump said.

"I prefer quality over quantity," she said.

Melania scoffs when asked if she had had a breast augmentation or other plastic surgery.

"I didn't make any changes," she has said. "A lot of people say I am using all the procedures for my face. I didn't do anything. I live a healthy life, I take care of my skin and my body. I'm against Botox, I'm against injections. I think it's damaging your face, damaging your nerves. It's all me. I will age gracefully, as my mom does."

Melania has said the key to the success of her marriage is separate bathrooms.

In March 2006, their son, Barron, was born. That same year, she "proudly" became a U.S. citizen, as the White House website says.

In an interview with *Parenting* magazine, Melania described herself as a "full-time mom." She said it was the "most important job ever." The fact that after Trump became president, she remained in New York with Barron until he finished the school year underscores that.

Melania's mother, Amalija, a timeless beauty with dark hair and sparkling eyes, and her father, Viktor, portly and friendly, with better English than his wife's, were always present in raising Barron. Viktor would take him fishing off the dock at Mar-a-Lago.

When Barron turned four and started school, Melania unveiled her line of jewelry and watches on the home shopping network QVC.

"She's got an amazing sense of design and an amazing level of intelligence," Trump told the *New York Times*. "She's got great ability, and I want her to run with it."

Melania also developed and marketed a skin-care line, and one of her favorite products was a moisturizer called Caviar Complex C6, which she rubbed on little Barron's body after his bath.

Taught by Melania and her Slovene parents, Barron speaks

Serbian, French, and some German, as well as English. Barron is as gregarious as his father. One day Barron, then age two, was sitting on the couch in the lounge area of Trump's Boeing 727-100.

"We're flying along, and Melania had given him a bottle," Mike Donovan, the pilot, remembers. "He took the bottle out of his mouth and said, 'Do you want some, Mike?'"

When greeted by a club member having breakfast on the esplanade overlooking the main Mar-a-Lago pool, which is heated to seventy-eight degrees like the second pool on the ocean, Barron, then around age seven, called back to her, "Enjoy your breakfast!" Barron's Mac and Cheese is always on the menu at Mar-a-Lago.

Every morning, Trump would read the papers with Barron, commenting on developments. Butler Tony Senecal remembers bringing breakfast to Barron, who was almost three, and to Melania's parents in the living quarters.

"Tony, sit down. We need to talk," Barron said.

Like his father, Barron did most of the talking—about his favorite subject, airplanes.

Senecal and Melania communicated by text. He texted her about Barron's comment.

"That doesn't surprise me," she texted Tony. "Doesn't surprise me at all."

The young Barron would bounce around Mar-a-Lago, telling a bartender to look up in the sky at a certain time for daddy's plane, which he would describe in great detail.

Years later, during his father's victory speech, Barron was understandably nodding off onstage at three in the morning. Based on that, a website started a rumor that he is autistic. Trump nemesis Rosie O'Donnell, a former host on ABC's *The View*, spread the rumor but later retracted it and apologized to

Melania. Schoolmates describe Barron as perfectly normal. Melania has described the boy as "very strong-minded . . . Sometimes I call him little Donald."

Barron understands the need for security and is respectful of Secret Service agents. In that respect, he emulates Chelsea Clinton, whom Secret Service agents considered a model first child. As he bounded out of the owner's quarters at Mar-a-Lago one afternoon, Barron checked in with his agent and gently tapped him on the back before heading off with him to Trump Spa, a towel over his shoulder.

In contrast to Barron, Jenna and Barbara Bush thought of Secret Service protection as a pain and treated agents as the enemy. Even though the agents dressed in casual clothes like shorts and jeans, and most people were unaware of their role, both girls resented having Secret Service agents around. Jenna would purposely try to lose her protection by running red lights or by jumping in her car without telling agents where she was going. As a result, the Secret Service had to keep her car under surveillance at the White House so agents could follow her—a complete waste of manpower. Similarly, when Barbara was attending Yale, she would sneak out of her dormitory and elude her agents.

"These girls didn't want protection," says a former agent who was on their details. "They would try to run from us and hide from us. They'd intentionally try to lose us, wouldn't tell us where they were going. They'd hop in a car and take off, not notify the detail they were leaving."

When you see Melania chatting with Trump at Mar-a-Lago and the couple enjoying themselves, you can tell this marriage will last. In person, the first lady is even more gorgeous than she appears in photographs or on television.

"I think Donald is so happy with her, and she dotes on him and their son, and they're just a beautiful couple," Norma Foerderer told me. "I've never seen Donald quite like this. He realizes how lucky he is. And he is. And she is too, mind you. They're just darling together, and they tease and they laugh. I think I've seen this more now with Melania than with any other wife."

Melania "doesn't have a vast army of friends, but she is such a good friend," Foerderer said. "She is very bright, and she doesn't broadcast her intelligence, it's just there. And she gives Donald good advice. If an issue is directed to her, she'll come up with an answer."

In a segment of Trump's former reality TV show *The Apprentice*, Melania and Trump showed off their lavish Fifth Avenue apartment. With Versailles-like gold leaf decor and breathtaking views of Central Park, the home boasts floor-to-ceiling windows, hand-painted ceilings, fountains, paintings, lots of marble, and two huge gold-plated entrance doors. Real estate experts estimate that the penthouse would sell for at least a hundred million dollars if it were to go on the market today.

Touring the apartment, one of the contestants said to Melania, "You're very, very lucky."

Melania, holding a glass of champagne and motioning toward her husband, smiled and said, "And he's not lucky?"

"I have my own mind," she told *Harper's Bazaar* in an interview. "I am my own person, and I think my husband likes that about me."

"Trump would ask her, 'Honey, do you think we should do this?'" Senecal says. "'Honey, do you think we should do that?' And she would say 'Yes, Donald, yeah.' They have a very equal relationship."

Even during the grueling campaign, Trump and his wife would talk on the phone several times a day.

While the media often portray Melania as brainless, moneygrubbing, spineless, or sickened by her husband, she speaks six languages—English, French, Italian, German, Slovenian, and Serbo-Croatian—and has tremendous influence on the president and his staff. She sits in on key meetings, summarizes the points others make, and has always given the correct advice, according to insiders. In fact, contrary to a report in *Vogue* that she did not want to be first lady, Trump has credited her with urging him to declare his candidacy rather than vacillate about whether to run for president. Otherwise, she said, the polls will not reflect his support because people would not believe that he was serious about running. And she said to him, "If you run, you're going to win."

After he and Melania, in a strapless white dress, descended the escalator at Trump Tower to announce on June 16, 2015, that he would make America great again, his campaign took off. A week later, a Suffolk University poll had him in second place in New Hampshire among the large 2016 Republican primary field.

Like the first ladies before her, Melania makes appearances to call attention to worthy causes. In West Virginia, she visited a day-care center for babies born addicted to opioids. She urged attendees at a United Nations luncheon to set good examples for children. She invited experts and people affected by drug addiction and opioid abuse to the White House for a listening session and told them she planned to "use my platform as first lady" to help as many kids as possible. She took her first solo trip—to Canada—to support Americans participating in an athletic competition for wounded service members and veterans.

Melania kept former first lady Michelle Obama's vegetable garden at the White House, where she encouraged the children helping her in the garden to make healthy eating a priority.

"I'm a big believer in healthy eating because it reflects on your mind and your body," she said before telling the group to "come with me and have some fun." She later pulled leeks from the ground and clipped an artichoke from a nearby plant. "I encourage you to continue and eat a lot of vegetables and fruits so you grow up healthy and take care of yourself. . . . It's very important," she told the visiting children.

Melania's promotion of worthy causes did not stop supposedly pro-immigrant liberals from making fun of her foreign accent as she recited the Lord's Prayer at a Trump rally in Melbourne, Florida. Pro-immigrant comedian Chelsea Handler chortled that Melania "can barely speak English."

Both Melania and Trump picked up on the fact that Angella Reid, who had been appointed chief usher by Obama, was difficult with the White House residence staff. An African American, Reid was the White House's first female chief usher, who oversees the operation of the residence portion of the White House. But Trump and Melania let her go. To replace Reid, Melania announced that Timothy Harleth would serve as chief usher, leaving his position at Trump International Hotel to oversee a residence staff of more than ninety people a seven-minute walk away along Pennsylvania Avenue. With more than a decade of hospitality and leadership experience, Harleth had supervised more than 110 employees as director of rooms at the hotel.

Saving taxpayers money, Melania employs just twelve aides, compared to Michelle Obama's twenty-four. Trump employs 377 people at the White House, compared to Obama's 476.

More than previous first ladies, Melania accompanies her

husband on trips to express empathy for victims of natural disasters such as Hurricane Harvey that hit Texas, Irma that hit Florida, and Maria that hit Puerto Rico. But Melania's most important role never comes out.

"She is a very powerful behind-the-scenes force," Sean Spicer tells me. "I don't think people fully recognize how influential she is and what a grounded political sense she has on her own." Spicer says, "There are times when you're in the room and see it, and she'll weigh in on a decision, and it's not just a yes or no. Instead, it's, look, based on this scenario, here's what makes sense. She always seems to have the pulse on the right move and the right person at the right time. When she weighs in, it's always spot-on. She knows where he is, where he should be, and how we could move an issue."

Whether in the Oval Office, on *Air Force One*, or in the residence, "When she's around and she feels strongly about an issue or an event or whatever it is, she'll make her position known," Spicer says. "The thing is she really thinks about his positioning. Melania knows how to sort of read him and read the situation. She will say, 'This is not good for you. This is not consistent with what you said.' She really has his best interests at heart. She knows when to pick her battles, and she's always entirely right."

Melania reads widely, both publications and articles on the Internet. As she said to me at Mar-a-Lago while sitting next to Trump at dinner, "I read every one of your articles," referring to the ones I send her.

Melania gives Trump both positive and negative articles that she thinks he should read. She also tips him off to people who come off well on TV in support of him.

An independent thinker, Melania does not necessarily take sides with one faction or another within the White House staff.

However, "Melania didn't want Ivanka or Jared or other people coming and seeing the president up in the residence for business. She definitely put her foot down on that," Bannon says.

"I think Melania does all the stuff of being a first lady because she's just very proud of it," Bannon says. "She's very low-key. She's not the type who's doing over-the-top waving. She never tries to draw attention to herself."

While Melania often agrees with the advice of aides, "Sometimes she'd be the first one to weigh in with a point," Spicer says. In some cases, she will let an aide know that she is on his or her side when that person is under attack from her husband and presumably will let Trump know how she feels as well.

Melania lets Trump know when her intuition tells her an unsavory character is trying to gain access or take advantage of him.

"Melania knows who the bullshit artists are," Bannon says. "She knows the promoters, the guys looking out for themselves and not Trump, and she lets him know it." He adds, "You could write something negative about the president. If it had justification, she'll show it to him."

"Those of us who have the privilege to know her and work with her also acknowledge and appreciate how brilliant she is," Kellyanne Conway says of Melania. "She has amazing instincts, political and otherwise. She reads people exceedingly well. Her own story as an immigrant who heard about this wonderful place called America is inspiring. She was a little girl in Slovenia and came to this country to pursue her dreams. She is a successful entrepreneur in her own right, and is a devoted wife and mother."

Stunning though she is, Melania is modest. "Great pictures!

But not the best of me," Melania wrote to me, using a smiley face, of a photo of the two of us at a Trump New Year's Eve party at Mar-a-Lago.

All first ladies influence their husbands and their admin- istrations to some degree. In the case of Laura Bush, "If it's a particular interest of the first lady, we will pay attention to the funding for those programs, and they will always prevail," Clay Johnson, George W. Bush's high school friend and Yale room- mate who became deputy director of the Office of Management and Budget, told me for my book *Laura Bush: An Intimate Portrait of the First Lady*. Johnson said Laura's influence extended beyond budgets. OMB routinely asked for her opinion or suggestions on appointments and on issues affecting agencies that deal with subjects of interest to her, such as education, the arts, women's rights, AIDS, libraries, the humanities, and juveniles with social problems.

Bush himself also bounced policy questions off Laura. "I don't believe he sits down with her and says, 'I have six policy items I want to go over with you,'" Johnson said. "Rather, is- sues come up in informal conversation. She is very smart and very wise and can give him an objective, big picture perspective that after an hour or so with the policy people, he may have lost. As an example, the president will talk to her about civil service reform issues. She will say, 'Do you really want to do that, or do you really want to make a change in leadership at a time like this?'"

Secret Service agents were dismayed to overhear Michelle Obama push her husband to be more aggressive in attacking Re- publicans and to side with blacks in police shooting controver- sies. Having listened to their talk in the presidential limousine, a former Secret Service agent says, "Michelle's agenda goes back to when she said about her husband running for president, 'For the first time in my adult lifetime, I am really proud of my country.'"

Unlike either Laura Bush or Michelle Obama, Melania interacts with aides and discusses policy questions, helping to focus policy or strategy. While Laura is a devoted reader of literary works, Melania devours articles on current events and policy issues. Melania also took control of events on the White House grounds, saying all planning and scheduling must go through her.

Melania has confided to aides that she tries to get Trump to cool it when he feels he is under attack and a counterattack will only make things worse, calling more attention to the problem. A prime example of his self-destructive tendencies was Trump's decision to bring pointless legal action to stop the publication of Michael Wolff's book *Fire and Fury*, hyping its sales. Sometimes Trump listens; most of the time he does not.

The one piece of advice Trump has never followed from Melania is her constant suggestion that he stop sending tweets to his forty million followers, the greatest number of any world leader.

"She would tell him that he shouldn't tweet so much, put the Twitter away, just do not tweet," Priebus says. "No tweeting. Stop tweeting. Slow down on tweeting."

"That might be one area where she won't win," Spicer says. "But that's probably the only one."

At his age, Trump is "not about to change," says Trump's friend Chris Ruddy, CEO of Newsmax Media and a member of Mar-a-Lago. "He won't stop saying things that rub people the wrong way. And he will not stop tweeting—nor should he—though perhaps there should be a process for reviewing his tweets before posting."

8

SCAM ARTISTS

On the 250th anniversary of President Jackson's birth, Trump honored the seventh president as a personal hero when he laid a wreath at his tomb in Nashville. Jackson "rejected authority that looked down on the common people," Trump said in his remarks.

Like Trump, Jackson faced a hostile press. But when it comes to Trump, it would be difficult to overemphasize just how biased and often dishonest the press has become. During the campaign, the *New York Times* ran a page-one story above the fold that depicted what it claimed was "a debasing face-to-face encounter between Mr. Trump and a young woman he hardly knew."

"Donald J. Trump had barely met Rowanne Brewer Lane when he asked her to change out of her clothes," the startling lede said of the 1990 encounter. The story quoted Brewer Lane as saying, "Donald was having a pool party at Mar-a-Lago. There were about fifty models and thirty men. There were girls in the pools, splashing around. For some reason Donald seemed a little smitten with me. He just started talking to me and nobody else."

Then, Brewer Lane said, "He suddenly took me by the hand, and he started to show me around the mansion. He asked me if I had a swimsuit with me. I said no. I hadn't intended to swim. He took me into a room and opened drawers and asked me to put on a swimsuit."

Brewer Lane, at the time a twenty-six-year-old model, did as Mr. Trump asked, the story said. "I went into the bathroom and tried one on," she recalled. "I came out, and he said, 'Wow.'"

All of that was true, except for one problem: The paper framed her quotes to make it appear that her positive experience with Trump was a profoundly negative one.

Two days after the story appeared, an infuriated Brewer Lane was on *Fox & Friends* to totally refute the story's implications. She told cohost Ainsley Earhardt that her agent had invited her to a pool party at Mar-a-Lago at the last minute. She did not have time after a photo shoot to go home before the party and grab a bathing suit. She said she got along with Trump nicely as they chatted around the pool.

"We started walking around the mansion," she said on Fox. "He started showing me the architecture. We were having a very nice conversation, and we got into a certain part of it, and he asked me if I had a swimsuit. I said I didn't."

Trump asked if she wanted one, and he gave her a bikini. As she changed in the mansion, he returned to the pool party. When she returned to the party, Trump said, "Now that's a stunning Trump girl right there."

"I was actually flattered," she said on Fox. "I didn't feel like it was a demeaning situation or comment at all," adding that was what she told the *New York Times*.

Indeed, contrary to the paper's claim that the encounter was "debasing," the story buried in the sixteenth paragraph the fact that after meeting Trump, the model began dating him.

On the TV show, Brewer Lane said the paper took her quotes and spun the May 14, 2016, story to create a negative connotation, when in fact she had told the paper that she enjoyed the encounter and Trump's "boyish charm." She said their relationship continued for several months.

"I did not have a negative experience with Donald Trump, and I don't appreciate them making it look like that I was saying that it was a negative experience because it was not," Brewer Lane said flatly.

In fact, contrary to the story's claim, Trump "never made me feel like I was being demeaned in any way," she said on TV. "He was very gracious. I saw him around all types of people, all types of women. He was very kind, thoughtful, generous, you know. He was a gentleman," Brewer Lane said.

Asked whether Trump ever mistreated women, Brewer Lane said, "Not that I've ever seen. Absolutely without a doubt, no." Moreover, she said, "I think Donald is doing a great job, and he is a very successful businessman. He's a great leader because of that." In fact, she said, ". . . I'm supporting him."

Decades ago, the two *New York Times* reporters who wrote the story would have been fired for writing a clearly dishonest article. But in today's media world, scam artists posing as journalists are not fired and even appear on TV without a sign of embarrassment to defend their bogus work.

Rather than try to refute Brewer Lane's denunciation of their article, Michael Barbaro and Megan Twohey, the *New York Times* reporters who wrote the story, spoke vaguely on CBS *This Morning* about their impressions and intent.

"I recall in my interview with her that she expressed some—she basically said 'I was taken aback by this,' and I think that's how we depicted it," Barbaro said. Twohey spoke of their desire to present "a variety of voices" in the piece. Nor did the paper retract the story after its subject appeared on TV to say its portrayal was false and completely the opposite of what happened.

"Ms. Brewer Lane was quoted fairly, accurately, and at length," a spokesperson for the paper said. "The story provides a lot of context for the reader, including that the swimsuit scene was the 'start of a whirlwind romance' between Ms. Brewer Lane and Mr. Trump."

What the statement failed to mention was that a reader would have to wade through 725 words of the story, headlined "Crossing the Line: How Donald Trump Behaved with Women in Private," before learning that rather than being offended by her encounter with Trump and demeaned by him, she began dating him. If that fact had been included in the lede, exposing the story as a fraud, it could not have been run.

Before the election, the media said Trump was a business failure and broke. After the election, the media said he was so successful and wealthy that his tentacles stretched all over the world, and almost anything he touched constituted a conflict of interest that would benefit him financially. In fact, unless a president keeps his assets in cash under a mattress, any decision he makes may affect his wealth. That is why Congress exempted the president from the federal conflict-of-interest statute. Rather than benefitting financially from his presidential run, Trump took off from his business to campaign for two and a half years and now donates his salary of $400,000 a year to worthy government programs like the fight against opioid addiction.

To further denigrate Trump, the media often claimed that his wealth was inherited. In fact, while his father early on would guarantee his son's construction loans, when Fred Trump died in 1999, Trump was already worth $1.6 billion, according to *Forbes*.

Stories on objections to Trump's plan to build a wall attacked the idea as racist but rarely mentioned that when they were in Congress, Barack Obama, Hillary Clinton, Joe Biden, and Chuck Schumer all voted to authorize construction of fencing and other barriers along the southern border.

On the Senate floor in October 2006, Obama said of the legislation, "The bill before us will certainly do some good." He praised the bill, saying it would provide "better fences and better security along our borders" and would "help stem some of the tide of illegal immigration in this country."

Nor do the stories mention Bill Clinton's comments in his 1995 State of the Union address when he spoke forcefully about the problem of illegal immigration and referred to "illegal aliens," not "undocumented" immigrants.

"All Americans, not only in the states most heavily affected but in every place in this country, are rightly disturbed by the large numbers of illegal aliens entering our country," Clinton said. "The jobs they hold might otherwise be held by citizens or legal immigrants. The public service they use impose burdens on our taxpayers." Moreover, Clinton said, "We are a nation of immigrants. But we are also a nation of laws. It is wrong and ultimately self-defeating for a nation of immigrants to permit the kind of abuse of our immigration laws we have seen in recent years, and we must do more to stop it."

When Trump says almost the exact same thing about illegal immigration, journalists and Democrats slam him as a contemptible racist. The same double standard applied to Trump's announcement that the United States considers Jerusalem the capital of Israel and that the U.S. Embassy in Israel would be relocated from Tel Aviv to Jerusalem. Presidents Clinton, Bush, and Obama all said the same thing and never followed through, but stories condemning Trump's decision as dangerous and foolish almost never mentioned the previous presidents' promise.

Stories condemning Trump's claim that enhanced interrogation, including waterboarding, works never mentioned that in December 2014, President Obama's CIA director John Brennan said, "Our review indicates that interrogations of detainees on whom EITs [enhanced interrogation techniques] were used did produce intelligence that helped thwart attack plans, capture terrorists, and save lives."

Stories on Trump's approval of the Keystone XL Pipeline cited objections from environmentalists but rarely mentioned that if approval was not given due to concerns that the crude oil would contribute to global warming, TransCanada would divert the oil from Alberta to China. There, refineries pose far greater risks to the environment. The stories never mentioned that the United States already has 185,000 miles of liquid petroleum pipelines, which are far safer than transporting it by truck or train. Nor did the stories mention that the protesters who purportedly wanted to preserve the environment destroyed fifty acres of grassland and left so much garbage that it took 250 garbage trucks to clean it up.

Media stories reamed Trump for revealing too much to Russian diplomats in an Oval Office meeting about the roll-up of ISIS's efforts to plant bombs in laptops to blow up airliners. In fact, because Russia and the United States cooperate with each other on counterterrorism matters, exchanging such information between the two countries is routine. But because the arrangements are kept confidential, the White House press office could not rebut the reports that Trump had grievously harmed national security.

Trump did not tell the Russians where the plot had been hatched, and initial reports did not say. But then, in an effort to expose how wrong Trump had been to mention the intelligence coup to the Russians, ABC News and NBC News revealed far more details to the entire world, including that the plot had been uncovered in Israel by an Israeli spy.

The media widely claimed that Trump's ban on travelers from seven countries was a Muslim ban, when in fact it was aimed at countries that do not have a reliable structure for allowing the United States to vet immigrants. Even within the United States, it is difficult for the FBI with a full background investigation to determine if an individual could pose a threat. With no reliable records or sources in a country like Libya, Somalia, Syria, or Yemen, it is impossible. Nor did the stories usually mention that the vast majority of the world's Muslims living in other countries were not included in Trump's ban.

"Newly released records show the trust agreement that Donald Trump used to put his adult sons in charge of his company allows him to draw money from it upon his request, illustrating the thin divide between the president and his private fortune," the *Washington Post* breathlessly reported, as if there were something nefarious about Trump dipping into his own funds.

The media reported Trump's controversial pardon of former Arizona sheriff Joe Arpaio, but both the *New York Times* and the *Washington Post* ignored Trump's comments at a news conference pointing out that Obama had pardoned Chelsea Manning, who was convicted of violations of the Espionage Act after disclosing to WikiLeaks nearly 750,000 classified or sensitive military and diplomatic documents. Nor did they pick up on Trump's reference to Obama's pardon of Oscar López Rivera. Rivera admitted engaging in seditious conspiracy, use of force to commit robbery, interstate transportation of firearms, and conspiracy to transport explosives with intent to destroy government property when he was one of the leaders of the Fuerzas Armadas de Liberación Nacional Puertorriqueña (FALN). FALN was a clandestine paramilitary organization devoted to Puerto Rican independence that carried out more than 120 bomb attacks on United States targets between 1974 and 1983, killing six.

Instead of reporting what Trump actually said, the *Washington Post* kissed off Trump's defense of his pardon by saying, "At the news conference, when asked about Arpaio, he began reading from a sheet of paper, rattling off other controversial pardons under former presidents Bill Clinton and Barack Obama."

"Top Trump Organization Executive Asked Putin Aide for Help on Business Deal," a *Washington Post* headline said. Not until the eleventh paragraph did the story say that the executive, Michael Cohen of the Trump Organization, said that the Russian project was abandoned for business reasons when Russian government permission was not secured and that the failed initiative had nothing to do with Trump's presidential campaign.

A *Washington Post* story declared Trump "the least popular president in modern times" based on a new poll. Buried in the second to last paragraph was the fact that the poll found that if the election were held again, Trump would still beat Hillary, not only in electoral votes but in popular votes.

The press reported any fleeting encounter by a low-level Trump campaign aide with a Russian as a huge story. But the stories never mentioned Brit Hume's statement on Fox News that he once saw Senator Dianne Feinstein, the Democrat from California who is a member of the Senate Select Committee on Intelligence, having lunch in the Senate Dining Room with Sergey Kislyak, the Russian ambassador to the United States.

Nor is Fox News immune to broadcasting misleading information. In an effort to support Trump's claim that he had been wiretapped in Trump Tower, Fox News judicial analyst Andrew Napolitano made the absurd claim that Obama had gone outside of normal channels and appealed to GCHQ, the British version of the National Security Agency, to intercept Trump's communications. That would have been a felony.

Fox ran interviews with experts like former attorney general Michael Mukasey and former federal prosecutor Andrew McCarthy saying that FBI counterintelligence cases, such as the one probing Russian interference in the 2016 election, do not result in criminal charges. Tell that to John A. Walker Jr., a Navy warrant officer; Jonathan J. Pollard, a spy for Israel; Ronald Pelton, a former NSA employee; former FBI agent Robert Hanssen; and Aldrich Ames, a CIA officer, all of whom went to jail on espionage charges as a result of FBI counterintelligence investigations.

The media castigated Trump for threatening North Korea with "fire and fury." Few stories mentioned that back in 1993, then-president Bill Clinton made a similar threat against Kim Il-sung, the grandfather of the current leader. During a trip through Asia, Clinton said about his policy toward North Korea, "We would overwhelmingly retaliate if they were to ever use, to develop and use nuclear weapons. It would mean the end of their country as they know it."

While some of Trump's comments may be misconstrued as racist, in fact they are usually a statement of fact: In announcing his presidential bid on June 16, 2015, at Trump Tower, Trump said, "When Mexico sends its people, they're not sending their best. . . . They're sending people that have lots of problems, and they're bringing those problems with us. They're bringing drugs. They're bringing crime. They're rapists. And some, I assume, are good people." Clearly, anyone who violates U.S. law by illegally crossing the border is more likely to engage in criminal activity than other immigrants.

The stories claiming that Trump is a racist rarely mention that for two years before meeting Melania Knauss, he dated African American model Kara Young. Nor do they quote Lynne Patton, an African American who, until she took a job in the Trump administration, was one of the Trump Organization's most trusted employees as a vice president of the Eric Trump Foundation and senior assistant to the Trump family. Sitting at Trump Grill, an upscale restaurant in the lower lobby of Trump Tower, a few months before the election, Patton told me that she is treated as a member of the family and that Trump is the furthest thing from being a racist or a misogynist.

When she released a video supporting Trump, she was prepared for the backlash she says she received.

"I read on a daily basis the vitriol that family members receive," Patton told me. "Every time they go on TV, it's everything from their looks, to what they were wearing, to what they said, to the color of their tie, to the way their hair is styled."

When the Trump administration named Patton to head the Department of Housing and Urban Affairs' New York and New Jersey office, the *New York Times* headlined the story: "Trump Family Wedding Planner to Head New York's Federal Housing

Office"—because as one of her duties, she had once helped with Eric Trump's wedding planning.

Nor do stories claiming that Trump is a misogynist quote Barbara Res. Trump hired Res in September 1980 to be in charge of building the sixty-eight-story Trump Tower on Fifth Avenue. Forget about female executives in the construction business then; they did not exist. But Trump put his faith in her and told her he wanted her to "treat everything as if it were my project and my money, and I would be his final word," Res told me.

Today, Trump and Melania send Barron to St. Andrew's Episcopal School in Potomac, Maryland, where 42 percent of children enrolled are students of color. Although this fact is listed on the school's website under the "About" tab, no major media outlet has cited it.

From minor to major stories, by my estimate, roughly half of the exclusives reported by the media about Trump have turned out to be wrong. White House staffers did not meet in the dark because they could not figure out how to turn on the lights in the Cabinet Room. Trump does not watch TV in the residence in a bathrobe. Trump did not call then-National Security Adviser Mike Flynn at 3 a.m. to ask him whether a strong or weak dollar is good for the economy. Trump did not hire security forces who were in conflict with the Secret Service at his rallies: They worked smoothly together.

Far more serious, FBI director James Comey did not ask for more funds for the FBI's investigation of Russian involvement in the election, allegedly leading to his being fired by Trump. The FBI never requests special funding for any investigation.

In a talk at a reunion of *Washington Post* employees held by former *Post* chairman Don Graham at the Hyatt Centric in Arlington, Virginia, *Post* reporter David A. Fahrenthold, who broke the story of the *Access Hollywood* tape, strongly implied that he got the audiotape from NBC executives, saying that in that case there was no need to check its authenticity.

"We knew it was valid," he told the more than three hundred former employees on September 28, 2017.

Yet NBC executives killed a story by Ronan Farrow that exposed Hollywood producer Harvey Weinstein's sexual attacks on women and the hypocrisy of the Hollywood elite. They have created an industry of sanctimoniously denouncing Trump at every turn as morally reprehensible but were aware of Weinstein's predatory behavior and did nothing about it.

When it comes to media hypocrisy, there was no better example than when the Associated Press revealed in 2012 that the CIA had developed an asset who was reporting on an al-Qaeda plot in Yemen to blow up airliners bound for the United States. AP's decision to run the story meant the end of the CIA's asset, potentially putting at risk the lives of hundreds of future airline passengers.

The story had no legitimate reason for running: No abuse or failure was involved. The CIA was doing its job to save American lives. Yet the press pounced on the Obama Justice Department when it tried to determine the source of the leak by obtaining AP phone records. It is difficult enough for the FBI to pinpoint the source of a leak for possible criminal prosecution. Yet as a result of the pressure from the media, Attorney General Eric Holder changed Justice Department policy to make it harder for the Justice Department to obtain media phone records in the future.

In September, October, and November 2017, broadcast evening news coverage of Trump was 91 percent negative, according to the Media Research Center. Stories on the remarkable unemployment numbers of the Trump administration and the fact that Trump's aggressive tactics against ISIS were paying off—with terrorists giving up because they had no food and were not being paid—were buried or were nonexistent.

"I think the media have been harder on Trump than any other president certainly that I've known about," former president Jimmy Carter told Maureen Dowd of the *New York Times*. "I think they feel free to claim that Trump is mentally deranged and everything else without hesitation."

In contrast, even though it was based on Air Force records obtained under the Freedom of Information Act, no one in the media picked up the fact that as vice president, Democrat Joe Biden had spent a million dollars of taxpayer funds flying back and forth to his Wilmington home often several times a week, sometimes making round trips from Wilmington just to play golf with Obama, as reported in my book *The First Family Detail: Secret Service Agents Reveal the Hidden Lives of the Presidents*. But the media had a field day running stories about Trump Cabinet officers flying on government or chartered planes for legitimate government business.

During Watergate, I sat next to Bob Woodward and Carl Bernstein at the *Washington Post* and later joined Woodward's investigative team at his invitation. I know the pressure we were all under from executive editor Ben Bradlee to be fair and accurate. Today, journalists in the mainstream media—where a Pew Research Center poll found liberals outnumber conservatives five to one—simply cannot bring themselves to write a positive story about Trump or to give decent play to his successes.

Honest journalism is not completely dead. The *New York Times*'s exposé of Hollywood producer Harvey Weinstein's predatory behavior toward women and the *Washington Post*'s exposé of Senate candidate Roy Moore's similar sexual conduct with teenage girls when he was a deputy district attorney represented journalism at its best. Contrary to Moore's defense, the women who accused him of preying upon them as teenagers did not suddenly decide to come forward just before the Alabama special election. Rather, *Post* reporters developing stories on his candidacy heard rumors about his sordid activities with teenage girls when Moore was in his thirties. They tracked down the women and persuaded reluctant victims of Moore's predatory behavior to tell their stories.

But when it comes to political reporting, the liberal media bias is pervasive and "all runs counter to President [Donald] Trump," says former National Public Radio CEO Ken Stern. "When you are liberal, and everyone else around you is as well, it is easy to fall into groupthink on what stories are important, what sources are legitimate, and what the narrative of the day will be."

9

DEAL MAKER

Back in May 1989, Trump invited Brad Blakeman, who was in charge of advance work for President George H. W. Bush's trips to New York, to join him for a cruise around Manhattan on his yacht the *Trump Princess*.

Borrowed by Hollywood for the James Bond movie *Never Say Never Again*, the 282-foot boat was originally named the *Nabila* by its owner, Saudi arms dealer Adnan Khashoggi, after his daughter. Time-Life books called it "the most opulent modern yacht afloat." When Khashoggi ran into financial problems, he sold the yacht to the Sultan of Brunei, who later sold it to Trump.

With chamois-leather ceilings and walls, the yacht is estimated to be worth $250 million. It has the requisite swimming pool, surrounded by lounges that rise into the air, allowing for better tanning, plus a discotheque, a sauna, a fully equipped operating room, a movie theater, and a helipad. It requires a forty-member crew and has eleven cabins for twenty-two passengers.

As they boarded the yacht at the Water Club dock on the East River, Trump greeted Blakeman and the twenty other guests. While drinks and hors d'oeuvres were being served, an aide told Blakeman that Trump wanted to talk to him.

"I know all about you," Trump said to Blakeman as he stood next to the captain on the bridge. "You handle all President Bush's trips to New York. I need a favor, and I was told that you can do it."

"What do you need?" Blakeman asked.

"I just bought the Plaza Hotel, and I would like that to be the official hotel of the president in New York. No more Waldorf," Trump said. "We'll roll out the red carpet. Anything the president needs, you'll get. We'll do a much better job than the Waldorf. The Plaza is a much finer hotel. Will you do that for me?"

"I'm sorry. That's not going to be possible," Blakeman said.

"Why? You're the guy in New York. You handle all his trips," Trump said.

Blakeman explained that when Bush was the U.S. ambassador to the United Nations, he stayed in the Waldorf's apartment for the American ambassador to the U.N. It was his second home. He knew the shoeshine man, he knew the telephone operators. He was not going to want to stay at another hotel.

However, Blakeman said he would let Bush know of the invitation. He also requested that the Secret Service and White House Communications Agency do a site survey of the Plaza Hotel. After that, the president's political staff agreed to hold a fund-raiser at Trump's hotel. When Blakeman let Trump's office know, an aide said Trump would be chairman of the fund-raiser.

"Mr. Trump was cochair of the event, inviting his friends and contacts, and it was tremendously successful," Blakeman says.

"I'm very appreciative of your help in making the hotel a presidential headquarters," Trump wrote to him afterward. "I'm sure that the Plaza Hotel with its outstanding staff will more than meet the expectations of the advance team."

Trump no longer owns the *Princess*, having decided that boats are too slow for his taste. He sold it to Saudi prince Al-Waleed bin Talal. But as president, he uses the gems of his kingdom—his crown jewel Mar-a-Lago, as well as the White House, *Air Force One*, and his golf courses—as no previous president has done to forge relationships and woo to his side congressional, business, and world leaders.

In June 2006, I asked Trump what would be the first thing he would do if he were president.

"As president, I would invite to my first state dinner all of the people who are our friends and many of the people who are enemies to see if we can work things out," he said.

Once in the White House, Trump put his game plan into action. By inviting Chinese president Xi Jinping to Mar-a-Lago in April 2017 for a two-day summit in an informal resort setting, Trump was able to establish a mutually beneficial relationship that eventually led in part to China's taking the unprecedented step of voting in the United Nations to impose sanctions on North Korea and to cut off banking ties with the rogue state. After meeting with the Chinese leader subsequently during his Asia trip, Trump and Xi Jinping announced more than $250 billion in deals between the two countries across industries such as energy, technology, and aviation.

Trump later said that it was at Mar-a-Lago, over the "most

beautiful piece of chocolate cake that you've ever seen," that he informed the Chinese leader about the fifty-nine cruise missile strikes he had just authorized against Syria.

Two months earlier, Trump had entertained Japanese prime minister Shinzo Abe at the estate and played twenty-seven holes of golf with him at Trump International Golf Club in West Palm Beach, a ten-minute drive from Mar-a-Lago, and at Trump National Golf Club in nearby Jupiter.

The press stirred a minor controversy by claiming that because the two leaders were seen peering at a laptop screen after dinner on the Mar-a-Lago terrace, they were discussing classified information about the missile North Korea had just launched toward Japan.

In an article headlined "Trump Turns Mar-a-Lago Club Terrace into Open-Air Situation Room," the *Washington Post* said, "Trump became president, in part, because of Democrat Hillary Clinton's neglect of information security."

But White House aides told me Trump had been briefed on the missile launch at a secure location, and the two leaders were discussing a joint statement they were about to issue. No classified material was being discussed.

As he did with other world leaders, Trump played cat and mouse with the Chinese leader, sometimes threatening to impose tariffs on Chinese imports or denouncing China's lack of cooperation in pressuring North Korea, sometimes praising the Chinese leader for progress in taking on North Korea.

Whether because of ignorance or bias, few in the media seemed to get the fact that Trump was a deal maker who candidly described his approach in his many books. In *How to Get Rich*, Trump said, "The best negotiators are chameleons. Their attitude, demeanor, approach, and posture in a negotiation will depend on the person on the other side of the table. A good tactic for negotiation is to distract the other side."

"The guy is fairer than hell," says Gary J. Giulietti, a longtime Trump friend who is a consultant to Trump on insurance issues as a partner of Lockton Cos., the world's largest privately held insurance brokerage company. "He wants the best for his properties, he wants a competitive price. But he treats everyone with respect. Whenever he has to honor anything, he does. Even if he disagrees, he will compromise. If you don't like him, he wants you to like him. Because of his bravado, I think people assume the worst."

When negotiating, Giulietti says, "He'll fight you like a dog, but when you make a deal, he'll find a way to make you his friend to work with you."

Even if he decides he cannot do a deal, "If he thinks you've done something for him and improved his lot, he'll find a fair way to show his appreciation for the work and effort you put in to making a proposal, either giving you business in the future or by some alternative means."

As with Mar-a-Lago, an invitation to the 132-room White House from Trump is a powerful tool. Being invited to a White House reception or hearing an assistant announce that "the White House is calling" has such a profound effect on people that presidents and White House aides must constantly remind themselves that they are mortal.

For the first family, servants are on call to take care of the slightest whim. Laundry, cleaning, and shopping, done. From three kitchens, White House chefs prepare meals that are top quality and exquisitely presented.

If members of the first family want breakfast in bed every day—as Lyndon Johnson did—done. A pastry chef makes everything from Christmas cookies to chocolate éclairs. If the first family wants, it can entertain every night.

Invitations—hand-lettered by five calligraphers—are rarely turned down. In choosing what chinaware to eat from, the first family has its pick of place settings created for other first families. Fresh flowers decorate every room. Lovely plantings—including the Rose Garden and Jacqueline Kennedy Garden—grace the landscape.

Over the years, the White House has been sacked and burned, gutted, extended, modified, improved, renovated, and redecorated. In 1902, Theodore Roosevelt officially changed the name of the president's home to the White House. That same year, the West Wing was added to house presidential offices. In 1909, the Oval Office—the president's office—was added at the southwest corner of the West Wing.

As if to purposely confuse, no one ever refers to the front or back entrance of the White House. Instead, they refer to a portico—an entrance with a roof supported by columns that protects it from the rain like a porch. In 1824, the South Portico was added to the rear of the house, and in 1829, the North Portico was added to the front. Then in 1942, the East Wing was built for the offices of the first lady as well as the White House military office.

When Margaret Truman's piano began to break through the second floor, the District of Columbia's commissioner of public buildings said the floor was "staying up there purely from habit." A renovation, finished in 1952, included gutting the inside of the house and installing a steel frame to support the floors. A balcony on the second-floor level of the South Portico was also built.

Other changes have reflected technological progress. When

John Adams, the second president, and his wife, Abigail Adams, first moved into the White House in 1800 with their eight servants, they had an outdoor privy. In 1803, Thomas Jefferson replaced the privy with two custom-made water closets. In 1834, indoor plumbing was installed. In 1845, the White House got its first refrigerator. Gas lighting came in 1848.

Four years later, a telephone was installed—the number was one—but it got little use because few people had the luxury of a telephone. In 1880, the White House got its first typewriter. To cool the fever of James Garfield as he lay dying from an assassin's bullet, a primitive air-conditioning system was invented for the White House in 1881. Ten years later, the White House got electric lights.

Today the White House is a five-star hotel complete with priceless paintings. In Nancy Reagan's memoir, *My Turn*, she detailed the perquisites that made the White House feel like a palace. "If we needed a plumber, we'd call the usher's office, and he'd be there in five minutes," she wrote. "There were people to wrap packages and wind clocks. And just as soon as the president took a suit off, it would be whisked away for pressing, cleaning, or brushing. The sheets are changed after every use, even a catnap."

Obama rarely invited members of Congress—Republicans or Democrats—to the White House or to ride with him on *Air Force One*. Trump makes it a regular practice to invite them, along with labor leaders, factory owners, police officers, farmers, and veterans.

Trump has had "more one-on-one meetings with congressmen and senators, and more dinners, and more lunches, in a short period of time than any president in history," Priebus says. "Plus he calls them." After several months, "He had had all these meetings with all these people, and he's gotten to know people pretty well," Priebus says. "He made all these phone calls to almost every House member, and that matters. He had had multiple meetings with every senator and lunches and dinners with many of them. He got to know these members like no one could ever possibly get to know them in the first four months of being the president."

Indeed, no president has shown such a willingness to participate in the process and get to know members of Congress, Priebus says. "He doesn't get tired of it," Priebus says. "The craziest thing about him is that he'll keep calling, picking up the phone and calling, picking up the phone. Access to a president and to Trump is at an all-time high."

Rather than being haphazard, Trump's bravado, exaggeration, and controversial comments are a means to an end.

"Through press statements and tweets, he's negotiating, whether it's with that moron in North Korea or the leader of Iran," Giulietti says.

As he learned at Goldman Sachs, "You can only get a deal if you take a hard line," Bannon says. "No, we're not prepared to sell the company under any circumstances. And then you figure out where your deal is. You need to open up a space in the middle for people to be able to negotiate, but you only do that after adamantly taking a stand for one hard position."

While the press likes to portray Trump as impetuous and impatient with details, when it comes to important decisions, he usually weighs options carefully. When Trump tweeted that he was reversing an Obama-era policy allowing transgender soldiers to serve in the military and have their sex-reassignment surgeries paid for by the government, it appeared to be a spur-of-the-moment decision. In fact, the White House had carefully developed options that Trump could choose from to change the Obama policy. After a succession of meetings, aides presented Trump with four options. They ranged from option one, which posed the least risk for legal challenges, to option four, which posed the greatest risk of litigation.

While tweeting a presidential decision was novel, the options had been vetted by the staff secretary and the Principals Committee, the National Security Council's Cabinet-level senior interagency forum that considers national security policy issues. Trump considered each option and made his decision.

Meanwhile, Trump rescinded an Obama administration policy that said students in public schools who are transgender had to be allowed to use the bathroom of their choice. The Obama measure created confusion and the potential for attacks on female students by men posing as transgender people using girls' bathrooms.

"Eighty percent of the time he followed the process, but twenty percent of the time he woke up in the morning and made a decision and tweeted it," a White House aide says. "That's what he does."

10

WINTER WHITE HOUSE

As Donald Trump tells it, he was on his way to a dinner party in Palm Beach in 1982 when he asked his limousine driver about properties for sale.

The driver mentioned Mar-a-Lago, the 110-room estate built by cereal heir Marjorie Merriweather Post. Post had left the property to the federal government in hopes that it would become an outpost for diplomats. But Jimmy Carter, who famously turned down the heat at the White House to sixty-eight degrees, thought the acquisition frivolous.

The deteriorating property reverted to Post's foundation, which could not find a buyer. It was the jewel of Palm Beach, but no one wanted to assume the cost of maintaining the mansion—a million dollars a year, including taxes.

The future president asked his driver to take him by the estate and was mesmerized. He arranged to tour it the next day.

His first offer of nine million dollars was rejected, but three years later, the foundation reconsidered and suggested he could buy the property for five million. He accepted and threw in another three million dollars for the furnishings.

At first, Trump used the estate as his private home, inviting his famous friends like Michael Jackson and Lisa Marie Presley to stay there. In 1995, Trump was able to open Mar-a-Lago as a club, retaining his private quarters as a second home.

Designed by Palm Beach architect Marion Sims Wyeth with help on finishing details from Joseph Urban, Mar-a-Lago is a 55,695-square-foot Mediterranean-style complex on South Ocean Boulevard. It has fifty-eight bedrooms, thirty-three bathrooms, three bomb shelters, a theater, a ballroom, a nine-hole golf course, tennis courts, and a private tunnel leading to the beach on the Atlantic. Atop the mansion sits a seventy-five-foot tower.

For fifty years, Marjorie Merriweather Post reigned as the queen of Palm Beach. Until her death in 1973, she presided over endless parties, supper dances, and balls that lasted until dawn. It was Post who remarked, "There is more money, more champagne, and, of course, more affluence in Palm Beach than all the rest of America put together."

To Trump, owning what would become the Winter White House in Palm Beach represented the pinnacle of success. If you consider the multibillionaires who maintain part-time homes in Palm Beach, it is easily the wealthiest town in the world.

With vigilant police, ubiquitous personal security staffs, and screens of tall ficus encircling every mansion, Palm Beachers protect their impossibly rich society from outside scrutiny. Behind the hedges, the games that Palm Beachers play—their affairs, scams, murders, snubs, intrigues, jealousies, pretenses, bigotry, and occasional generosity—make the seamiest TV shows look like nursery tales.

Beautiful people are everywhere—blondes wearing white tank tops and micro-miniskirts and long-haired, blue-eyed brunettes with bodies that make men's heads spin. The men are handsome, tan, and very fit. Beauty is the coin of the realm, a lesson in evolution. People who do not consider themselves very attractive or very successful do not show up on the island. Those who do are assumed to be wealthy, part of the club.

"If you're here at all, that says something," says Kirby Kooluris, who was for many years a walker, escorting wealthy women to balls.

Accomplished at little more than consuming, the socialites who populate the island look to external trappings to lend meaning to their lives, creating an artificial hierarchy as a way of measuring their own success. Based on wealth, breeding, manners, and dress, they determine who is in and who is out, who will be invited to the top parties, and who will achieve the crowning distinction of having their phone number listed on the twelve-inch-by-sixteen-inch card sent out by the Fanjul sugar barons with holiday greetings. As in high school, those who are excluded—who are "unclubbable," as Palm Beachers say—are devastated. In Palm Beach, people are judged not by their accomplishments but by the quality of their balloon decorations.

The town has only one supermarket—the Publix at 265 Sunset Avenue, where valet parking is free. When an elderly Palm Beach resident lost control of her car in the parking lot, she hit a Rolls-Royce, a Mercedes, a Porsche, a Cadillac, and an Isuzu pickup truck. Alongside the celery and Pampers, Publix sells beluga caviar and Cristal champagne at over $200 a bottle.

One evening at Ta-boó, Palm Beach's trendiest restaurant and bar on Worth Avenue, a waiter rushed to the night manager with an urgent request.

"I have to have some Twinkies," the waiter said. "This guy at table four is going to pay me $500 [equal to almost $1,000 in today's dollars] if I can get him Twinkies in half an hour."

"Cut me in, and I'll send for the Twinkies," Kevin O'Dea, the night manager, said.

When the Twinkies arrived, the pastry chef put the Twinkies on a large plate and surrounded them with raspberry sauce and whipped cream.

"He not only paid $500 for the Twinkies, he tipped $175 on a $600 check," O'Dea said.

In her office on Sunrise Avenue, Ann Zweig, a Palm Beach caterer, laughingly recalled what happened when she mentioned to an heir to a major fortune in Palm Beach that Ivana Trump needed a butler.

"Ivana Trump needs a butler? Me! I always wanted to make it with Ivana Trump," the man said.

" 'My God. You don't know how to be a butler,' " Zweig said.

"What do you mean?" the man said. "I've had one all my life."

The trust fund baby applied for the job and was hired. He donned a white jacket and white gloves for a party.

"Amongst the guests was his mother," Zweig said. "He didn't stay long."

For some, the socializing can be a strain. Charles H. "Carl" Norris Jr. blamed commuting to Palm Beach during the season for the breakup of his sixteen-year marriage to Diana Strawbridge Wister.

Wister, who at the time was worth $900 million from Campbell's Soup Co. stock, had met Carl when he worked on her legal affairs when he was with a Philadelphia law firm. At the time, she was married to a fox hunter.

Besides a home on Lake Worth in Palm Beach, the couple had a house in Vail, a sprawling estate called Runnymede Farm in Coatesville, Pennsylvania, and property in Mount Desert Island, Maine, a summer haunt of blue bloods.

During the divorce proceeding, Diana testified that each home was staffed at all times with social secretaries and servants in case she dropped by. In some years, she conceded, the couple spent $600,000 on clothing alone.

Asked why she failed to answer her door at her Palm Beach home when a deputy sheriff arrived to serve her with divorce papers, Diana was perplexed. Then she smiled as the meaning of the question dawned on her. It would never occur to her to answer a doorbell.

"That is the duty of the household staff. I've never answered a door," she said.

Joseph P. Kennedy, the founder of the Kennedy dynasty, had his home in Palm Beach at 1095 North Ocean Boulevard. Until his death in 1969 at the age of eighty-one, Joe would be described in print as a Horatio Alger hero and chaste Roman Catholic, a saloonkeeper's son who rose from East Boston to become one of the richest men in America. Usually, he would be pictured with his wife, Rose, and one or more of his nine children. The pictures never showed his well-sculpted, green-eyed Hyannis Port secretary, Janet Des Rosiers, who was his mistress for nine years.

The safety, the money, the sunsets, the lushness, the balmy weather, the unblemished streets, the lack of purpose all combine to create a feeling of floating. Instead of discussing the latest horror in Washington, Palm Beachers chat about the weather forecast or the traffic problems caused by Trump's winter visits to Mar-a-Lago. Sheltered on what Cleveland Amory called "an island of privilege, in many ways the most remarkable one left in this country," they tend to be trusting, open, almost childlike. When choosing jurors, prosecutors in the Palm Beach County State Attorney's Office told me they try to avoid Palm Beachers: They are too cut off from reality. Only the daily paper and television offer a reminder that most married couples do not own matching Rolls-Royces.

As part of the research for my 1999 book *The Season: Inside Palm Beach and America's Richest Society*, my wife, Pamela Kessler, a former *Washington Post* reporter, and I flew down to Palm Beach with Trump on his plane and spent the weekend with him at Mar-a-Lago. On the way down, Trump imitated the nasal, constricted tones of members of Palm Beach's blue blood WASP Old Guard who condemned his club because it admitted blacks and Jews.

Letting his guard down for once, Trump explained, "I want to be loved and enjoy sticking it to them."

To this day, there are clubs in Palm Beach that will not admit minorities as members.

"There's nothing like the Everglades Club anywhere in the country," Trump told me. "If you're Jewish and marry a gentile member, forget it. You can only be a guest. They wouldn't let Estée Lauder come in with C.Z. Guest." Asked about the club's policy on Jews, an Everglades Club president declined to comment.

If the members of the Palm Beach Town Council had had their way, there would be no Mar-a-Lago Club. Trump believed that prejudice by Palm Beach Town Council members, some of whom belonged to those clubs, was in part behind their opposition to his plan to turn Marjorie Merriweather Post's 1927 estate into a private club that would not discriminate.

Providing insight into how Trump operates as president, to overcome the town's opposition and get his club approved, Trump used the carrot and the stick. His Florida lawyer, Paul Rampell, who had come up with the club idea and over a period of a month persuaded Trump to accept it, sent DVDs of *Gentleman's Agreement*, a movie about anti-Semitism in the 1940s, and *Guess Who's Coming to Dinner*, about antiblack prejudice, to the mayor and each of the town council members when they tried to impose crushing restrictions on the club.

Their limits on membership, traffic, party attendance, and even photography would have made it virtually impossible for Mar-a-Lago to operate as a club. None of those restrictions had been applied to those clubs in town that discriminated.

The message behind sending the movies was clear: Trump was accusing the town council members of bigotry. On top of that, presaging the way he labels opponents today, Trump publicly referred to the trust fund babies who opposed his plans for Mar-a-Lago as the "lucky sperm club." For good measure, he sued the town for fifty million dollars.

At the same time, Trump unleashed a charm offensive. Guided by Rampell, who is Jewish and a lifelong resident of the town, Trump invited members of the town council to play golf or tennis with him. He invited them to glittering events at Mar-a-Lago, promising the men that gorgeous young women would be in attendance.

For town council members, sending the movies depicting prejudice was the last straw. "It's like saying the emperor has no clothes," Rampell tells me. "Discrimination by clubs was an unmentionable. They expected Trump to bow to them. Donald was the extreme in the other direction."

The town was horrified at Trump's intrusion. Trump represented everything Palm Beach society claims to hate. Trump was not only nouveau riche, he was aggressive and flamboyant. Instead of the conventional Rolls-Royce costing up to $450,000, Trump drove a red Lamborghini, which can zoom up to 180 miles per hour. Instead of wearing the approved blue blazer with no tie, Trump wore tailored suits with white shirts and ties. In contrast to the Old Guard, Trump was not shy about having money. Nor was he afraid to poke fun at the town's traditions and unique culture.

"It's amazing," Trump said of the International Red Cross Ball, which he has attended every year and is the highlight of the season. "It's from a hundred years ago. It's like a religion to them," he told me. "They worry about this 365 days a year. It's incredible. Only in Palm Beach."

Trump spent millions renovating Mar-a-Lago. He employed Richard Haynes, whose father originally gilded Mar-a-Lago, to do nothing but replicate and restore the estate's artistic touches. Using gold leaf thinner than tissue paper, Haynes regilded forty rams' heads that jut from the roof line. Trump spent $100,000 on four gold-plated bathroom sinks near the ballroom.

Showing off his bedroom, Trump said to me, "This is Marjorie's room. It's exactly as it was. Central air-conditioning has been put in."

Melania has redecorated the bedroom and the rest of the private quarters, which Trump calls the owner's wing. She arranged to buy the draperies in the forty-five-room John Kluge estate in Charlottesville, Virginia, and had them hung in the bedroom. Trump later bought the Kluge estate, which was once listed for sale at a hundred million, for $6.7 million and turned it into a bed-and-breakfast called Albemarle Estate at Trump Winery. A room goes for $405 a night in the spring. Trump already owned the vineyard, winery, and much of the land surrounding the house, which he also purchased for a fraction of their value about a year earlier. Trump now features the estate's Trump Sparkling Blanc de Blanc at his Mar-a-Lago New Year's Eve party.

As in the White House, Trump is a hands-on manager who pays attention to detail. When we stayed at Mar-a-Lago for the book on Palm Beach, Trump was developing plans to build a second pool with cabanas and a grill along the beach on the ocean. Besides steaks, hamburgers, and hot dogs, the menu for what Trump calls the Beach Club includes Jared's Chopped Salad, a delicious mix of crisp romaine lettuce, roasted corn, chickpeas, avocado, Swiss cheese, roasted red peppers, and tomatoes with choice of dressing. He also designed a ballroom to replace the tent used for shows and social events. The problem was how to present the plan to the town of Palm Beach. Because Mar-a-Lago has been designated a historic site, the town has to approve every detail of any construction. As we sat in on a meeting with his lawyers and architects at Mar-a-Lago, Trump objected to calling the ballroom a ballroom.

"The word 'ballroom' is a hard word to get approved," Trump said to his lawyers. "'Pavilion' is a softer word. Use pavilion."

Trump looked at the architectural drawings. He asked for a black felt-tipped pen. "Here's what I would do," he said to an architect, drawing on the plans. "I would add this—another bay," meaning an alcove.

Trump asked how large the new ballroom would be. He said

Trump and his staff debated whether he should emerge from
his limousine after his inauguration.

First Lady Melania Trump weighs in on policy and strategy.
Trump's aides consider her judgment impeccable.

Trump wants to project a tough-guy image and vetoes releasing official White House photos that betray unguarded moments, as in this photo.

Trump's executive orders rolling back regulations signaled to businesses they could expand and hire more workers, boosting the economy.

Kellyanne Conway is known as the number one
White House leaker. At right is Steve Bannon.

Jared Kushner and Ivanka Trump are the Teflon aides, pushing the most
disastrous decisions of the Trump presidency yet remaining in place.

Reince Priebus, at left, presided over many of the successes
of the Trump presidency.

Former U.S. Marine Corps General John F. Kelly brought a semblance of
discipline to the Oval Office. At left is Sarah Huckabee Sanders.

Trump tells friends that billionaires are constantly asking him
to fix them up with Communications Director Hope Hicks,
a former model, but he refuses.

"I've gotten a sense he always feels under attack,"
Sean Spicer says of Trump.

Unlike Jenna and Barbara Bush, Barron Trump treats his
Secret Service agents with respect.

Trump uses Mink hair spray on his famous hair.

Trump and Melania have long attended the annual International Red Cross Ball at Mar-a-Lago. "It's like a religion to them," Trump says. "They worry about this 365 days a year. It's incredible. Only in Palm Beach."

The author and his wife, Pamela Kessler, have attended Trump's New Year's Eve party at Mar-a-Lago for two decades.

Trump uses Mar-a-Lago as the Winter White House to forge relationships with congressional and world leaders.

Aside from playing golf, Trump works almost all the time at Mar-a-Lago, never following his wife, Melania, to one of the two pools.

he wanted it to be even bigger than originally planned—twenty-two thousand square feet. "It will be the best in Palm Beach," he said. "Do it."

Trump drove a Durango SLT four-wheel-drive vehicle to the site of a thirty-five-foot waterfall being built for his new Trump International Golf Course in West Palm. On the ground were samples of rocks ranging in color from white to red.

"I like the lighter color," Trump said. "I don't like the red. To me, a red rock is more like granite from New England." He asked the construction crew which color they liked, then he asked his staff, Pam, and me. He seemed genuinely interested in everyone's opinions, and when most said they preferred the reddish samples, he decided to go with them.

Now at the Sunday night buffet, while watching football playoffs on big-screen TVs at Trump International Golf Course, 350 to 400 club members devour oysters on the half shell, stone crabs from Joe's Stone Crab in Miami, gigantic cocktail shrimp, lump crabmeat, prime dry-aged steaks grilled to order, barbecued ribs, rack of lamb, veal chop, steamed four-pound lobsters cracked open on the spot, and every dessert from apple crisp to make-your-own hot fudge sundaes, which Trump especially savors.

Still, Donald's favorite food is meatloaf, which is always on the menu at Mar-a-Lago. And when my wife Pam and I sat with Trump at his table at the Golf Club buffet, Jared and Ivanka ate kosher hot dogs.

Like a proud maître d', Trump greets guests and asks if their steak was done properly. A germophobe, he used to avoid shaking hands but now only avoids it when dining.

Rather than being a white elephant, Mar-a-Lago has thrived. It now costs $200,000 to join—up from $100,000 before Trump became president—plus $15,000 a year in fees. In addition, the roughly 450 members pay for dining, shows, and suites where they can stay at $1,000 a night and up. The club opens every year with a Halloween party and closes after a Mother's Day brunch.

One weekend, Jackie Evancho, the young singing marvel who gained popularity on *America's Got Talent*, performed. David Foster, who has won eighteen Grammys and worked with Mariah Carey, Donna Summer, Kenny Rogers, and Céline Dion, introduced her.

Referring to Trump's ego, Foster said, "Out by the pool today, I mentioned to Donald that the weather was beautiful. Donald replied, 'Thank you.'" The host laughed along with everyone else.

Fronting on both sides of the idyllic 3.75-square-mile island, Mar-a-Lago with its furniture and artwork is insured for $700 million. The club brings in $37 million a year in income for Trump. As he wrote in *The Art of the Deal*, Mar-a-Lago "may be as close to paradise as I'm going to get."

While the press hammers Trump for enjoying himself at Mar-a-Lago, the fact is, as he did before he was elected, he works almost all the time, never even following his bikini-clad wife Melania to the pool on the ocean, the one she prefers over the main pool at the mansion. Unlike Obama, who played golf almost exclusively with White House or campaign staffers as well as Joe Biden, Trump plays golf with congressional and world leaders to forge relationships that help achieve results.

"Even before he had any political desires, Trump would come to Mar-a-Lago on a Friday evening, get off the jet, and he was working," his friend Gary Giulietti says. "He was always carrying paperwork. He'd work tirelessly. Next thing you know, he'd have taken a shower, put on a new suit, and come out and would greet everybody there. Whether it was your wedding or you're just having dinner with some friends, he did it every time."

"Work, to me, is going on a two-week vacation," Trump has said. "If somebody says, you have to go away for two weeks, you're going to Africa on a safari. There's not going to be any phones. You know, get me out of here, right?"

At a recent New Year's Eve party held in the same ballroom where Trump and Melania held their wedding reception, the nearly seven hundred guests paid $1,200 per couple to attend. First came hors d'oeuvres and Trump champagne, which has become quite impressive, on the terrace overlooking the pool, cocktail shrimp, stone crab claws, cold lobster, oysters on the half shell, sushi, and caviar lovingly dished onto blini. At a previous New Year's Eve party, the hors d'oeuvres included foie gras seared to order and risotto with white truffles.

After the champagne and hors d'oeuvres, the guests swanned over to the ballroom for dinner and dancing. No one would be hungry for dinner, which included truffle and ricotta ravioli and filet mignon and scallops.

The band Party on the Moon kept the Mar-a-Lago pavilion rocking as guests donned party hats they found at their table. Even Trump's usually reserved wife Melania sported a black paper top hat.

To safeguard the billionaires who attend such events, Mar-a-Lago managing director and executive vice president Bernd Lembcke hires four town firefighters and emergency technicians to stand by. Originally from Germany, Lembcke was the Breakers Hotel's food and beverage manager before Trump hired him at Mar-a-Lago. When Trump began running for president, Lembcke proudly told me he had become a U.S. citizen. Polished and urbane, Bernd has a sophisticated understanding of How Things Work.

In contrast to past New Year's Eve parties, after Trump's election as president, guests for the party ushering in 2017 were screened for weapons, as Secret Service agents struggled to open bejeweled clutch purses. Stony-faced Secret Service agents stood at key locations in the ballroom wearing identifying pins, their hands clasped in front of them so they could react quickly and grab their guns. Other agents were not so obvious, mixing in with the guests and not wearing the traditional audio earpiece.

Sitting on a sofa overlooking the main Mar-a-Lago pool four days before the party, I asked Trump how he likes being protected by Secret Service agents.

"It's great," he said. "I have agents all around me as I'm playing golf, and they are all looking in different directions, so when I miss a shot, they don't see it!"

If Donald had wanted to invite them, he could have attracted some of the biggest celebrities in the country to the New Year's Eve bash. But his guests were old friends—including my wife Pam and me, who are honorary members of Mar-a-Lago, sitting with Donald and Melania at the head table. The rest were club members such as Gianna Lahainer and her husband Guido Lombardi. As revealed in *The Season*, Lahainer's previous husband, Frank, indulged her every whim: He bought her a twenty-five-carat engagement ring from Harry Winston, a white Rolls-Royce Corniche, a thirty-two-carat sapphire, and a twenty-six-carat emerald. In time, Frank contracted leukemia, and he died in Palm Beach at the age of ninety. His fortune was estimated at $300 million. Frank left everything to Gianna.

It was poor timing. Frank died inconveniently during high season, which runs from January through March. Gianna decided to postpone the funeral so she wouldn't miss any of the glittering parties, balls, and receptions that give Palm Beach residents their reason to exist. Instead of having him buried, she had her husband embalmed and stored at the Quattlebaum-Holleman Burse Funeral Home for forty days, until the season was over.

"I wanted to go to the parties," Gianna told me. "He was ninety. I am sixty. So why should I wait? I did everything for my husband. I did his injections. I was faithful."

Three days after Frank's death, Gianna threw a party complete with beluga caviar and Dom Pérignon champagne.

"I went to a party at the Breakers, I went to a party on a yacht with Ivana Trump, I went to a party at Mar-a-Lago," she said. "My new life was going on," she said. "Why should I wait? I would miss the season."

11

MOGUL

On March 17, 2016, Lara Trump, the wife of Trump's son Eric, was in the kitchen of the couple's apartment on Central Park South in New York when she opened a letter just before seven p.m. To her horror, white powder spilled from the envelope onto the kitchen table.

Fearing for her life, Lara grabbed her keys and Charlie, the couple's miniature beagle, and ran the three blocks to Eric's office on the twenty-fifth floor of Trump Tower. By 7:15 p.m., New York City police and Emergency Services teams were swarming Eric's office. They seized Lara's clothing and sent a team to their apartment to confiscate the envelope for testing. A note inside warned, "If your father does not drop out of the race, the next envelope won't be a fake."

Trying to develop leads, Secret Service agents joined the detectives as they interviewed Lara, as well as Eric, who is executive vice president of the Trump Organization, and Lynne Patton, then a vice president of the Eric Trump Foundation and senior assistant to the Trump family.

The powder turned out to be harmless, and the perpetrator was never found.

Typically, Trump gets six to eight threats a day, about the same number as Presidents Obama and George W. Bush received. The threats come in by letter, email, phone, tweet, and fax as well as on social media sites that Secret Service agents monitor. The Secret Service investigates each threat, and if the culprit can be located, the Protective Intelligence and Assessment Division places the suspect into one of three categories. Those considered Class III threats are the most dangerous. They appear to have a serious intention of carrying out an assassination and have the means to do it. For example, they may have had firearms training.

Close to a hundred people are on the Class III list. These individuals are constantly checked. Courts have given the Secret Service wide latitude in dealing with anyone who may be an immediate threat to the president.

"We will interview serious threats every three months and interview neighbors," an agent says. "If we feel he is really dangerous, we monitor his movements almost on a daily basis. We monitor the mail."

If the president is traveling to a city where a Class III threat lives, before the visit Secret Service agents show up at the perpetrator's door. Intelligence advance agents warn him to stay away from the president. They ask if the individual plans to go out and, if so, what his destination is. They then set up surveillance of his home and follow him if he leaves.

"If they aren't locked up, we go out and sit on them," former agent William Albracht says. "You usually have a rapport with these guys because you're interviewing them every quarter just to see how they're doing, what they're doing, if they are staying on their meds, or whatever. We knock on their door. We say, 'How're you doing, Freddy? President's coming to town, what are your plans?' What we always want to hear is 'I'm going to stay away.'"

Class II threats come from suspects whose intentions are serious but who may not be capable of carrying out an assassination. Often, they are in jail or mental institutions.

"He may be missing an element, like a guy who honestly thinks he can kill a president and has made the threat, but he's a quadriplegic or can't formulate a plan well enough to carry it out," an agent says.

A Class I threat may be someone who blurts out in a bar a desire to kill the president and, after interviewing the suspect and investigating his or her background, the Secret Service concludes that the individual was not serious.

"You interview him, and he has absolutely no intention of carrying this threat out," an agent says. "Agents will assess him and conclude, 'Yeah, he said something stupid. Yeah, he committed a federal crime. But we're not going to charge him or pursue that guy.' You just have to use your discretion and your best judgment."

In most cases, a visit from Secret Service agents is enough to make anyone think twice about carrying out a plot or making a public threat again.

When a suspicious call comes in to the White House, operators are trained to patch in a Secret Service agent. The agent may pretend to be another operator helping out.

"He is waiting for the magic word [that signifies a threat to the president]," a Secret Service agent explains. "He is tracing it."

The Forensic Services Division matches a recording of the call with voices in a database of other threat calls. No threat is ignored. If it can locate the individual, the Secret Service interviews the suspect and evaluates how serious a threat he may be. Agents try to differentiate between real threats and speech that is a legitimate exercise of First Amendment rights.

"If you don't like the policies of the president, you can say it. That's your right," a Secret Service agent assigned to the vice president's detail says. "We're looking for those that cross the line and are threatening: 'I'm going to get you. I'm going to kill you. You deserve to die. I know who can help kill you.' Then his name is entered into the computer system."

Since 1917, threatening the president has been a federal crime. As later amended, the law carries a penalty of up to five years in prison and a fine of $250,000, or both. The same penalty applies to threatening the president-elect, vice president, vice president-elect, or any official in the line of succession to become president.

When assigning code names to protectees, the Secret Service starts with a random list of words, all beginning with the same letter for each family. The code names were once necessary because Secret Service radio transmissions were not encrypted. Now that they are, the Secret Service continues to use code names to avoid confusion when pronouncing the names of protectees. In addition, by using code names, agents prevent anyone overhearing their conversations from recognizing the subject.

Generated randomly by a White House Communications Agency computer, the list of code names excludes words that are offensive or may easily be mistaken for other words. However, those under protection may object to a code name and propose another.

Both Donald Trump and Melania came up with their own code names. The president chose Mogul, while the first lady chose Muse. Priebus came up with Badger after his home state of Wisconsin. Vice President Mike Pence is code-named Hoosier for his home state of Indiana, while his wife, Karen, is Hummingbird.

After she was sent a suspicious white substance, Kellyanne Conway began receiving Secret Service protection. As the winner of the 1982 New Jersey Blueberry Princess pageant, Conway chose Blueberry as her Secret Service code name. In addition to receiving the white substance, Conway received threats.

"Most of them are online," she says, "and most of them are very explicit and graphic, and they're sometimes people who have a history of following through but for whatever reason weren't prosecuted." However, she is no longer under protection.

While not protected by the Secret Service, Sean Spicer accepted the agency's proposed code name of Matrix, which Sarah Huckabee Sanders inherited after Spicer left. Even though they are not under Secret Service protection, the White House press secretary and cabinet officers, who may be protected by their own agency's security details, are assigned Secret Service code names to assist in maintaining continuity of government and coordinating protection of those in the line of succession to the presidency.

Unlike Hillary Clinton, who is so nasty to her Secret Service agents that being assigned to her detail is considered a form of punishment, both Trump and his wife treat agents with respect and consideration. In that way, they emulate Barack and

Michelle Obama, who would sometimes invite agents to parties or to share meals with them.

The President's Protective Detail consists of 300 agents, including those protecting the president's family, and assigns twenty-five to forty agents to the president per shift. There are 150 agents on the Vice President's Protective Detail.

As the president moves about in public, six agents surround him. They include a shift supervisor and a detail leader. When the president is advancing, the agents form a box configuration, and if he's moving down a narrow corridor, they form a diamond configuration. Other agents stand post at access points.

As with the president and vice president, agents allow the first lady and first kids a comfort zone: Agents do not sit in on classrooms, for example, but will station themselves around a school and down the corridor from a classroom. In the same way, agents are not stationed in the residence portion of the White House. However, as with the president and vice president, agents accompany the first lady and first kids wherever they go—to soccer practice, to friends' houses, and to vacation spots.

If a president's child is going to a birthday party in a private home, agents scout out the house beforehand. Given that the host vouches for the young guests by inviting them, agents will not screen them with magnetometers or conduct background checks. During the party, agents station themselves in an adjoining room or the basement and sit outside in Suburbans. If an event is an "off-the-record movement" where no one knows that the president's children will be attending, agents likely will not check out the premises beforehand.

While the president makes the last call on his protection, the Secret Service advises him if it believes a venue is unsafe. That happened when Trump wanted to attend the Congressional

Baseball Game after a gunman attacked Republican players at their practice and gravely wounded Representative Steve Scalise from Louisiana. Instead, Trump sent a video message.

Before the president stays at a hotel, an entire floor is reserved, plus the two floors below. Agents sweep the area for explosives, bugging devices, and radioactive material or other contaminants. They check carpeting for concealed objects. They examine picture frames that could be hollow and conceal explosives. They install bulletproof glass on windows, and they plan escape routes from every room that the president may enter.

As many as twenty-five vehicles could compose the president's motorcade. A helicopter hovers overhead, and no aircraft are allowed in the area. For an overseas trip, military cargo planes airlift in more than fifty support vehicles. Fighter jets fly overhead so they can intervene quickly if a plane gets too close to the president's location on the ground. As many as six hundred people could be included on an overseas presidential trip, including military personnel and up to fifty Secret Service agents. Including the White House doctor and other administration personnel, two hundred to three hundred people travel on a domestic presidential trip.

Often, the first limousine in the motorcade is a decoy; the second limousine is a backup. The president could actually be in a third limousine or in any other vehicle in the motorcade. The number of cars in the motorcade depends on the purpose of the trip. For an unannounced visit to a restaurant, seven or eight Secret Service cars, known as the informal package, make the trip. For an announced visit, the formal package of up to forty vehicles goes out, including cars for White House personnel and the press.

When Trump boards *Air Force One*, the military aide carrying the nuclear football can be seen trailing him. The nuclear football is a leather-covered titanium business case weighing forty pounds. Secured with a cipher lock, it contains a variety of secure phone capabilities and options for launching nuclear strikes that the president may authorize.

The president authenticates his identity with codes found on a small plastic card he carries with him. An identical nuclear football is assigned to the vice president to be used in case the president is incapacitated or has died.

Contrary to the lore, the football does not operate like an ATM, with the president or vice president inserting the authenticator card and punching in launch codes to authorize a strike. Instead, along with written options, the nuclear football contains a secure phone to open up communications with the National Military Command Center at the Pentagon. During a conference call, the president or vice president reads the codes from the authenticator card to verify his identity. Military leaders and White House national security advisers then brief the president or vice president on the nature of the threat and the options for retaliating.

"As part of the conference call, the president is told how many seconds or minutes remain if the president would wish to respond, before he might not be able to do so because nuclear weapons will hit the White House or his current location," says retired Navy vice admiral John Stufflebeem, who was the military aide to President George H. W. Bush and later oversaw the top secret program himself when he was deputy director for global operations assigned to the Joint Chiefs of Staff.

If the president or vice president wants to consult the written options, he may do so. If he then chooses a retaliatory option or options, his command is read back to him. When he confirms it, the command center uses the military's launch authorization codes to release nuclear missiles.

Since Trump or Pence would likely have fifteen minutes or less to respond to an impending attack from a country like China, Russia, or North Korea before the United States could be wiped out by nuclear-tipped missiles, the military aide who carries the satchel is supposed to accompany the two leaders wherever they go. Staying over at hotels, the military aide sleeps in a room adjoining the president's or vice president's room.

When Secret Service agents script an arrival or departure from a hotel or office building, they make sure the military aide rides the elevator with the protectee. In motorcades, the military aide travels in the vehicle right behind the president's or vice president's limo. In the event the president or vice president comes under attack during a public appearance, Secret Service agents have standing instructions to evacuate the military aide together with the protectee.

Unlike Joe Biden, Trump never allows the military aide with the nuclear football to get more than a few feet away from him. As vice president, when Biden visited his home in Wilmington often several times a week, he would order the limo with the military aide to keep a mile behind his motorcade. The reason was that Biden wanted to preserve his image as a regular Joe and did not want to be seen with a long motorcade. But if Obama had been taken out and the United States was about to be obliterated by a nuclear attack, even with no traffic, the military aide with the nuclear football could not have caught up to Biden in time for him to unleash a counterattack. For Biden, his image came first.

12

INTRUSION

Prior to the inauguration, Trump and his aides debated whether he and his family should emerge from their limousines during the inaugural parade from the steps of the Capitol to the White House. The Secret Service assured Trump that he would be safe.

As with previous inaugurations going back to Jimmy Carter's, agents chose locations where Trump and his family could emerge from their limousines far away from office buildings. The Secret Service could station countersniper teams and counterassault teams armed with semiautomatic Stoner SR-16 rifles and flash-bang grenades for diversionary tactics at locations flanked by federal office buildings, such as FBI headquarters.

The presidential limousine, known as "the Beast," is a 2009 Cadillac put into service for Barack Obama's inauguration. The Beast lives up to its moniker. Built on top of a GMC truck chassis, the vehicle is armor-plated, with bulletproof glass and its own supply of oxygen. It is equipped with state-of-the-art encrypted communications gear. It has a remote starting mechanism and a self-sealing gas tank. The vehicle can keep going even when the tires are shot out. It can take a direct hit from a bazooka or grenade. The car's doors are eighteen inches thick, its windows five inches thick. The latest model has larger windows and greater visibility than the Cadillac first used by President Bush for his January 2005 inauguration.

But, as I told Trump at Mar-a-Lago just before New Year's Eve, the Secret Service could not guarantee that if he emerges from the Beast, he would not be a target of drones armed with explosives or biological or radiological weapons. While screened with metal detectors, individuals in crowds along the route could have secreted plastic explosives or biological or radiological weapons.

When I urged Trump not to emerge from his limo, the president turned to his detail leader standing beside him and asked him what he thought. Predictably, the agent assured Trump that the Secret Service could handle any problem. Back and forth Trump went between me and the agent, quizzing us on the possible threat.

While most aides were against it, Bannon pushed for the president to emerge from his limo.

"I said, 'You've got to walk down the street,'" Bannon says. "I was a big advocate of that. I was a little surprised it actually happened because I didn't think it was going to happen because so many guys had said, don't do that. But then he said, 'Yeah, I'll walk down the street. Look at Melania. She looks so amazing, and she will be fantastic. I'll be fine.'"

Looking strong and tough is a big secret to Trump's success, Bannon says.

"Not backing down, not being weak," Bannon says. "The worst thing you can tell Trump is that he's weak."

Although more briefly than at previous inaugurations, Trump and his family twice got out of their limousines to walk along the parade route. But two months later, evidence emerged that the Secret Service was shockingly inept and could not be trusted to assure anyone of his or her safety.

At 11:38 p.m. on March 10, 2017, surveillance video recorded a man jumping a fence near the Treasury Building next to the White House security fence. He hid behind a White House pillar before heading for the South Portico. The man, identified as Jonathan T. Tran from Milpitas, California, even peered into a White House window before Secret Service Uniformed Division officers, who guard the White House, recognized what was happening. For more than sixteen minutes, the twenty-six-year-old wandered on the White House grounds. Wearing a backpack, he was armed with two cans of Mace.

Asked if he had a pass, Tran said, "No, I am a friend of the president. I have an appointment," according to a complaint filed in U.S. District Court in Washington. Tran carried a letter addressed to Trump, who was in the White House at the time.

The letter mentioned "Russian Hackers" and said he had relevant information. Tran wrote that his "phone and email communications [had been] read by third parties," and that he had "been called schizophrenic."

Until CNN broke the story a week after the intrusion, the Secret Service covered up what had really happened. When announcing Tran's arrest, the agency never mentioned the embarrassing fact that Tran had managed to wander the White House grounds for more than sixteen minutes before being caught. In the same way, the Secret Service lied when announcing the arrest of Omar J. Gonzalez in 2014, claiming he had not penetrated the White House itself and was not armed. In fact, he had penetrated all the way into the White House and was armed with a knife.

At least a dozen times a year, intruders try to jump the reinforced steel fence around the White House. Typically, half of them actually succeed in entering the White House grounds before Secret Service Uniformed Division officers take them down with dogs or, if they refuse to put down their weapons, kill them. But until September 19, 2014, no intruder had succeeded in scaling the seven-foot, eight-inch-high fence and making it into the White House itself.

Underscoring the agency's arrogance, then-Secret Service director Julia Pierson claimed that uniformed officers exercised "tremendous restraint" in not killing Gonzalez. In doing so, she appeared to think that the public could be duped into accepting the Secret Service's failure as a success. But the agency was not fooling the FBI. Senior FBI officials were horrified by the handling of the matter and found laughable the Secret Service's effort to cover up its own failure by brazenly hailing the officers' "restraint."

Gonzalez not only entered the White House but was able to run through most of the main floor, passing by the staircase to the residence portion and entering the East Room. Finally, a uniformed officer managed to tackle Gonzalez and take him to the ground near a door to the Green Room on the south side of the White House.

Pierson approved statements saying that Gonzalez had been

quickly detained at the door and that a search determined he was unarmed. The statements were false. When arrested, Gonzalez was armed with a knife.

In the more recent incident, if Tran had been armed with explosives or weapons of mass destruction, the intrusion could have resulted in President Trump's assassination. A Secret Service investigation that was never made public found that, besides officers who were not paying attention during the latest intrusion, sensors around the White House grounds had been turned off because squirrels or birds were triggering them and they were considered a nuisance. Other sensors had been relocated to save money.

"We make do with less" is part of a Secret Service culture that has led to one scandal after another. Since the Department of Homeland Security took it over from the Treasury Department in 2003, the Secret Service has had a lax, corner-cutting, cover-up management culture that punishes the agency's brave and dedicated agents for reporting problems and telling the truth about the agency's many deficiencies and promotes agents who ignore the problems and reassure presidents like Trump that they are safe.

Indeed, nothing has changed within the Secret Service since the party-crashing Salahis went prancing into the White House state dinner back in 2009, or since I broke the Secret Service prostitution scandal in 2012, or since Gonzalez was able to penetrate all the way into the White House armed with a knife before being apprehended in 2014. Going back even further to 1981, under pressure from Reagan White House staffers, the Secret Service allowed unscreened spectators to get within fifteen feet of Reagan as he left the Washington Hilton, enabling John

W. Hinckley Jr. to shoot him and almost take the president's life. Given the laxness and cover-up culture, agents say it's a miracle there has not already been a recent assassination.

On April 25, 2017, Trump appointed Randolph D. "Tex" Alles to be the twenty-fifth director of the Secret Service. Pushed by General John F. Kelly, then secretary of Homeland Security and later White House chief of staff, the appointment seemed ideal. Alles had both federal law enforcement and military experience, having been a major general in the Marine Corps and then-acting deputy commissioner of U.S. Customs and Border Protection.

Trump had had another nominee in mind, George Mulligan, a sharp veteran agent who is chief operating officer of the Secret Service. But "General Kelly wanted him [Alles] in the worst way, and nobody else wanted him," Bannon says.

When he interviewed Alles, Trump was not impressed. Alles volunteered that he knew next to nothing about the Secret Service. Apparently it was too much trouble to read books and articles about the agency or to check out the Secret Service website before meeting with the president. Agents are also unimpressed by Alles and largely ignore him. Alles seems more interested in making friends with agents than fixing the problems that plague the once-proud agency. Apparently co-opted by Secret Service management, Alles proved to be the exact opposite of what was needed to reform the Secret Service.

Alles not only retained the same senior management that produced so many scandals, he has done nothing to change the agency's culture that has led to those scandals and the low morale that results in a shockingly high turnover rate.

Despite the chief recommendation of President Obama's own Department of Homeland Security blue ribbon four-person panel that he appoint a director from outside the agency to change the culture and shake up the agency, Obama chose Joe Clancy, a veteran agent, who did nothing to change that culture. Indeed, Clancy proudly proclaimed in November 2014 after the Gonzalez intrusion that the Secret Service would have a new, more secure fence built around the White House in three years. That fence has yet to be built. In contrast, six months after Trump took office, contractors were offering prototypes for the wall to be built on the southern border.

While Alles indeed came from outside the agency, instead of reforming it, he left its failings intact. As I wrote in *The First Family Detail: Secret Service Agents Reveal the Hidden Lives of the Presidents*, when the White House announced Clancy's appointment as director, "Obama guaranteed that the Secret Service would continue to lurch from one security lapse to another." Instead of one man wandering the White House grounds for sixteen minutes with two cans of Mace, thirty al-Qaeda or ISIS terrorists could have penetrated the White House grounds armed with explosives and WMD.

The latest intrusion was the result of Obama's and Trump's failure to heed the warnings of the DHS panel. If Alles ever read those recommendations, he has ignored them.

The media made much of the extra costs of protecting Trump family members and covering the president on trips. For a family trip in June 2017, Don Trump Jr. and his wife, Vanessa, dropped protection for their family, which includes five children. Vanessa was said to be annoyed at the headache of coordinating the children's schedules with their Secret Service details. But after the trip, their Secret Service protection remained intact. That left forty-one Trump aides and family members under protection, the same number as under Obama. In reporting on the costs, the media rarely mentioned that during his eight years in office, the cost of Obama's Secret Service and Air Force travel expenses came to $106 million, according to documents obtained by Judicial Watch.

At one point, Alles actually proposed the possibility of saving money by withdrawing Secret Service protection of some Trump family members and some aides unless they had actually received a threat. Throughout history, none of the assassinations or assassination attempts has been preceded by a threat.

The entire cost of the Secret Service is roughly two billion dollars a year, about the cost of one Stealth bomber. About a third of the budget is devoted to investigations of financial crimes, and the rest goes for protection of the president, vice president, their families, the White House, national security events like inaugurations, and visiting foreign leaders. Given that an assassination nullifies an election, it's a small price to pay for protecting democracy.

One of the Secret Service's failings is its ingrained attitude that "we make do with less." Instead of reversing that attitude, Alles had bought into it. Instead of visualizing what it would be like if al-Qaeda or ISIS took Ivanka Trump hostage, Alles was worried about deploying some of the agency's thirty-two hundred agents to protect her.

Horrified White House staff immediately shot down Alles's proposal to cut back on protection. Especially given the hatred directed at Trump and his family, the idea that the director of the Secret Service would entertain dropping protection of the president's family members is itself a scandal and all anyone needs to know about why Alles should be replaced before a tragedy occurs.

13

MOOCH

Despite his persona on *The Apprentice*, Donald Trump almost never fires anyone himself. Instead, he makes their lives miserable.

Having given his chief of staff virtually no authority, the president periodically complained to aides about Priebus's effectiveness. Despite the fact that some of his own tweets were most damaging to his presidency, Trump blamed Priebus for not stanching the constant leaks to the press.

Rumors that Priebus was on his way out circulated for months. Trump fed the rumor mill, asking friends and other advisers to evaluate Priebus's performance and tossing around names of possible replacements. Like almost everything else in the Trump White House, it all leaked to the press and provided a constant stream of negative White House stories. Jared contributed by telling associates he believed Priebus was doing a poor job.

But Trump never gave Priebus the power to get it done. Priebus felt the internal chaos was unsustainable. He was frustrated that he could not assert full control over basic White House functions, such as policy development, communications, and even formal announcements, which sometimes were made impulsively by the president.

As in his business, Trump acted as his own chief of staff.

"We kind of run a little bit like a mom-and-pop in that sense," Don Trump Jr. said in a 2011 deposition in a lawsuit involving a Florida development. "I guess there is an organizational chart, but in theory, there is not too many levels." He added, "Could I make one? Yes. Is there one officially? Not that I'm aware of."

But the U.S. government is not a family business. "You can't have a structure where nobody reports to the chief of staff and everybody feels free to pursue their own agenda," Spicer says. "It just doesn't work."

Matters came to a head when Trump in July 2017 named hedge-fund magnate Anthony Scaramucci communications director, bypassing Press Secretary Sean Spicer. Scaramucci joined Goldman Sachs's investment-banking unit after graduating from Harvard Law School. He started his own hedge fund, SkyBridge Capital, in 2005 and remained a comanaging partner until January 2017, when the firm was sold to the investment company RON Transatlantic and HNA Capital, the financial services arm of the Chinese HNA Group.

Jared and Ivanka pushed Trump to hire Scaramucci, who had no experience in the realm of public relations. Being neophytes, neither Jared nor Ivanka saw through Scaramucci's slick self-promotion.

After meeting with Ivanka, Trump announced that Scaramucci would become communications director. Scaramucci, known as "the Mooch," made it clear in a press briefing that he would report to Trump, not Priebus.

In Bannon's opinion, the move to hire Scaramucci was another ploy by Jared and Ivanka to dump both Spicer and Priebus. It was an example of Trump's adopting bad advice. Ironically, Trump had previously rejected several attempts by Scaramucci to join the White House.

"Scaramucci was always shot down by Trump," Bannon says. "Trump said, 'He never supported me. He's a promoter, and I have no interest.'"

Trump pointed out that Scaramucci did not back him in the campaign. He bounced from supporting Governor Scott Walker of Wisconsin, to former Florida governor Jeb Bush, to Florida senator Marco Rubio.

In the early days of the race, Scaramucci called Trump a "hack politician" on Fox Business Network and savaged him for his bombastic and controversial rhetoric. Calling Trump anti-American, Scaramucci said, "And I'll tell you who he's going to be president of. You can tell Donald I said this: the Queens County bullies association."

However, Jared and Ivanka persuaded Trump to come around to hiring Scaramucci as communications director. According to Bannon, Ivanka urged her father to hire him, saying, "We need good press coverage for Jared. Nobody in the press office is supporting Jared."

Scaramucci had been going on TV and defending Trump, which is the way many Trump supporters try to endear themselves to the president. Then Scaramucci got into a spat with CNN over its report linking him to a Russian investment fund managed by a Moscow-controlled bank. The network subsequently retracted its report, and three journalists who were involved in developing the story left the network as a result.

Trump had watched Scaramucci act as a surrogate for him on TV. Based on that, he heaped lavish praise on him to advisers. Above all, Trump relished the fact that Scaramucci was able to get a retraction from CNN.

After that triumph, Ivanka brought Scaramucci into the White House, meeting with him and her father in the late afternoon. On the spot, the president hired him as the communications director, a vacant position.

That furthered Jared's and Ivanka's goal of getting rid of Spicer as press secretary, who they felt was failing to promote them. As part of that effort, they had made sure Spicer was not on the list to meet Pope Francis when Trump traveled to the Vatican. A devout Catholic, Spicer was hurt. Trump tried to tell him that it was a mistake, but the slight was purposeful.

"It was a hundred percent Jared and Ivanka," Bannon says. "They were trying to run Sean out of the White House. They were trying to humiliate him."

What the president did not seem to appreciate was how important it was to Sean to be included in the visit and that it was a slap in the face to exclude him.

In front of Scaramucci, Priebus, Spicer, Jared, and Ivanka, Bannon told Trump that Scaramucci would be a disaster. Priebus and Spicer seconded that declaration.

"I told Scaramucci I totally disagree with his appointment," Bannon says. "You have no skills to be a comms director. It's a skill set and a profession."

Scaramucci gave a White House press briefing that went smoothly. But he ramped up the drama by threatening to fire "everybody" in the White House press office if leaks to reporters did not stop. Scaramucci had once offered Priebus the job of chief operating officer of his company and an ownership interest. Priebus had hooked him up with Scott Walker's campaign, for which he served as finance chairman, yet Scaramucci began disparaging Priebus.

Apparently, Scaramucci blamed him for the fact that he had not been offered a White House job earlier. In fact, Priebus had been holding up a job offer because under ethics rules, he could not hire him as an assistant to the president until the sale of Scaramucci's company SkyBridge Capital was complete and the ethics office signed off on his hiring.

"Scaramucci perceived me as the guy who was solely responsible for hiring, so he thought I was responsible for him not getting a job, not the fact that we had an ethics obligation before we bring people in," Priebus says. Priebus and Bannon had put Scaramucci on speakerphone to try to explain to him why he could not yet be hired for the White House staff, but Scaramucci never seemed to accept the explanation. He seemed to think Priebus was screwing with him. But instead of hiring him for the White House, Priebus arranged for Scaramucci to be hired by the Ex-Im Bank, where the conflict-of-interest rules were not as stringent as for a high-ranking White House aide.

In an interview on Fox News while still in his White House job, Scaramucci complained about leaks and Washington's backstabbing culture. "What I don't like about Washington is people do not let you know how they feel," he said. "They're very nice to your face and then they take a shiv or a machete and they stab it in your back. I don't like it. I'm a Wall Street guy, and I'm more of a front-stabbing person, and I'd rather tell people directly how I feel about them than this sort of nonsense."

For Trump, the final straw was a phone interview Scaramucci gave to Ryan Lizza of the *New Yorker* immediately after a White House dinner with Trump and Fox News people.

"On Wednesday night, I received a phone call from Anthony Scaramucci, the new White House communications director," Lizza wrote. "He wasn't happy. Earlier in the night, I'd tweeted, citing a 'senior White House official,' that Scaramucci was having dinner at the White House with President Trump, the first lady, Sean Hannity, and the former Fox News executive Bill Shine."

Scaramucci demanded to know who had leaked the news of the dinner, Lizza wrote. When Lizza refused to tell him, he responded by threatening to fire the entire White House communications staff.

"What I'm going to do is, I will eliminate everyone in the comms team, and we'll start over," Scaramucci told Lizza, saying that the leak of the dinner was "a major catastrophe for the American country." In Scaramucci's view, Lizza wrote, the leak proved that his rivals in the West Wing—particularly Priebus—were plotting against him. He told Lizza that Priebus would be fired shortly.

On CNN, Scaramucci compared his relationship with Priebus to that of the fratricidal brothers Cain and Abel. Later, in an expletive-laced rant to the *New Yorker*, he described the former Republican National Committee chairman as a "paranoid schizophrenic, a paranoiac."

In the same interview, Scaramucci disparaged Bannon. "I'm not Steve Bannon. I'm not trying to suck my own cock," he said. "I'm not trying to build my own brand" on the president's coattails. "I'm here to serve the country," he added.

In a tweet minutes after talking with Lizza, Scaramucci

claimed that his financial records showing that he had assets of eighty-five million dollars had been "leaked" to the press. Tweeting about the so-called leak, he listed Priebus's Twitter handle, suggesting that he was blaming the chief of staff for what he called a felony. When stories took note of the fact that he seemed to be blaming Priebus, Scaramucci tweeted, "Wrong!"

When going on TV, Scaramucci never missed a chance to work in that he had graduated from Harvard Law School. Yet in talking about the "leak," he claimed he was going to report the "felony" to the FBI and Justice Department. In fact, the financial disclosure filings listing his assets were public records that were online. Even if they were not public records, the FBI would not become involved unless the leak was of classified material affecting national security.

14

ACCESS

With the hiring of Scaramucci, both Spicer and Priebus had had enough. After Scaramucci's position as communications director was announced at a senior staff meeting, Spicer went into the Oval Office and told the president he disagreed with the pick and quickly resigned.

Given his long background as a press spokesman for the RNC and then the White House and Scaramucci's lack of any experience in that profession, Spicer saw it as a personal affront to work for him. He told the president the arrangement couldn't work. Once he had turned over the podium to Sarah Huckabee Sanders, Spicer had assumed his role would evolve into more of a full-time communications director.

Spicer had an impossible job. It was difficult to respond to Trump's misstatements without contradicting him. No communications plan could stay on track because of the president's

Twitter finger. The warring factions of the White House made it impossible to know exactly what was going on.

On the one hand, Trump wanted him to be combative, but then Trump would say he was too combative. Spicer could never get past that first day's briefing, when Trump pressured him to nitpick at a press briefing about the inauguration crowd size. Spicer was also kept out of the loop on why Trump fired FBI director James Comey. He then gave the explanation that Deputy Attorney General Rod Rosenstein had written a memo saying he had no faith in Comey because Comey, instead of leaving it to senior Justice Department officials, had taken it upon himself to decide whether to indict Hillary Clinton. However, Trump undercut Spicer by contradicting that version, saying he had previously decided to fire the FBI director.

"Everyone just assumed, oh, there's no way that anyone would walk," Spicer says. "And I think that was what shocked people, is that I said this is ridiculous. Do what you want, but I'm not going to be a party to it."

Spicer told Priebus, whom he had worked for at the RNC, that he had resigned. A week later, Priebus told Trump that he was leaving as well.

For Priebus, the final straw was when Scaramucci announced he would be reporting directly to the president. Communications was perhaps the most important job in the White House. What was the point of being chief of a staff he could not control?

The president was alone in the Oval Office when Priebus walked in and told him he was resigning. Trump asked him what he thought of General Kelly, the secretary of Homeland Security, as a new chief of staff. Priebus said he thought Kelly would be a good choice. Trump had talked with Kelly the previous evening but did not offer him the job at that point.

Priebus would have liked to have stayed on for a year or two. But he knew what he was getting into before he accepted the job. As Priebus saw it, rather than being ineffective, he was the one who had made the White House work under very difficult circumstances.

"I actually had product that I was responsible for," Priebus says. "There was a product every day. There was the schedule, the meeting, the vetting. There was a product every day that had to be produced. Then there was this speech over here, and the right people were in the room, and the executive orders and proclamations were properly vetted through the usual White House review process."

But the job became a nightmare. For all the chaos that Trump presided over, no one questioned that the logistics, meetings, speeches, vetting, and appointments that Priebus oversaw went smoothly. But when it came to hiring decisions, Ivanka would bring up a comment about Trump someone had made years ago and underscore it with her father. Yet Trump hired Democrats like Gary Cohn on the spot as well as Scaramucci, who had belittled Trump. And Kellyanne Conway, who had no job description except to appear on TV, made it a practice to deride Priebus to reporters on a background basis.

Priebus said in a statement, "It has been one of the greatest honors of my life to serve this president and our country. I want to thank the president for giving me this very special opportunity. I will continue to serve as a strong supporter of the president's agenda and policies. I can't think of a better person than General John Kelly to succeed me, and I wish him God's blessings and great success."

Going back to his days at the military academy, Trump had been drawn to military leaders—"my generals," he calls them—

and by appointing Kelly, the president hoped to bring military discipline to his often unruly West Wing. As secretary of Homeland Security, Kelly had formed a bond with the president that was fortified when he aggressively defended the travel ban policy. Trump told aides that he saw Kelly as someone who dutifully followed through on his agenda—including a border security crackdown and sharp reduction in illegal immigration—and would not cause him problems.

"He is a Great American and a Great Leader," Trump tweeted about Kelly. "John has also done a spectacular job at Homeland Security. He has been a true star of my administration."

After his exit, Priebus gave classy interviews to Wolf Blitzer of CNN and Sean Hannity of Fox News, refusing to criticize anyone. Finally, with Kelly as the new chief of staff, Trump, who was troubled by Scaramucci's profanity-laden interview with Lizza, dismissed him as White House communications director. He had lasted ten days.

Kelly is a no-nonsense leader who does "not suffer idiots and fools," in the words of one colleague. Born in 1950 to an Irish Catholic family in Boston, Kelly enlisted in the Marine Corps in 1970.

As a condition to taking the job, Kelly made it clear to Trump that he expected aides to report to him. Before Kelly took over, aides would either walk into the Oval Office unannounced or gather outside, hoping that Trump would see them and summon them in. Staffers would drift into the Oval Office to push their points with Trump as if it were a Turkish bazaar. That traffic diminished with Kelly, who imposed some order to having access to the president. Aides can no longer linger outside the chief of staff's office, either. White House staff waiting to see Kelly or other senior advisers in nearby suites are asked to remain in the lobby, where White House visitors sit on couches and can read a selection of daily newspapers.

Like the majority of Trump's cabinet picks, Kelly was more impressive than many Cabinet officers in previous administrations. While many like Priebus and Pence were part of the Republican establishment that Trump had railed against during his insurgent presidential campaign, Trump had long ago come to recognize that if he wanted an outstanding Cabinet to move his agenda, he would have to pick candidates with solid experience either in government or in the private sector. At the same time, as part of his promise to "drain the swamp," Trump imposed a five-year ban on executive branch officials engaging in lobbying the government after leaving their jobs. Former government officials were banned entirely from lobbying the United States on behalf of a foreign government.

Kelly devoted his first three weeks to determining how to create a less chaotic environment around the president. In two memos, signed by Kelly and Robert Porter, the assistant to the president for policy coordination and staff secretary, Kelly codified rules and procedures that a White House typically sets at the outset of an administration. While Priebus had done the same, given his lack of authority, they were often disregarded.

One of Kelly's memos told White House aides that all material prepared for the president was to undergo a vetting process first, reaffirming what Priebus's instructions to the staff had been. Then Kelly would sign off on it before it landed on Trump's desk. But as happened under Priebus, those orders were not always obeyed.

The new chief of staff instructed the often-feuding factions in the White House to "get their act together" before bringing an issue before Trump. As was the practice with Priebus, Kelly listens in on the line when Trump makes a call.

At the same time, Kelly made it clear that he would not seek to directly control the president's behavior. Just before Election Day, Trump had blown up publicly on Twitter after the *New York Times* reported that his aides had succeeded in keeping him off Twitter for the final stages of the campaign. Nor did Kelly succeed in controlling Trump's impromptu comments, as when he doubled down at Trump Tower on blaming "both sides" for the racially charged violence in Charlottesville. Kelly had advised Trump to deliver a more somber, traditional statement. He and other advisers also had urged the president to avoid taking questions from the news media at Trump Tower, a request that the president ignored.

As before under Priebus, the draft of an executive order goes through several stages of development, involving the White House Counsel's Office and vetting by relevant staff and agency officials. Then Kelly gives it final approval before it goes to the president.

Kelly is also supposed to control access to Trump in the Oval Office. The exceptions are Melania and the president's son, Barron, as well as Ivanka if she is speaking to her father as his daughter. But Jared and Ivanka can still lobby the president outside the White House.

In one senior staff meeting, Kelly made clear that any policy issues on Capitol Hill must all run through Marc Short, Trump's director of legislative affairs, who had previously seen his authority undermined by conflicting messages from within the West Wing.

As Kelly was wrapping up a meeting in the Oval Office,

National Security adviser H. R. McMaster approached the president to further discuss an issue they had been debating. Infuriated, Kelly got into H. R.'s face. As their noses came within an inch of each other, Kelly screamed at him that the meeting had concluded and that he needed to leave.

"Everyone acknowledges that Kelly is clearly in charge, and they don't want to run afoul of him," Spicer says. "Authority is two things, the reality of it and the perception of it, and in his case, he has both."

"Kelly has brought order and discipline where there once was chaos," Kellyanne Conway says. "Kelly understands how to literally exercise command and control over large structures. He exemplifies and expects of us the major qualities that he has exemplified in his forty-five years of public service—integrity, focus, discipline, performance, results, team cohesion."

While Trump privately expressed appreciation for the order Kelly imposed, he has also said he has mixed feelings about the restrictions Kelly has placed on daily access to him, particularly when they encroach on Jared's and Ivanka's ability to see him. While no one can keep Jared and Ivanka from influencing the president outside of the White House, their vendetta against Bannon, Priebus, Spicer, and other White House aides had backfired because Kelly put a crimp in their power. Yet given the fact that they were behind the worst decisions of Trump's presidency, they remained the Teflon aides.

Nor did Kelly's strictures stop the leaks or impinge on Trump's Twitter habits. In the middle of Senate deliberations over his tax plan, Trump retweeted videos from an anti-Muslim group in Great Britain that purported to show a Muslim migrant beating up a Dutch boy on crutches and a Muslim destroying a statue of the Virgin Mary. But the assailant in one of them was not a "Muslim migrant," and the other two showed four-year-old events with no explanation.

In an opinion piece titled "Trump's 'Muslim Video' Retweets Go Too Far," Joel Pollak, Breitbart News's senior editor at large, wrote that one of the tweets "simply refers to a 'Muslim' shown destroying a statue of the Virgin Mary." Another tweet "refers to a 'Muslim migrant.' These references seem intended to conflate the misdeeds of one person with the behavior of a group as a whole."

Thus, by branding the vast majority of peace-loving Muslims as terrorists, Trump's retweets not only were unfair and inflammatory, they undercut the FBI's efforts to counter terrorism. As William H. Webster, the former FBI director and former director of Central Intelligence, told me, conflating terrorists with all Muslims is dangerous because the United States is "trying to build relationships with Muslims now in order to be sure that their good citizens help us in keeping terrorist attacks from happening. We need the people who are most likely to know about a plot in time to do us some good, and they are often the people that will be blackened because of their religion or ethnicity."

In other respects, nothing changed. Trump continues to play one aide against another and erupts in screaming tirades, as he once did with his new chief of staff, General Kelly. After a rally in Phoenix, Trump was in a cantankerous mood when staff members gently suggested he refrain from injecting politics into the day-to-day issues of governing. He reacted by lashing out at Kelly, the most senior aide giving him this advice. Kelly kept his cool, but he later told other White House staffers that during his thirty-five years of service to his country, he had never been spoken to like that. In the future, he told them, he would not abide such treatment.

The paradox of Trump was that he could be generous, sup-portive, and considerate and at other times treat his aides like dirt. In effect, some aides felt, Trump manages through chaos by pounding someone down to the ground to build someone else up for a couple of weeks. While the team-of-rivals game sparks competition, it also stirs resentment among the staff.

When it came to his tirades, Trump seemed to lack empathy, aides thought. While Trump could make an aide feel like a mil-lion bucks, at other times he seemed incapable of understand-ing how his humiliation of them made them feel. Yet if Trump treated an aide rudely, an hour later he acted as if nothing had happened, as if the incident had vanished from his brain. Since he did not view the humiliation of an aide as awkward or strange, it did not exist in his head.

Despite Kelly's calming influence, Trump continued to fume on a daily basis about the Russia investigation and to bypass some of the processes Kelly had tried to impose.

"It is very distracting to the president, as it would be to any citizen, to be investigated for something, while at the same time trying to carry the weight of what being president of the United States means on his shoulder," General Kelly told Fox News. Kelly said the investigation prompted "multiple conversations a day, generally in the morning when we first talk." Many days begin with a "general conversation" about the investigation be-fore they start other business, "but it is very distracting for him."

After Priebus left as chief of staff, he and Trump continued to talk, exchanging advice. As with other trusted aides, Trump would invite Priebus to lunches in the White House. The fact that Trump never forgave Priebus for saying he should drop out of the race and finally pushed him out of the White House yet, once he was gone, still continued to treat him as a friend and adviser was one of the many mysteries of Donald Trump.

To be sure, Trump was operating strategically, forestalling criticism by maintaining good relations with his former aides. But Trump also seemed to enjoy staying in touch with those who had helped him, valuing their advice and displaying loyalty, even if he had treated them at times with disdain. In keeping former aides close, Trump is thinking long term, Priebus says. "He thinks long term a lot."

15

HOPESTER

Trump eventually replaced Scaramucci with Hope Hicks, who had handled public relations since the beginning of the campaign. With an office ten feet from the Oval Office, better than any other staffer, Hicks understands Trump and how he wants to communicate.

"Hope is the gatekeeper in chief," Spicer says. "She knows him probably better than anybody in terms of the staff, and she will fight for him on every issue."

Hicks's decisions were often spur of the moment.

"Whether she granted an interview with Trump just depended on who you are and what the moment was," Spicer says. "If it was like a good day, she'd say, 'We've had five calls for interviews. Here are two that I think you should do.' But on another day, the same reporter could call, and it could go to a black hole, too."

A native of Greenwich, Connecticut, Hicks is the daughter of Paul B. Hicks III, the National Football League's former executive vice president of communications who was Roger Goodell's right-hand man.

A stunning former model, Hicks graduated from Southern Methodist University in 2010. Her connection to the Trumps began two years later, when she joined New York public relations powerhouse Hiltzik Strategies and began working on accounts related to Trump's real estate, hospitality, and fashion ventures. In August 2014, she joined the Trump Organization, working for Ivanka Trump, helping expand her fashion label and modeling for her online store.

Five months later, Trump made Hicks, who was twenty-six years old, his press secretary. In January 2015, while planning for his potential presidential run, Trump summoned Hicks to his office.

"Mr. Trump looked at me and said, 'I'm thinking about running for president, and you're going to be my press secretary,'" she says.

Initially Hicks was the White House director of strategic communications. After Trump fired Scaramucci, she became interim communications director. In September 2017, Trump named her communications director.

Trump calls Hicks the Hopester; she calls him Mr. Trump. She never appears on TV and has given only a few short interviews over the years.

Hicks issued her personal description of him after Trump, in a news conference at Trump Tower shortly after he won the White House, announced that he would be putting his companies into a trust that his two older sons would run during his presidency.

"I hope at the end of eight years, I'll come back and say, 'Oh, you did a good job,'" Trump said, as his sons looked on. But he couldn't resist a final tweak—half joke, half warning: "Otherwise, if they do a bad job, I'll say, 'You're fired.'"

Hicks noted that Trump was simply joking.

"President Trump has a magnetic personality and exudes positive energy, which is infectious to those around him," Hicks said. "He has an unparalleled ability to communicate with people, whether he is speaking to a room of three or an arena of thirty thousand. He has built great relationships throughout his life and treats everyone with respect. He is brilliant with a great sense of humor and an amazing ability to make people feel special and aspire to be more than even they thought possible."

Trump has told friends that billionaires are constantly asking him to fix them up with Hicks, who is consumed by her work and until recently was never seen with a date. Trump says he refuses.

Hicks is known as a Trump whisperer, letting aides know when it is a good time to speak to the president.

"She can help give readouts on conversations the president has had with legislators," says Marc Short, Trump's director of legislative affairs. "If there's something that's happening in urgent fashion, she's able to convey that information quickly to the president and get back with the answer that we need."

In letting aides know Trump's moods, Hicks performs the same function as did longtime Trump aide Norma Foerderer and her successor, Rhona Graff, a senior vice president of the Trump Organization who had worked for Trump for thirty years by the time he became president.

Everyone who knew Trump knew that Norma Foerderer was his right hand. When Jay Leno wanted to invite Trump on his show, he called Foerderer. When Jack Nicholson tried to call

Trump, he went through Norma first so she could verify that he was who he claimed to be.

Before joining Trump in February 1981, Foerderer had been a junior State Department political officer based in Africa. She then joined a nonprofit, which she quit abruptly after her boss yelled at her for not catching a typo.

Out of a job, she saw a classified ad in the *New York Times* for a secretary. It turned out that the ad had been placed by Ivana Trump, who first interviewed her. After Foerderer passed that test, Donald interviewed her one Saturday morning.

"There was Donald, in the office, perched on the reception desk . . . with his coat slung over his shoulder in a cape fashion and wearing a tie," Foerderer recalled. "And so there he was, swinging his leg. I arrived on the stroke of nine. He said, 'I'm glad to see you're on time.' Punctuality has always been a big thing with him. And I said, 'Oh, my God.'"

After interviewing her for two minutes, Trump hired her and gave her a raise after three weeks. Foerderer thought Ivana, who dubbed her husband "the Donald," was more interested in Donald's hiring a secretary than he was. In fact, Foerderer found that Trump had no files. He kept everything in his head. His lawyer kept copies of contracts.

"Donald is such a man of vision," Foerderer said. "He allows you to do whatever you want. Soon, I was doing all the purchasing. I did all the human resources. I screened his mail, I looked for special projects, did the preliminary research on them, and then would give him the results so other staff members could investigate further. I arranged special events and press conferences, I did his PR. It was the kind of job that just grew because I was there and available."

Somehow, Foerderer said, "Donald instills in you the desire

to do more and more and more, and you want to please him. And yet he rarely criticizes. I mean he would if you did something stupid. He allows you to expand, if you come in with an idea, he'll say, 'Fine, run with it, and see what you do.' This motivates and challenges you even more, and you want to please him because you admire him so much."

Foerderer often sat in on meetings with lawyers or architects who were amazed at the ideas Trump came up with.

"Everybody stands around like dummies, because they didn't realize this could be done," she said.

Trump would say, "Norma's a good negotiator."

"Well," she said, "I learned from the master. I got him really wonderful deals for commercials. What did I do? I would sit tight and say, 'I want a million.' They'd say, 'Start lower.' My response would be, 'Look, you're getting Donald Trump, and there's only one of him. I can't recommend a lower price for him. You're getting a bargain.' I'd just talk and talk and talk, and joke with them. And before you know it, bingo. I'd be just as surprised as anybody else that it happened. But I just knew that I had to persevere the way he does."

Above all, Trump demanded candor from his executives, Foerderer said.

"I was good with him because I was completely honest with him," Foerderer said. "I'm not a sycophant in any way. I thought Donald was a tremendous man, and I admire him enormously, but there was no way I was going to let him believe I agreed with him when I did not. If I disagreed with something, I would be the first to say to him, 'Donald, I don't think so.'"

Foerderer made an appearance on Trump's show *The Apprentice*, recommending against finalist Amy Henry, who was quickly fired in favor of Bill Rancic. Before Trump would fly to Mar-a-

Lago, Foerderer would let butler Tony Senecal know the arrival time and any special requests the boss had.

One day, Foerderer warned Senecal that Trump was "in a mood like a bear with a sore ass." She said Trump had just read a *National Enquirer* article reporting that a police officer had caught his then-wife Marla Maples having sex with her bodyguard Spencer Wagner on the beach near Mar-a-Lago at 4 a.m. on April 16, 1996.

The officer had spotted Wagner's car parked illegally. He found Wagner, thirty-four years old, hiding under a lifeguard stand on the beach. Wagner claimed he was there alone until Maples, then thirty-three, emerged from underneath the stand wearing tight, black spandex leggings and a skimpy jogging top. The officer issued a parking ticket and told the pair to move along.

After the heads-up from Foerderer, Senecal bought all 127 copies of the *National Enquirer* with the article reporting the encounter from Main Street News, then Palm Beach's only newsstand. After giving the manager twenty dollars to keep quiet, Senecal stashed the papers in the trunk of his car.

The next morning, Trump saw him reading a newspaper in the pantry.

"What are you reading?" Trump asked

"The Shiny Sheet," Senecal said, using the local moniker for the *Palm Beach Daily News*. "I already read the *National Enquirer*," Senecal told the boss. Then the butler told him about the 127 copies of the paper stashed in his car trunk.

The Palm Beach social arbiter, the *Palm Beach Daily News* is known as "the Shiny Sheet" or simply "the Shiny" because it is printed on smudgeproof high-quality paper, supposedly in deference to the Palm Beach socialites who don't want to get their hands dirty. The paper runs pages of photos, taken at balls and private parties, often of couples grimacing through extreme plastic surgery jobs.

No news is too trivial to escape the Shiny Sheet's notice. "Unlocked bike stolen from Publix," one headline said. The story reported that a midnight-blue bike had been stolen from the supermarket's parking lot. The story noted that only one of the bike's twelve gears was working.

Although the paper doesn't print everything it knows, it understands the readership. One day, a banner headline screamed across the front page: "Eggs Over Easy: Caviar Prices Jump, Supply Dwindles." Another more recent headline said, "Gold Louis Vuitton Toilet on Sale for $100,000." When Rolls-Royce announced that Palm Beach was one of the few locations in the country where its new Bentley Continental Sedanca Coupé (top speed 155 miles per hour) would be unveiled, the story and accompanying photos filled nearly all of the top half of the front page.

After the story of her liaison with her bodyguard ran in the *National Enquirer*, Maples told the media she had been caught short and had to take a bathroom break. Wagner denied claims of an affair, too. But as media reports of the incident continued to circulate, Trump fired the bodyguard four months later. After he was fired, Wagner came forward and said he had slept with Maples after their "passion boiled over."

A year later, Trump and Maples split, and in 1999 they divorced. In contrast to Melania, Maples resented his work ethic and his golfing. She opposed turning Mar-a-Lago into a club, saying she did not want to share the estate with others. Aside from their daughter Tiffany Trump, her one positive contribution was urging Trump to create Trump Spa, complete with complimentary fruit, fresh juices, and trail mix, just off the main pool. Trump promptly installed as the spa manager Angelia Savage, a stunning former Miss Florida who was third runner up in the 1996 Miss USA contest.

Trump's thoughtful side manifested itself when Foerderer began having a problem with her eyes and had to stay at home. Trump called her every week and sent her baskets of gourmet food. When Foerderer died in September 2013, Trump attended her funeral and tweeted, "I have just lost my beautiful & elegant long time exec. assistant Norma Foerderer. She passed away yesterday—a truly magnificent woman."

Rhona Graff originally worked with Foerderer as Trump's second assistant and took her place as a senior vice president after Foerderer retired. She graduated from Queens College, from which she also received a master's degree in education. Like Foerderer, Graff appeared on a few seasons of *The Apprentice*.

When it came to fending off the constant requests she received to see Trump, Graff had a velvet touch, treating everyone with respect. But when Trump thought someone was infringing on his territory—perhaps using his name for promotion—Graff could turn steely.

Describing Graff, Trump told *Real Estate Weekly*, "She is bright, articulate, extremely efficient and has proven herself to be responsible and loyal on every level."

Graff was happy in New York and had no desire to follow her boss to the White House. During the transition, she trained the president's new executive assistant, Madeleine Westerhout. At age twenty-six, Westerhout became a familiar face in late 2016, when cameras focused on her guiding an array of Trump poohbahs through the lobby of Trump Tower into an elevator or into the main entrance of Trump's New Jersey golf club.

Dubbed the "elevator girl" by some media outlets, Westerhout is originally from California and holds a bachelor's degree
in political science from the College of Charleston in South Carolina. She worked as an assistant to Republican candidates at
the state and federal level and took time off from college in 2012
to intern for Mitt Romney's presidential campaign.

Westerhout later became an assistant to the Republican National Committee's chief of staff Katie Walsh and found herself
assisting the president-elect's transition team after Trump won
the election. While Trump often dials numbers himself, Westerhout also places calls for him and helps schedule his appointments. Besides his landlines, the Secret Service issued him a
mobile phone that encrypts conversations.

SOCRATIC METHOD

Trump regularly calls friends to bounce off ideas and ask for their input. The smarter they are, the more he likes them.

Most of them billionaires, they include New England Patriots chairman and CEO Robert Kraft, former New Jersey governor Christie, Continental Resources CEO Harold Hamm, developer Richard LeFrak, Vornado Realty Trust chairman Steve Roth, private equity real estate investor Tom Barrack, real estate brokerage executive Howard Lorber, former campaign chairman Corey Lewandowski, Reince Priebus, former deputy campaign manager David Bossie, Newsmax CEO Chris Ruddy, former House Speaker Newt Gingrich, Fox News scion Rupert Murdoch, and investor Carl Icahn. Early on, Trump would call Rudy Giuliani, but the relationship seemed to fade.

At other times, Trump calls people spontaneously when he sees them on TV or when he reads an article quoting them. But some who are described in the press as friends or advisers, such as his former strategist Roger Stone, who purport to convey the latest information from the Oval Office, actually never talk with Trump or just briefly say hello to him at Mar-a-Lago.

"The men influencing Trump include Roger J. Stone, a self-proclaimed dirty trickster and longtime Trump confidant who himself has been linked to the FBI's Russia investigation," the *Washington Post* erroneously reported, apparently based on Stone's own claims. But Stone's only contact with Trump was in a meeting that lasted under ten minutes in December 2016, when Stone presented Trump with his book *The Making of the President 2016*.

"Trump was very dismissive," says Bannon, who was in on the meeting. "He hates when he thinks guys are feeding off him to make a living. He doesn't take his calls."

Promoting her book *Raising Trump*, Trump's first wife, Ivana, claimed that she and the president speak "about once every fourteen days." In fact, like most divorced couples, they never speak with each other. Ivana also claimed that she turned down Trump's offer to be the Czech ambassador.

"My ex said, 'Ivana, if you want it, I give it to you,'" the first Mrs. Donald Trump told the *New York Post* from her front-row seat at the Dennis Basso fashion show. She claimed she turned down the offer because she did not want to give up her jet-setting lifestyle.

"She was never promised the Czech Republic post," a Trump aide says.

Whether negotiating or seeking advice, with his habit of making asides, Trump encourages candor, as he did with the press at Mar-a-Lago after his meeting with China's Xi Jinping.

"We had a long discussion already. So far, I have gotten nothing. Absolutely nothing," he said to laughs from the delegation.

"How am I doing? Am I doing okay? I'm president. Hey, I'm president," Trump said boyishly in a Rose Garden talk. "Can you believe it?"

In the same way, one of Trump's strengths is that to a remarkable degree, he encourages open, candid debate among his staff. When choosing both staff and friends, Trump values two things: intelligence and candor.

"Everyone openly argued and shared ideas about everything," Priebus says. "We would get in a big semicircle around his desk all the time and discuss and argue. We discussed and argued over the events of the inauguration, who to call and who not to call, as well as real policy issues."

Trivial though it may seem, even the use of the honorific "Mr. President" can intimidate aides, stifling honest feedback.

"Few people, with the possible exception of his wife, will ever tell a president that he is a fool," President Ford lamented in his book, *A Time to Heal*. "There's a majesty to the office that inhibits even your closest friends from saying what is really on their minds. They won't tell you that you just made a lousy speech or bungled a chance to get your point across. Instead, they'll say they liked the speech you gave last week a little better or that an even finer opportunity to get your point across will come very soon. You can tell them you want the blunt truth; you can leave instructions on every bulletin board, but the guarded response you get never varies."

"People are circumspect when speaking to the president," says Bradley Blakeman, who was George W. Bush's deputy assistant to the president for appointments and scheduling. "You're respectful of the office, and you restrain criticism because it's the president. So I was pleasantly surprised when I heard that people are so direct with President Trump and open in their criticism because it takes a special type of person to give it and to receive it. If they know that they can be blunt with the president and in some cases brutally honest and the president takes it in the spirit it's given as being constructive, that's hugely important."

The fact that Trump's aides were an amalgam of populist nationalists, hard-line conservatives, establishment Republicans, and a few Democrats demonstrated that he wanted to hear competing views. Rather than cloister himself with White House aides, Trump solicits opinions from almost anyone, from chambermaids to Secret Service agents to Mike Pence, who has a knack for retreating into the woodwork when Trump causes a controversy.

"He encourages disagreement in order to get everyone's best thought out and then makes a decision based on everyone's arguments," Priebus says. His aides' differing positions on free trade versus restricted trade are an example.

Priebus thought making Romney secretary of state an intriguing idea, and both Joe Scarborough and Bannon came up with the idea as well. Bannon liked the fact that Romney was a hawk on China.

"But Romney came for the first meeting with Trump, and he doesn't really know anything," Bannon says. "I mean it was kind of shocking. He actually said he didn't think it was serious for him to become the secretary of state so he said, 'Hadn't prepared.'"

For subsequent meetings, Romney brushed up on world affairs. Trump liked the fact that Romney looked the part, and they hit it off, but Trump decided not to name him to the position. Aides pointed out that it would be a slap in the face to Rudy Giuliani, who wanted the secretary of state job and had strongly supported Trump during the campaign, if Trump offered the job to Romney, who had castigated him during the campaign, calling Trump a "phony, a fraud."

But Trump also was not convinced Giuliani would be suitable as secretary of state. Trump went with his gut, and his gut told him Rudy was not cut out for the job. Instead, he offered him the post of attorney general, but Giuliani declined the offer.

"Giuliani only wanted secretary of state," Bannon says. "He said, 'Look, I'm seventy-two years old. Attorney general is too much work. I can't do it. No way. I'm making ten million dollars a year.' Giuliani said he would take secretary of state. Other than that, he was not interested."

Contrary to popular impression, Trump began to have doubts during the transition about his choice of Michael Flynn as national security adviser. That was well before the former director of the Defense Intelligence Agency lied to Pence when he told him he had only exchanged holiday greetings with Russian ambassador Kislyak, prompting Trump to fire him.

As with Giuliani, Trump had reservations about appointing Sessions attorney general. But in his case, everyone around Trump said Sessions would be perfect for the job. Besides having been a member of the Senate Judiciary Committee, Sessions had previously served as a U.S. attorney and attorney general of Alabama. Given the fact that Sessions was the first senator to endorse him back in February 2016, Trump felt a loyalty to him he did not feel toward Giuliani. For that reason, he overcame his gut feeling. But despite Sessions's aggressive effort as attorney general to carry out Trump's agenda, Trump continued to question the decision. He privately called Sessions weak, and he told aides he regretted appointing him.

In the end, Trump chose Rex Tillerson, the CEO of Exxon, as secretary of state. Condoleezza Rice, the secretary of state under George W. Bush, had proposed him. However, whether on North Korea, Afghanistan, or Iran, Tillerson and Trump had fundamentally different positions, Tillerson being more moderate. Aides felt that Tillerson thought that as secretary of state, he was going to be the CEO of foreign policy. He was mistaken.

"Tillerson and Trump have just a terrible relationship," Bannon says. Tillerson is more moderate than Trump. When Trump overrules him, "Tillerson kind of rolls his eyes," Bannon says. "He's been terribly disrespectful in meetings. He will say sarcastically, 'Okay, you're the boss. It's your deal. Just tell me what you want done.'"

Trump, not for the first time, publicly contradicted his chief diplomat on a major foreign policy issue when he tweeted that Tillerson was "wasting his time trying to negotiate with Little Rocket Man," using his nickname for North Korea's leader, Kim Jong-un. "Save your energy, Rex, we'll do what has to be done," Trump said, referring to a possible military strike against North Korea.

"On financial policy, you had Gary Cohn, the U.S. trade representative, Bob Lighthizer, Wilbur Ross, and Steve Mnuchin, all offering different opinions," Priebus says. "He [Trump] brings on disparate arguments to learn from. That's the way he conducts business and learns and makes decisions."

But Trump's tolerance for dissent did not extend to public declarations. He let several senators know of his frustration with Gary Cohn, who went out of his way to publicly criticize Trump after his "both sides" comments concerning the violent events of

Charlottesville. Cohn had been hoping to succeed Janet Yellen as chairman of the Federal Reserve, but Trump made it known that he had no chance in hell. The position ultimately went to Jerome Powell, a member of the Federal Reserve Board of Governors.

In soliciting advice in the White House, Trump employs the Socratic method, Bannon says.

"What he does is he questions nonstop," Bannon says. "He goes back and forth and asks a thousand questions. Sometimes he asks it of the doorman. Sometimes he'll ask it of a general. Sometimes he asks it of somebody from Mar-a-Lago. But he's just picking up more and more information and part of it is patterning. He's looking to graph where the critical mass is."

"There are some things that are fundamental to what he believes, and he is very clear about that," Sean Spicer says. "And then there are some issues where he may seek a lot of input from different folks, then kind of listen to all sides, and then kind of come to a very decisive final answer."

In other cases, Trump has made up his mind but double-checks with a range of people to try to see if they will reinforce his gut instinct.

"He'll ask people all the time about a person or an individual," Spicer says. "That's not necessarily always part of the decision-making process. That's more of the sounding-board process. At the back of his mind, he may know what he wants to do. But he wants to make sure that he's hearing a bunch of other people telling him the same thing. At the back of his mind, he knows the answer is A, and he's trying to validate what he has decided."

At times, Trump will bat a question back and forth between two individuals as in a quiz show.

"This president's method of managing is by him personally curating points of views from a diverse group of people in whom he has some trust and credibility," said Trump's longtime friend Thomas Barrack Jr., who ran his inaugural festivities, to the *New York Times*. "And he very rarely accepts one course of action or one suggestion without laundering it amongst all of them. And what happens in that process is confusion amongst those from whom he's seeking advice. What works for him is that, out of that milieu, his instincts take him to the right answer."

Calling Trump a pragmatic problem solver, one of his lawyers told me: "I have observed Donald Trump during the past twenty years in rooms filled with lawyers, architects, CPAs, and other professionals for all sorts of planning. He listens, surveying everyone's opinions, encouraging thorough debate, and welcoming positions challenging to him or to conventional wisdom. He then decides, reversing his previous positions if he thinks it's warranted."

In the days leading up to his New Year's Eve party celebrating 2017, when I chatted with Trump at Mar-a-Lago about problems in the Secret Service and other matters, Trump asked my opinion on Israeli settlements and the two-state solution. I know as much about the Middle East as Trump knows about the Talmud, but I gave my opinion. Indeed, that was the way Trump had first learned about Mar-a-Lago, chatting with his limousine driver and asking about properties for sale.

When Paul Rampell, Trump's Florida lawyer, proposed turning the Mar-a-Lago estate into a private club, Trump called him almost every day over the course of a month, sometimes several times a day. As he does in the White House, Trump consulted a range of other people. He told Rampell that friends who are in real estate told him the idea would never work. Several other law-yers also threw cold water on the idea. But Trump went ahead.

Trump would ask his longtime security chief Keith Schiller, a former New York City police detective, for his take on almost any matter. Two decades ago, Schiller was at the Manhattan prosecutor's office when he noticed Trump's wife Marla Maples. She was reporting an alleged theft by a former employee. With Maples was her bodyguard.

Describing how he came to work for Trump as his chief of security, Schiller told his high school classmate Rich Siegel in a videotaped interview that he was not impressed by the man's physical stature. "A light goes off. I said: 'Bodyguard, I can do this . . .' I'm no stranger to putting my hands on people," according to Schiller.

Fellow police officers admired Schiller for his size and strength. When raiding an apartment to make an arrest, he would volunteer to carry the sixty-pound battering ram up a flight of stairs, then slam the ram himself.

Schiller reached out to Trump and started working for him part-time in 1999. After his retirement from the police depart-ment in 2004, Schiller became the Trump Organization's director of security. Schiller followed Trump onto the campaign trail, pro-viding security in the months before the Secret Service took over.

At one rally, when a man jumped onto the stage to attack Trump, Schiller beat a Secret Service agent by seconds to grab Trump and shuffle him off the stage. Contrary to press reports that portrayed Trump's private security as Gestapo-like, Schil-ler, who was never armed, and former FBI agents hired to help maintain security at rallies worked smoothly with Trump's Se-cret Service detail.

In August 2015, I urged Trump to request Secret Service protection, saying private protection was useless at that point. He finally did request it in October of that year, and his Secret Service protection began on November 12, 2015. Schiller then continued to provide an added layer of protection, not hesitating to keep reporters away from the candidate or venture into rally crowds to confront protesters.

Schiller was a good gatekeeper, and Trump would sometimes take his advice over the advice of other aides. Schiller was critical of FBI director Comey, telling Trump that the FBI was not aggressive enough in investigating Hillary Clinton's use of a private email server. His views helped shape those of his boss.

In fact, it was Comey who decided to investigate Clinton in the first place and to castigate her and her aides at a press conference before the election as "extremely careless in handling of very sensitive, highly classified information," hardly indicating that he wanted to go easy on her. Aside from the legal issues and whether a jury in Washington would convict her, Comey then fell victim to endless misinformation about the investigation, including from some former FBI agents.

Critics said the FBI should have recorded its agents' interview of Clinton, that she should have been placed under oath, that she should have been given a polygraph test. They maintained Comey should have recommended impaneling a grand jury so that subpoenas could have been issued for pertinent evidence. They said the FBI should have interviewed her at the start of the investigation rather than at the end so her statements could be compared with what agents later uncovered.

But except in unusual circumstances, the FBI only records interviews when a subject is in custody after an arrest. Lying to the FBI is a crime, so there is no need to place a subject under oath, and the FBI does not do so. Proving a case using the statute prohibiting lying to the FBI is far easier than proving a perjury case for lying under oath. Since Clinton was cooperating, subpoenas were not necessary and could have resulted in delays if Clinton's lawyers challenged them in court. Polygraphs are voluntary. Clinton, whose FBI interview was voluntary in the first place, never would have consented to being polygraphed.

Whether the FBI conducts an interview near the beginning or end of an investigation is a judgment call based on the case. In a complex investigation of this kind, where the subject likely would not consent to an interview unless she thought the FBI had already gathered extensive damaging evidence, it is more likely that the FBI would conduct an interview at the end of an investigation when all the facts had been amassed.

Along with Comey, for some reason Schiller never liked George Gigicos, Trump's longtime advance man, even though Gigicos was one of a handful of aides who were the organizing force behind the hundreds of rallies Trump held throughout his campaign. Whenever the slightest thing went wrong, Schiller would be on his case.

Watching TV in his Phoenix hotel room in August 2017, Trump saw shots of an empty venue an hour and a half before his rally was about to start. Irate at what he saw on TV, Trump asked Schiller, who was the director of Oval Office operations, why the crowds were scarce. Schiller asked Gigicos, who explained that while TV correspondents were live early, the rally wouldn't start for several more hours and crowds had just begun to trickle in.

Soon after, Trump called Gigicos, saying that the venue better be full by the time he arrived. It was crammed with people. Yet a few days later, Gigicos got a call from the Trump campaign's executive director, Michael Glassner, who informed him that Trump did not want him working on his rallies anymore.

"George was batting like a thousand. Arranging all those rallies during the campaign. He did every one of them," a Trump aide says. "It's hard to do, but he had a capacity crowd in almost every one of them. And it turned out the one in Phoenix was a pretty good crowd."

17

<hr>

RUSSIA

When it comes to Trump and the question of collusion with Russia, there is indeed a smoking gun. But it's not the June 2016 meeting that Don Trump Jr., along with campaign chairman Paul Manafort and Jared Kushner, held in Trump Tower with a Russian lawyer.

The lawyer, Natalia V. Veselnitskaya, duped Don into setting up the meeting by claiming to have dirt on Hillary Clinton. In fact, the meeting was a bait and switch. It turned out the lawyer had no meaningful information to offer on Hillary. Rather, she wanted to interest the Trump team in a Moscow initiative to allow American families to adopt Russian children.

The meeting, which lasted twenty minutes, was the sort any political campaign or media outlet would have agreed to. Like investigative reporters, political operatives want to obtain tips, even if most of the time the proffered information turns out to be of no value. In this case, nothing came of the meeting. In contrast, Hillary Clinton's campaign actually helped pay for a dossier of almost entirely false accusations about Trump, some of which a British former intelligence official obtained from Russian contacts.

According to journalistic standards that existed decades ago, the fact that such a meeting took place would not have even been a story. The reason it became public was that Kushner, in an amended filing, disclosed it as a contact he had had with a foreign national. The pretext for the meeting was a hoax, and nothing came of it. To suggest by running a story that there was something nefarious about it was unfair. But in today's politically charged media world, the meeting became an immediate sensation as part of a narrative—pushed by the media and Democrats—suggesting that the Trump campaign illegally colluded with Russia.

On its face, the claim is bogus: Even if the campaign had colluded with Russia, that would not have been a violation of law, as former Harvard Law professor Alan Dershowitz, who voted for Hillary Clinton, pointed out in TV interviews. Campaigns are free to obtain information and coordinate with any source, foreign or domestic, just as Hillary's campaign did when funding the dossier on Trump. Moreover, after he became president, Trump demonstrated that he is no pawn of Russia: In response to its chemical attack, Trump sent missiles into Syria, an ally of Russia. Against Russian interests, he approved the largest U.S. commercial sale of lethal defensive weapons to Ukraine since 2014 to help Ukrainian forces fight a Russian-backed separatist movement in two eastern provinces.

Tongue in cheek, Jared told congressional interns that Trump's campaign team was too disorganized to collude with Russia. He could well have been speaking about himself. Invariably, when Kushner filed a disclosure statement about contacts with foreigners, he had to subsequently amend the document because he had left something out. Instead of filling out the forms himself, he often gave the task to aides to carry out.

In congressional testimony, both the FBI and the CIA said that while Russia clearly meddled in the U.S. election by attempting to sow dissension and mistrust of both Trump and Hillary Clinton, they saw no sign of collusion. If that message did not make an impact on the public, it's because the media largely ignored it.

The *Washington Post* ran a story reporting former CIA director John Brennan's congressional testimony that the CIA had alerted the FBI to a troubling pattern of contacts between Russian officials and associates of the Trump campaign. Not until the third paragraph did readers learn that Brennan testified that he saw no proof of collusion.

Indeed, Brennan affirmatively said in his testimony that the contacts may have been benign. The *Post* did not report that comment, and the *New York Times* saved it for the seventh paragraph of its story on Brennan's testimony. The *Wall Street Journal* buried Brennan's statement that he didn't know if these contacts by people tied to Trump's campaign amounted to collusion in the thirteenth paragraph of its story.

Not to be outdone, the *Washington Post* did not report until the eighteenth paragraph of a story about campaign operative Carter Page's possible contact with Russians that Trump aides and Page said that he had never actually met Trump and that Page left the campaign in August 2016. The story left out the fact that in a December 2016 letter, Trump attorney Don McGahn told Page to "immediately cease" claiming that he was a Trump adviser.

"You were merely one of the many people named to a foreign policy advisory committee in March of 2016—a committee that met one time," McGahn said in the letter.

The *Washington Post* ran a story saying a close Trump aide— identified by some publications as Kushner—is a "person of interest" in the FBI's Russia investigation. The story was bogus on its face because the FBI uses that term only in violent crime cases, never in counterintelligence cases.

Rather than acknowledge that there was no actual substance to the claims of collusion, papers like the *Washington Post* and *New York Times* ran elaborate charts with lines drawn between campaign aides and Russians. Democratic members of Congress got TV time by couching their remarks as questions and prefacing their accusations by saying, "If it's true that . . ."

Nor did firing Jim Comey constitute obstruction of justice, as many TV analysts claimed, since Trump did not order that the investigation be stopped, he was not a target of an FBI investigation, and his action did not entail corruptly covering up, destroying evidence, or making false statements, as happened during Watergate.

It turns out that in all the thousands of stories about collusion, there was indeed a smoking gun—in reverse. It established definitively that there had been *no* collusion and that the entire effort by the media and Democrats to try to tie the Trump campaign to Russia was a fraud. That evidence was an August 14, 2017, *Washington Post* story citing campaign emails demonstrating conclusively that top campaign officials, including Chairman Paul Manafort, had no interest in obtaining any kind of cooperation from Russia.

The idea for obtaining help from Russia came from a one-time campaign adviser, George Papadopoulos. For six weeks of work, Papadopoulos had been paid $8,500 before he was let go from the campaign.

Three days after Trump named his campaign foreign policy team in March 2016, Papadopoulos offered to set up "a meeting between us and the Russian leadership to discuss U.S.-Russia ties under President Trump," according to an email he sent to seven Trump campaign officials with the subject line "Meeting with Russian Leadership—Including Putin." He said his Russian contacts welcomed the opportunity.

"The proposal sent a ripple of concern through campaign headquarters in Trump Tower," the *Washington Post* story said. "Campaign co-chairman Sam Clovis wrote that he thought NATO allies should be consulted before any plans were made. Another Trump adviser, retired Navy Rear Admiral Charles Kubic, cited legal concerns, including a possible violation of U.S. sanctions against Russia and of the Logan Act, which prohibits U.S. citizens from unauthorized negotiation with foreign governments."

Indeed, "Among those to express concern about the effort was then-campaign chairman Paul Manafort, who rejected in May 2016 a proposal for Trump to do so," the *Post* story said. Moreover, on March 24, Clovis, the campaign co-chairman who also served on the foreign policy team, reacted to one proposed Russia meeting by writing, "We thought we probably should not go forward with any meeting with the Russians until we have had occasion to sit with our NATO allies."

In the same email chain, Kubic, the retired admiral, reminded others about legal restrictions on meetings with certain Russian officials, adding, "Just want to make sure that no one on the team outruns their headlights and embarrasses the campaign."

Finally, Manafort responded to one email about an invitation from a Russian organization official to set up a meeting by saying in an email to his associate Richard Gates: "We need someone to communicate that DT [Donald Trump] is not doing these trips."

Gates agreed with Manafort and told him he would make sure that no one in the campaign would respond. He would do that, he said, by instructing "the person responding to all mail of non-importance" that any communication about a Russian overture is to be ignored by everyone in the campaign.

There could be no clearer evidence that the Russia collusion story was a sham than the emails, which were among more than twenty thousand pages of documents the Trump campaign turned over to congressional committees. But rather than putting an end to the conspiracy theories, the story was largely ignored by the media, which continued to run stories about alleged Russian collusion as if the emails had never existed. Indeed, the *Washington Post* story that demonstrated conclusively that there was nothing to the Russia collaboration claims was headlined "Trump Campaign Emails Show Aide's Repeated Efforts to Set Up Russia Meetings."

The eventual indictment of Papadopoulos by Special Counsel Robert S. Mueller III charged him with lying to the FBI about his contacts with the Russians. Since his efforts to obtain help from the Russians were not illegal—any more than the Clinton campaign's collection of information from Russians—he was not charged in connection with anything having to do with that activity. But the indictment stated plainly that no meeting between the Trump campaign and the Russians arranged by Papadopoulos ever took place.

Nonetheless, when Papadopoulos was indicted for lying to the FBI, the media played up the nonstory that the low-level aide had *wanted* to set up meetings between the Trump campaign and the Russians, while largely ignoring the fact that the campaign wanted nothing to do with any Russians. Instead of enlightening the public, the press had turned into a propaganda tool.

As with Papadopoulos, Mueller indicted Michael Flynn, whom Trump had named to be his national security adviser during the transition, for lying to the FBI about his conversations with Sergey Kislyak, the Russian ambassador to the United States. Flynn agreed to plead guilty. According to the indictment, Flynn lied when he told FBI agents that he did not ask Kislyak in a December 29, 2016, telephone conversation to refrain from escalating the situation in response to sanctions the United States imposed on Russia. He lied again when he told agents that he did not ask Kislyak in a December 22 phone call to defeat or delay a United Nations Security Council resolution.

Flynn's indictment triggered endless speculation by the media that he was about to spill the beans about Trump or his White House aides. A scowling Carl Bernstein suggested on CNN that Flynn could be another John Dean, Nixon's White House counsel who played a major role in exposing the Watergate cover-up. But what if there were no beans to spill? And what was the crime in the first place? Both Republican and Democratic lawmakers were only too happy to join in the speculation, giving them air time. Never have so many words been uttered about so little.

Besides the indictments of Flynn and Papadopoulos, Mueller issued indictments of Manafort and his associate Richard Gates. The indictments focused on their personal business dealings long before Manafort had joined the Trump campaign. The tax and money laundering case against Manafort described a complicated scheme in which he lobbied for a pro-Russia party in Ukraine and its leader, Viktor F. Yanukovych, and allegedly hid proceeds in bank accounts in Cyprus, the Grenadines, and elsewhere. Prosecutors said he laundered more than $18 million and spent the money extravagantly.

Back in June 2006, when I asked Trump how he would operate if he were elected president, he said, "There would be fewer scandals in my administration because I don't tolerate scandal." Immediately upon seeing a wire service report about Manafort's dealings in Ukraine and allegations of millions of dollars in cash payments and secret lobbying, Trump fired him as campaign manager. Similarly, seeing reports that Tom Price, the secretary of Health and Human Services, had racked up roughly a million dollars in flight costs on private and military aircraft since taking office, Trump let him go.

Having lied to Pence about his conversations with Kislyak, Flynn served in the White House for only twenty-four days. If Trump had left it at that, the matter would have faded from view. But obsessive as he is, Trump could not leave well enough alone. He knew he had not colluded with the Russians. How could the FBI not see that?

Trump's security chief Keith Schiller had been bad-mouthing Comey, and Jared told Trump he should fire him. Ivanka supported the idea as well. Trump was already down on Comey for not indicting Hillary Clinton. What Trump did not understand was that without evidence of criminal intent, the existing laws would not support an indictment over Clinton's handling of her classified emails.

Aside from the FBI agents and prosecutors who worked on the case, no one is in a better position to explain Comey's decision not to prosecute the former secretary of state than John L. Martin. After leaving the FBI as a special agent, Martin became a Justice Department prosecutor. For twenty-five years he was in charge of prosecuting all the espionage laws, including Section 793(f) of the federal criminal code, the pertinent statute in the Clinton investigation. Among the seventy-six spies Martin prosecuted were John A. Walker Jr., Jonathan Pollard, and Aldrich Ames. All but one of the prosecutions resulted in convictions.

During those years, Martin tells me, he never used Section 793(f) alone because, while that law makes it a felony to handle material relating to the national defense with "gross negligence," it is unlikely a jury would convict a defendant on that charge alone without a showing of criminal intent. Thus, in the case of former CIA director David Petraeus, besides charging him with a violation of Section 793(f), the Justice Department charged him with lying to the FBI, an indication of criminal intent. Petraeus agreed to a plea disposition.

Besides the absence of provable criminal intent, Comey had to consider the fact that some jurors could give Clinton a pass simply for being a presidential candidate. Did Comey want the FBI to be responsible for throwing the presidential election into chaos if, in the end, the prosecution resulted in a dismissal by the court, a hung jury, or an acquittal?

While Comey's decision to make the call himself rather than leave it to Justice Department officials on whether to prosecute

Clinton can legitimately be argued either way, "Comey did the right thing," Martin says. "He put the facts out to let the people decide."

It seemed to aides that Trump was looking at what to do about Comey from the day he won the election. Within the first few days of his presidency, he began contemplating whether he should keep him or fire him. Comey had been in the press continuously during the campaign in connection with the Clinton email investigation. But then he ultimately decided that he wasn't going to charge her even though he laid out all the elements of the appropriate charges.

Trump groused that Comey was not doing enough to investigate leaks of classified information. But the FBI does not announce its leak investigations. The Bureau routinely pursues them whenever an intelligence agency reports a leak to the Justice Department and the FBI determines that it has a reasonable chance of tracking down the leaker. By November 2017, Sessions revealed in a congressional hearing that the FBI had twenty-seven ongoing leak investigations in progress. The number compared with an average of three investigations undertaken each year under Obama but mainly reflected the explosion of seriously damaging leaks after Trump became president.

Trump also did not like the fact that in congressional testimony in May 2017, Comey had misstated the number of Hillary's classified emails that were on the laptop of her aide Huma Abedin. Comey said that Abedin forwarded "hundreds of thousands" of emails involving her boss to her husband's computer. The FBI immediately sent a letter to the Senate Judiciary Committee correcting the error. It said that about 49,000 emails potentially relevant to the investigation into Clinton's use of a private email server had been found on Anthony Weiner's laptop.

However, only a "small number" of these had been forwarded by Abedin. "Of those forwarded to Weiner, only two email chains contained classified information," the FBI said.

Anyone who has been on TV knows how easy it is to misstate a fact. But that controversy reignited the president's thoughts as to whether or not Comey should continue as FBI director. Trump began discussing internally whether Comey should be replaced.

At his Bedminster golf club, Trump discussed the matter with Jared and Ivanka. Both played to Trump's sense of grievance, and both were for firing Comey. After spending the weekend at the golf club, Trump returned to the White House and made his decision that he was going to fire Comey. Back in the White House, Trump told Pence and several senior aides—Priebus, Bannon, and White House counsel Donald McGahn—that he was ready to move on Comey.

First, since Attorney General Jeff Sessions and Deputy Attorney General Rod J. Rosenstein, to whom Comey reported directly, were coming in for a meeting, McGahn said Trump should confer with them before firing Comey. As it turned out, both said Comey had erred in deciding on his own not to indict Hillary, something they had previously discussed between themselves. As a result, they told Trump, they had lost confidence in him as FBI director. Trump asked them to give him a memo to that effect. That sealed Comey's fate. But Priebus cautioned Trump to wait and talk to Comey in person.

Even though Trump told aides he was intent on firing Comey, they believe that if Rosenstein had said he and Sessions supported Comey instead of saying that they had no confidence in him, Trump would have changed his mind and kept Comey on as FBI director. Instead, they helped trigger the firing.

Going on NBC, Trump told Lester Holt, "And, in fact, when I decided to just do it [fire Comey], I said to myself, I said 'you know, this Russia thing with Trump and Russia is a made-up story, it's an excuse by the Democrats for having lost an election that they should have won.'"

While that statement sounds as if Trump, in his usual truncated fashion, was saying he fired Comey because the FBI director was pursuing the Russia investigation and he wanted to stop it, Trump made it clear to aides afterward that he meant the opposite—that he was aware that firing Comey could prolong the Russia investigation. His comments to Holt immediately following that statement confirm Trump's claim.

In the interview, Holt asked Trump if he was "angry with Mr. Comey because of his Russia investigation."

"I just want somebody that's competent," Trump responded. "I am a big fan of the FBI, I love the FBI."

Trump said in the interview that he supported a full investigation into Russian interference in the election. He said he never tried to pressure Comey into dropping the FBI probe of the Trump campaign and insisted, "I want to find out if there was a problem in the election having to do with Russia."

Trump added, "As far as I'm concerned, I want that thing to be absolutely done properly. Maybe I'll expand that, you know, lengthen the time [of the Russia probe] because it should be over with, in my opinion, should have been over with a long time ago. 'Cause all it is, is an excuse, but I said to myself, I might even lengthen out the investigation, but I have to do the right thing for the American people."

In other words, in confusing fashion, Trump was saying that rather than trying to end the FBI's Russia investigation, he recognized that by firing Comey, he may have been prolonging it. The media largely ignored those statements. Nor, in all the endless stories about the Russia investigation, did the media point out that Trump never asked anyone to stop the investigation. It was a point that Comey, Rosenstein, and Sessions all confirmed.

In contrast, during the Watergate scandal, President Nixon actually took steps to try to suppress the FBI's investigation of his role and his aides' involvement in a cover-up of the White House's orchestration of a break-in at Democratic National Committee headquarters. The most damaging tape of Nixon's Oval Office conversations recorded Nixon telling his chief of staff, H. R. Haldeman, to have the CIA concoct phony national security reasons to divert the FBI from pursuing crucial leads in the Watergate investigation. Nixon's ploy resulted in a delay in the FBI's investigation of only a week. Except when J. Edgar Hoover was director and engaged in massive abuses, including keeping blackmail files on presidents and members of Congress, the FBI has never bent to political pressure.

"By referring to 'the Russia thing,' Trump meant he did think about the Russia investigation and said, hey, I need to make this move, but actually by getting rid of Comey, this is going to make the Russia situation even longer and potentially more problematic," an aide notes. "But I have to do it. I have to get rid of this guy. It was the opposite of what he's been accused of."

Comey, who at the time was visiting the Los Angeles field office, learned he was fired in an embarrassing manner—in public, from the television, in full view of his staff. As Comey was delivering a speech to FBI field office employees, he initially laughed as news that he had been fired flashed across the TV screens.

"How'd you guys do that?" Comey said to his staff.

The FBI director assumed he was being pranked by his

underlings. He had to be told by his team that the headlines were no joke. He had been dismissed, effective immediately.

For those who lived through Watergate and remember how Nixon tried to stifle the FBI's investigation of his role in a cover-up, Trump's action, delivered to FBI headquarters by Trump's security chief and Comey nemesis Keith Schiller, cast a pall on his presidency, raising legitimate questions about any later action he took in connection with the FBI or Justice Department.

To be sure, Trump had the right to fire any government executive. But the fact that Comey was overseeing an FBI investigation that could conceivably lead to charges against the president himself or his aides made it look as if the United States had become a banana republic.

"I said to Trump, you can fire Comey, but you can't fire the FBI," Bannon says. "The one thing the president's head was not comprehending was that this is not a city of personalities. It's a city of institutions. These institutions have long histories, and they have incredible institutional memories."

Early on, Bannon advised Trump that if he were going to fire the FBI director, he should do it immediately upon taking office. But Trump took no immediate action, eventually inviting Comey to dinner and saying, "I need loyalty, I expect loyalty," according to Comey. Comey hedged his response.

Once Trump seemed set on firing Comey, Bannon stayed away from the Oval Office for two days. "I gave my best advice. I said my piece," Bannon says. " 'You're president of the United States, go for it.' "

Bannon notes that Jared was pushing Trump to fire him. "It was his idea, and he got it in his head," Bannon says. "I got in Jared's face about it."

Since Comey had decided not to indict Hillary, Jared thought

Democrats would love the idea of firing the FBI director. It didn't work out that way. Democrats attacked Trump over firing Comey. While that was motivated in part by partisan politics, they had a legitimate point.

In Bannon's view, "Jared represented a lethal combination of arrogance and incompetence that ends administrations."

Exasperated with Jared and Ivanka, aides felt they simply had no idea of what they were doing and no understanding of the jobs and the responsibilities and the qualifications of a lot of those jobs. Their attitude seemed to be that if they could just get a bunch of these smart people to tell all these dumb people in government what to do, they'd fix it all. They had no understanding of the basic fundamentals of how government works, how a campaign works, how politics works. Most of all, they had no understanding of the political consequences of their actions.

Ivanka and Jared were pushing for Trump to fire Comey without understanding that it would be impossible to get a new nominee through the Senate, an aide says. "They didn't understand the basics of why Scaramucci wasn't qualified," the aide noted. "And in the end, they would run away from the decision. They have no accountability for any of the decisions that they advocate for."

Indeed, when the backlash over firing Comey began, Jared and Ivanka blamed Spicer and the communications team, as if they could somehow undo the damage Trump had done to himself. Pushing Trump to hire Scaramucci, they cited the bad press over Comey's firing. Their track record was perfect: From pushing to fire Comey to proposing to hire Scaramucci, they were responsible for the worst decisions of Trump's presidency. And during the campaign, Jared criticized then-campaign manager Corey Lewandowski for not being a "team player" by not supporting campaign chairman Manafort, who later was charged with a range of criminal violations, according to Lewandowski's and David Bossie's book *Let Trump Be Trump*. Trump eventually removed Lewandowski as campaign manager because he was seen as too combative and bombastic.

Neither Jared nor Ivanka had had any experience in government. Unlike Trump, who also had no experience in government, they lacked the judgment necessary to maneuver in Washington. The fact that both Jared and Ivanka were thirty-six years old did not explain their naiveté. Neither Ivanka nor Jared had the savvy to understand why firing the FBI director or hiring Scaramucci would be an unmitigated disaster.

While Trump privately acknowledges that they are a problem, and tells them they should have remained in New York, he can't bring himself to fire them. Trump almost never fires anyone himself, and as a devoted family man, he would have even more trouble firing his own daughter and her husband.

18

SPECIAL COUNSEL

After Trump fired Comey, Bannon told Trump that firing the FBI director was "the dumbest move in modern political history." Trump never outright admits a mistake. But several times, he asked Bannon, "What do you think? Do you think firing Comey was a mistake?"

As if that misjudgment were not enough, Trump began a crusade to get Jeff Sessions to resign as attorney general because two months earlier, Sessions had recused himself from making decisions about the FBI investigation.

Under Justice Department guidelines, Sessions had no choice but to recuse himself. After Watergate, Congress passed a law requiring "the disqualification of any officer or employee of the Department of Justice . . . from participation in a particular investigation or prosecution if such participation may result in a personal, financial, or political conflict of interest, or the appearance thereof." Implementing this language, the Justice Department imposed a rule barring employees from participating in investigations when they have a personal or political relationship with "any person or organization substantially involved in the conduct that is the subject of the investigation or prosecution" or which they know "has a specific and substantial interest that would be directly affected by the outcome of the investigation or prosecution."

When aides explained the guidelines to Trump, he raged that as attorney general, Eric Holder Jr. had ignored congressional subpoenas for documents related to the Justice Department's response to Operation Fast and Furious. In fact, the recusal requirement is clear-cut. Whether an attorney general is required to comply with a congressional subpoena in a particular matter is not. In the end, a federal judge sided with Holder, declining to hold him in contempt over the issue.

Nonetheless, Trump was enraged at Sessions.

"Look at what Holder went through," Trump said to aides. "He got destroyed left and right year after year and he hung in there and he was tough. Say what you will, he was a great attorney general for Obama."

After Sessions's recusal, Deputy Attorney General Rosenstein took over the Russia investigation, leading to the appointment of Robert S. Mueller III, a former FBI director, as special counsel. That provoked even more presidential rage—not to mention legal fees in the millions.

In an interview with the *New York Times*, Trump went public with his hostility toward Sessions, saying he would not have picked Sessions as his attorney general if he had known he was going to recuse himself. But because Sessions did not know during the confirmation process the exact scope of the FBI investigation into Russian interference during the campaign, he did not know until he was sworn in as attorney general in February 2017 that the investigation included individuals associated with the Trump presidential campaign. Sessions had worked on the campaign, and he clearly had personal and political relationships with probable subjects of the investigation. They included former national security adviser Michael Flynn, former campaign manager Paul Manafort, and possibly others. After becoming attorney general, Sessions then realized that he was obligated to recuse himself from the FBI's Russia investigation.

The irony was that despite Trump's sniping, as the nation's top law enforcement official Sessions made a notable mark on the Justice Department, rolling back some of the Obama administration's signature policies while emphasizing his own agenda.

From attacking sanctuary cities that allow illegal aliens who have committed felonies to go free, to tearing up agreements that discourage police from acting proactively to catch criminals, Sessions implemented the conservative agenda Trump had promised during the campaign.

Sessions directed federal prosecutors to pursue the toughest possible charges and sentences in all criminal cases, overriding the previous guidance from Holder, who sought to ease penalties for some nonviolent drug offenses and reduce prison sentences for such crimes. Sessions reversed another controversial policy by further empowering the police to seize the personal property of people suspected of crimes but not charged. And Sessions ordered a resumption of the transfer of surplus weapons, vehicles, and other equipment from the nation's military to state and local law enforcement agencies.

That revived a program which Obama had sharply curtailed

on the nonsensical grounds that protecting police from violent protesters aggravated the protesters, spurring on their violence. Obama said in 2015 that "militarized gear sometimes gives people a feeling like [police] are an occupying force as opposed to a part of the community there to protect them." In other words, not offending protesters is more important than saving police officers from injury or death.

The same thinking had led Obama to avoid referring to militant Islamic extremism as the main terrorist threat. The vast majority of Muslims are peace-loving, but referring to militant Islamic extremism makes the point, distinguishing between radical elements and the rest of the 1.8 billion Muslims in the world. If you are afraid to name the enemy, how can you fight it or expect others to rally to your side?

To be sure, the FBI has been frustrated by the unwillingness of Islamic leaders to help the Bureau with tips on possible terrorists. A handful of terrorist plots have been rolled up by the FBI based on tips from Muslims. But what the FBI finds disturbing is that Muslim leaders by and large are reluctant to let the Bureau know of radicals within their community. The FBI is not about to publicize this. But Arthur M. "Art" Cummings II, who was the FBI's executive assistant director in charge of counterterrorism and national security investigations, opened up to me about the problem.

The FBI has outreach programs to try to develop sources in the Muslim community and solicit tips, but Cummings found little receptivity. He found that while Muslims have brought some cases to the FBI, Muslim leaders in particular are often in denial about the fact that the terrorists who threaten the United States are Muslims.

"I talked to a very prominent imam in the U.S.," Cummings

said. "We would have our sweets and our sweet tea. We would talk a lot about Islam. I would say we understand Islam and where they're coming from. We'd tell him what our mission is, trying to keep people from murdering Americans or anybody else, for that matter."

Months later, the FBI found out that the man's mosque had two extremists who were so radical that the mosque's leadership kicked them out. Clearly, those two extremists would have been of interest to the FBI. If they only engaged in anti-American rhetoric, the FBI would have left them alone. More likely they were planning action to go with their rhetoric.

Cummings asked the imam, "What happened?"

"What do you mean?" the imam asked.

"Why didn't you tell me about this?" the agent said.

"Why would I tell you about this?" the imam said. "They're not terrorists," he said of the radicals. "They just hate the U.S. government."

At one meeting, a Muslim group suggested having a photo taken of their members with the FBI director to show that their community is a partner in the war on terror. Cummings responded, "Let me make a suggestion: When you bring to my attention real extremists who are here to plan and do something, who are here supporting terrorism, and I work that based on your information, then I promise you, I will have the director stand up on the stage with you."

To Cummings's amazement, the answer was: "That could never happen. We would lose our constituency. We could never admit to bringing someone to the FBI."

"Well, we've just defined the problem, haven't we?" Cummings told them.

While Muslims will occasionally condemn al-Qaeda, "rarely

do we have them coming to us and saying, 'There are three guys in the community that we're very concerned about,'" Cummings said. "They want to fix it inside the community. They're a closed group, a very, very closed group. It's part of their culture that they want to settle the problem within their own communities. They've actually said that to us, which I then go crazy over."

On one hand, "They don't want anyone to know they have extremists in their community," Cummings observed. "Well, beautiful. Except do you read the newspapers? Everyone already knows it. That horse has left the barn. So there's a lot of talk about engagement, but realistically, we've got a long, long way to go."

As with his opposition to giving police military armaments, Obama wanted to close the prison at Guantánamo Bay in Cuba on the grounds it only sparks more violence by serving as a recruiting tool for terrorists. But the prison never was a chief recruiting tool for terrorists, and in any case terrorists will use any symbol of America as a recruiting tool. If prisoners were moved from Guantánamo Bay to a prison in the United States, by Obama's logic, the new prison would become a recruiting tool. While Obama signed an executive order on the second day of his presidency to close the prison at Guantánamo Bay, he never did close it. Trump proclaimed that it would remain open and take in more prisoners.

On the day Mueller was appointed special counsel, the president was interviewing candidates to replace Comey as FBI director. Sessions was with him briefly but made it a point not to participate in the interviews. Sessions left the Oval Office to go to the Cabinet Room to take a phone call. On the phone, Rod Rosenstein told him that he had just appointed Bob Mueller special counsel. Sessions returned to the Oval Office and told Trump of the appointment.

Mueller was admired by all sides for his integrity and effectiveness as FBI director. A former Marine and prosecutor, Mueller took over an FBI that had been rocked by scandals directly attributable to decisions of former FBI director Louis Freeh: the Richard Jewell case, the Wen Ho Lee case, the problems with the FBI Laboratory. Because Freeh had no use for technology, FBI agents had to double up on computers that had green screens and did not connect to the Internet. No one would take the machines even as donations.

Freeh froze the normal, collaborative decision-making processes of the FBI. He punished anyone who brought him bad news or disagreed with him.

"Freeh took away from the SACs [special agents in charge] the desire to make decisions because they feared repercussions," says Anthony E. Daniels, whom Freeh named assistant FBI director to head the Washington field office. "They were terrified of him. Freeh had contempt for management."

"Freeh said he wants everything straight. The first person who told it to him straight, he cut his head off. If an agent brought him bad news, he killed the messenger and pushed him out," says Weldon Kennedy, whom Freeh appointed associate deputy director for administration.

Days after he took office as director, Mueller ordered thousands of new Dell computers.

Like a giant ocean liner, the FBI does not change course quickly. Mueller had to deal with a bureaucracy that often resisted change and did not always give him straight answers.

Early on, Mueller removed Sheila Horan as acting director of the Counterintelligence Division. Besides finding that she was generally not on top of the subject, he felt she did not appropriately brief him on a Chinese counterintelligence case involving FBI agent James J. Smith in Los Angeles and had failed to warn him of problems with the case.

More than anything else, Mueller's removal of Horan defined the difference between the new director and Freeh. While Freeh had the habit of punishing anyone who disagreed with him or brought him bad news, Mueller banished those who failed to give him the facts.

Mueller was not a diplomat. Back when he headed the Justice Department's Criminal Division, Mueller would throw office parties at his home. He would signal that the festivities were over by flicking the lights. As a former Marine, Mueller expected his orders to be carried out to the letter. There would be no hand-holding. At the same time, he would go out of his way to offer condolences to FBI officials when they lost loved ones.

"He comes off as your central-casting ex-Marine—tough, no-nonsense, and not suffering fools gladly," says Michael R. Bromwich, a former Justice Department inspector general.

Mueller charged Art Cummings with shifting the FBI's emphasis to intelligence and rolling up future terrorist plots. Of course, the FBI always wanted to prevent attacks and often did. But as in the case of the first World Trade Center bombing, the Bureau would often close a case and move on to another without trying to develop sources and leads on future plots. Cummings would tell agents that by making an arrest, they could be jeopardizing the national security. They needed to cultivate suspects to pinpoint and stop the next attack.

To uncover terrorists and bring them to justice, the FBI deployed secret Tactical Operations (TacOps) teams—FBI agents who case a home or office, then break in to plant bugging devices and leave without getting caught and shot as burglars. Shown to me at FBI headquarters, the bugging devices are the size of postage stamps and will record for twenty hours or transmit as instructed remotely.

As revealed in my book *The Secrets of the FBI*, to prevent dogs from giving them away, before a break-in, TacOps agents show a photo of any dog that might be on the premises to a veterinarian who is on contract. He prescribes just the right amount of tranquilizer to shoot into the dog with a dart gun. On the night of the break-in, if the target is an office and closed for the night, agents conduct surveillance at the homes of anyone who might work there. If anyone tries to return to the office, agents will delay them by staging a phony accident, issuing a traffic ticket while dressed as police officers, or opening a fire hydrant and closing off the area.

Cummings devised trip wires that would warn the FBI of a terrorist plot. Under Cummings's direction, the FBI in effect reverse-engineered a terrorist operation. It looked at a potential terrorist incident and then worked backward to pinpoint all the elements a terrorist might require to achieve his goal. The FBI then had a road map of possible clues to an impending plot. As an example, the FBI asked companies or laboratories that supply certain chemicals or biological materials to report any suspicious purchases to the FBI or police.

Trip wires led to the arrest of Khalid Ali-M Aldawsari, a twenty-year-old college student from Saudi Arabia who allegedly was planning to blow up the Dallas home of former president George W. Bush. He was convicted and sentenced to life in prison. In another case, a nursery notified the FBI of large purchases of castor plants. The FBI found that the purchaser was planning to make ricin from castor beans and send it to a judge.

The results were palpable. Because of the change in emphasis and proactive programs Cummings put in place under Mueller's direction to detect possible plots, the United States has not had a successful attack by a foreign terrorist network since 9/11.

Trump and many Republicans jumped on the FBI because agent Peter Strzok, who was on both the Russia and Hillary investigations, had texted anti-Trump, pro-Hillary messages to FBI lawyer Lisa Page, with whom he was having an affair. But the fact that one agent had acted unprofessionally was no reason to cast aspersions on the entire Bureau. Judges, FBI agents, and journalists all have political opinions. The fact that Strzok voiced those opinions in strident fashion using FBI phones made him unsuited to investigate the Trump administration. But in the end, Mueller and Comey, both originally Republicans, made the decisions. What counts is that Mueller removed the agent from the Russia probe as soon as he heard about the messages.

It later came out that a text message from Strzok to another FBI colleague expressed skepticism about the Russia probe, saying he was hesitant to join the Mueller investigation because "my gut sense and concern is there's no big there there." But Republican members of Congress conducting oversight investigations never blinked. They continued a witch hunt against the FBI that was as baseless as the witch hunt against Trump and his alleged collusion with Russia.

Media outlets and Republican legislators spread the notion that the FBI obtained a warrant from the Foreign Intelligence Surveillance Court (FISA) to "spy" on the Trump campaign based on information in the dossier compiled about Trump with funding from Hillary's campaign. Putting aside the fact that Comey as FBI director described the dossier as "salacious and unverified," the notion that the FBI would rely on any third-party report to obtain a court order and that a federal judge would approve the request is ludicrous.

Given the power of the FBI, Americans and the media must remain vigilant when it comes to possible misuse of its authority. My reporting revealing the abuses of William S. Sessions in my book *The FBI: Inside the World's Most Powerful Law Enforcement Agency* led to his dismissal as FBI director by President Clinton. But the vast majority of FBI agents work incredible hours and often risk their lives to keep us safe. If your son or daughter were kidnapped, you would want the FBI on your side.

Despite Mueller's accomplishments and reputation for integrity, Trump lit into Jeff Sessions in the Oval Office because he blamed the appointment of Mueller on Sessions's recusal. Trump hurled a volley of insults at him, telling the attorney general it was his fault they were in the current situation. Saying that Sessions should resign, he said that choosing him to be attorney general was one of the worst decisions he had made and called him an "idiot."

Ashen and emotional, Sessions agreed to quit. Sessions later told associates that the demeaning way the president addressed him was the most humiliating experience in his decades of public life.

White House counsel McGahn informed Priebus that the special counsel had been named and that Jeff Sessions had just resigned. Priebus and McGahn agreed they could not let that happen. Sessions was already in the parking lot. Priebus ran after him and brought him to his White House office overlooking the North Lawn. Priebus, McGahn, Pence, and Bannon calmed him down. They told Trump that accepting Sessions's resignation would only sow more chaos inside the administration and rally Republicans in Congress against him. Having served in the Senate for two decades, Sessions was widely liked and admired in Congress. Moreover, Sessions was taking on every task Trump wanted him to pursue.

Trump relented, eventually returning the resignation letter Sessions sent him, adding a handwritten response making it clear he wanted Sessions to continue in his job. After interviewing a number of candidates, Trump chose Christopher Wray as the new FBI director. A partner at King & Spalding, Wray had a distinguished record as principal associate deputy attorney general from 2001 to 2003 and assistant attorney general for the criminal division from 2003 to 2005 under President George W. Bush. The Senate confirmed him in a ninety-two to five vote. But given the hard feelings Trump had stirred up within the FBI over his firing of Comey, who was widely admired throughout the Bureau, the FBI told Trump that even though he was officially invited, it would be better if he did not attend Wray's swearing-in ceremony.

19

SOVEREIGNTY

As deputy assistant to the president for national security strategy, Nadia Schadlow is on the cutting edge of Trump's foreign policy agenda. As such, Dr. Schadlow, who previously was with the Smith Richardson Foundation, interacts with world leaders and diplomats, listening to their concerns and explaining Trump's worldview.

As with the economy, Trump is changing the rules of the game in the world arena. And that has many offended, upset, or enraged, she says.

"Donald Trump challenges the traditional view of world order," Schadlow says. "He was elected on a platform that put American sovereignty first. The concept of sovereignty upsets many in Washington. They interpret it as America alone. But sovereignty does not mean America alone."

The United Nations is composed of sovereign states—defined territories with independent, centralized governments.

"Sovereignty is the foundation of democracy," Schadlow says. "You can't have democracy without sovereignty. Because then you end up in these amorphous global governance-type institutions that are often, over time, undemocratic. So I think it's almost fun to challenge this prevailing viewpoint."

America first means America forward.

"It's thinking about how you protect American interests more effectively," Schadlow says. "How you advance American values more effectively. It's not about isolating ourselves. It's about just being a more effective and confident advocate for the United States."

While Trump wants to reassert America's power, "He wants to cooperate, but to cooperate with reciprocity," Schadlow notes. "If we're going to help give you aid, we want you to come to the table with something as well. Even if you're a poor developing country, come to the table with a commitment to reform, or to reduce corruption. That is reciprocity."

The goal is to advance American influence. "The government should enable and not block prosperity or the growth of American businesses abroad," Schadlow says.

Under Trump, the National Security Council staff has been cut in half to about two hundred. Instead of trying to micromanage agencies, Trump wants to "devolve authority back to the departments, which is consistent with his effort to decentralize government and cut regulations," Schadlow says.

Thus, instead of approval from the NSC or the president himself, field commanders now have authority to initiate strikes. Under Obama, by the time approval was given, at least half the time the target had disappeared. At the same time, by withdrawing from Iraq and undermining combat efforts in Afghanistan by repeatedly announcing when U.S. troops would be withdrawn, Obama allowed ISIS to form and the Taliban to gain power.

Having written *Dereliction of Duty*, a book about the failures of leadership during the Vietnam War, U.S. Army lieutenant general H. R. McMaster had the perfect background to become Trump's national security adviser. He replaced Michael Flynn, whom Trump had fired after he was not truthful about his conversation with the Russian ambassador.

Born in Philadelphia, McMaster graduated from the U.S. Military Academy in 1984, and later earned a PhD in American history from the University of North Carolina at Chapel Hill. His PhD thesis was critical of American strategy and military leadership during the Vietnam War and served as the basis for his book.

In his book, McMaster cited historical evidence to show how military leaders failed their troops and their country by remaining silent during the escalation of the Vietnam War in Southeast Asia. But it was ultimately President Johnson who stubbornly pursued a course leading to defeat. In a June 11, 1964, memo to McGeorge Bundy, Johnson's national security adviser, John McCone, the director of Central Intelligence, debunked the "domino theory," Johnson's rationale for prosecuting the war. "We do not believe that the loss of South Vietnam and Laos would be followed by the rapid, successive communization of the other states of the Far East," McCone wrote.

In April 1965, McCone hand-carried a memo to Johnson. "I think we are . . . starting on a track which involves ground force operations [that will mean] an ever-increasing commitment of U.S. personnel without materially improving the chances of victory," McCone wrote. "In effect, we will find ourselves mired in combat in the jungle in a military effort that we cannot win, and from which we will have difficulty extracting ourselves."

As tens of thousands of Americans lost their lives fighting a fruitless war, Johnson ignored the CIA's conclusions.

McMaster twirls his class ring from West Point on the ring finger of his left hand. He has big hands and wears a proportionately big watch and the big ring. He may wear a suit to meetings now instead of his three-star-general uniform, but he still sports the big ring, symbol of the military academy's perpetual bond of "the long gray line."

Like most generals you can think of, McMaster is not fooling anybody with the suit. His military bearing gives him away. His bald head fairly gleams with authority. As he speaks, he constantly looks around. His pale eyes, deep set under a determined ridge of brow line, scan the faces of his listeners. He's an energetic speaker, his command of the facts instantaneous.

Under McMaster's and Schadlow's direction, the Trump administration rolled out a fifty-six-page national security strategy that upends Obama's passive, lead-from-behind approach. Mandated by Congress, the document identifies China and Russia by name as "revisionist powers" that seek to dominate their regions and "challenge American power, influence, and interests." It names Iran and North Korea as rogue states that "are determined to destabilize regions." Finally, it spotlights "transnational" threats like jihadists and criminal syndicates that pose cyber and terror risks.

"Previous national security strategies you could say were aspirational in nature," McMaster told me. "The president views the world as it is and recognizes that America has to compete.

He is a competitor. He's advocating for American security and interests and prosperity every day, and I think that's an important overarching point." In sum, Trump is "looking at the world as it is" and "has helped us regain our strategic confidence," McMaster notes.

As one example of the more aggressive, far-reaching approach to protecting national security, Trump blocked a China-backed investor from buying Lattice Semiconductor, an American semiconductor maker, over national security concerns. The White House said the U.S. government relies on the company's products, and the integrity of the semiconductor industry is vital.

Another big change is allowing commanders in the field to trigger strikes against the enemy rather than waiting for approval from the Pentagon and White House.

"Allowing the military to fight the way they need to fight, improving the agility of our armed forces and the speed of action, allow us to seize and retain the initiative over enemies—whether it's ISIS in Syria and Iraq or the Taliban, ISIS, and al-Qaeda in Afghanistan," McMaster says. That has contributed to the almost total defeat of ISIS and almost total removal of the ISIS caliphate from Iraq and Syria, McMaster says.

Contributing to the American success is the fact that Trump "ended that practice of announcing our plans and timelines," McMaster says. "We are no longer going to announce our plans to the enemy. We no longer are going to adhere to artificial timelines."

By demanding that North Atlantic Treaty Organization (NATO) members pay their agreed upon share of the organization's costs and by cutting funding to the anti-Israel, anti-U.S. United Nations, Trump demonstrated that America would not be pushed around in the international arena. And Trump suspended security assistance to Pakistan over its failure to combat terrorist networks within its borders.

Nowhere is the contrast between Obama's approach to foreign policy and Trump's more evident than on Iran. Intent on achieving a nuclear deal with Iran even if its provisions would expire ten to fifteen years after it was signed in 2015 and even if the United States handed over to Iran a hundred billion dollars in assets that had been frozen by America, Obama remained mute during the 2009 Green Movement protests. If the protests had grown, they could conceivably have led to the overthrow of the regime, as happened with other protest movements in the Middle East. When similar protests broke out in Iran in January 2018, Trump spurred on the demonstrators, denouncing the regime as "brutal and corrupt."

Contrary to Bannon's claim that McMaster wanted to increase the number of troops in Afghanistan to fifty thousand or ninety thousand, McMaster, along with Defense Secretary James Mattis, recommended adding four thousand troops to the eighty-four hundred troops already there. He believed the influx would help the Afghan army stabilize a fast-deteriorating security situation.

Despite what McMaster brought to the table, Trump complained about him, as he did with almost everyone else in his orbit with the exception of Melania. Trump told other aides that McMaster was too regimented. He imitated McMaster saying "no, sir"; "yes, sir."

Bannon recruited two businessmen—Erik D. Prince, a founder of the private security firm Blackwater Worldwide, and Stephen A. Feinberg, cofounder of Cerberus Capital Management—who wanted to propose plans to substitute private military contractors for American troops in Afghanistan. Both men owned companies that supply contractors and potentially would have profited from such a policy.

"Afghanistan and the Afghan people are not worth one American kid's life," Bannon told me.

Aside from the fact that private paramilitary forces are also Americans, if the United States were to withdraw from Afghanistan, wouldn't that lead to the creation of new terrorists, as happened when President Obama decided to withdraw from Iraq and ISIS took hold?

"Well, we'd have to go back and kill them," Bannon replied. "But I'm not into American troops staying there a long time, long term."

In keeping with his general aversion to American military entanglements, Trump had long opposed the war. As a private citizen, he repeatedly called on Obama to withdraw the troops.

"It is time to get out of Afghanistan," Trump wrote on Twitter on February 27, 2012, when he was beginning to think about running for president. "We are building roads and schools for people that hate us. It is not in our national interests." That summer, he ratcheted up his calls after a series of attacks by Afghan soldiers on American troops. "Why are we continuing to train these Afghans who then shoot our soldiers in the back?" he wrote on August 21, 2012. "Afghanistan is a complete waste. Time to come home!"

But once he became president, Trump created a national security team with long histories in Afghanistan. Mattis, his defense secretary, is a retired Marine Corps general who lost troops in fierce combat there early in the war. McMaster ran an anticorruption task force that worked with the Afghan government. Still, Trump's top national security officials were taken aback at a meeting in the Situation Room when an angry Trump began ripping apart their latest proposal to send thousands of additional American troops to the country.

"We're losing," the president declared. He complained that the plan was vague and open-ended, with no definition of victory. "What does success look like?" he asked.

Trump never forgot mistakes the United States made in Iraq. He rightly criticized George W. Bush for mishandling the aftermath of the invasion. But when it came to the decision to invade Iraq, what Trump did not realize was that during seven months of secret debriefings before his execution, Saddam Hussein admitted to FBI agent George Piro that to impress Iran, he purposely created the impression that he had weapons of mass destruction. He would refuse to allow inspectors into his palaces, for example. And as reported in my book *The Secrets of the FBI*, Saddam admitted to Piro that he had planned on developing a nuclear weapon within a year when he expected U.N. sanctions to be lifted, in part because he was paying off U.N. inspectors.

An Arabic speaker, Piro found that Saddam had a fondness for baby wipes, the disposable moist cloths used when changing a baby's diaper. If Saddam had enough baby wipes, he would use them to clean food like apples before he ate them. Piro realized that, as a way of manipulating him, he could control how many baby wipes Saddam received.

Ironically, while he disagreed with its policies, Saddam admired America, and he especially liked Americans. He disliked President Bush and his father but was not fixated on them. He liked President Clinton and thought Ronald Reagan was a good president.

When it was time to say good-bye before Saddam's execution, Piro bought two Cuban Cohiba cigars, Saddam's favorite brand, the FBI agent told me. They said good-bye in the traditional Arab manner: a handshake and then a kiss to the right cheek, a kiss to the left, and a kiss to the right again. Saddam appeared shaken and became teary-eyed.

Today Iraq is a democracy and no longer could be a nuclear threat under the control of a dictator who murdered three hundred thousand of his own people. In defending his decision to invade Iraq, for unknown reasons Bush never cited Saddam's admission to the FBI that he had planned on developing a nuclear weapon within a year.

The day before the meeting on Afghanistan troop levels, Trump invited four soldiers who had served there to the White House for lunch. His exchanges with these enlisted men impressed upon him how deliberative he had to be about sending more soldiers into combat and confronting the prospects for turning around a war that had dragged on for some sixteen years.

Illustrating his ability to change course based on the advice he is given, Trump asked tough questions the next day. He finally announced a broader strategy for Afghanistan, one that would require 4,000 more American troops but place more conditions on the Afghan government. In the end, Trump accepted the logic that a big military approach was needed to prevent Afghanistan from again becoming a launch pad for terrorism against the United States.

At a meeting of the National Security Council's principals committee, Bannon clashed with General McMaster, who had taken the lead in developing the Afghanistan policy. Their relationship deteriorated as Bannon and others on the far right waged war within the White House and outside it against Trump's national security adviser.

"It turned into an ugly campaign to smear McMaster's character," says Victoria Coates, a former national security adviser to Senator Ted Cruz who is special assistant to the president and senior director for international negotiations for the National Security Council. "This guy is an American hero. I don't care what you think of General Mattis, General Kelly, or McMaster in terms of their policies. These are people whose lives have been spent in the service of the country."

McMaster took it all with a sense of humor. Coates was moderating a roundtable discussion with McMaster when she had to cut it short.

"I'm sorry, General. I'm going to have to give you the hook," she said. "This has to be the last question."

"Oh, yeah, I'm sorry, guys," McMaster said. "I got to go meet George Soros." The room broke up.

When it came to North Korea, Trump and McMaster knew to be bogus the constant refrain of pundits that there are no good options for taking out the regime to stop its nuclear program. The pundits claimed that Kim Jong-un would obliterate South Korea if the United States took military action against North Korea. But the United States has an array of capabilities to neutralize the regime—from cyberwarfare to robots the size of insects.

The U.S. Air Force has developed missiles that zap electronics with high-power microwaves (HPM). That capability has been advancing secretly ever since the Air Force successfully tested a missile equipped with HPM in 2012.

The missile is called the Counter-Electronics High Power Microwave Advanced Missile Project (CHAMP). Built by Boeing's

Phantom Works for the Air Force Research Laboratory, the Boeing missile emits high-power microwaves (HPM) that disable computer chips. As a result, any electronic device targeted by the thirty-eight-million-dollar missile is rendered inoperable.

The test of the CHAMP missile took place in October 2012. The missile flew over a two-story building on the Utah Test and Firing Range and zapped the compound's entire spectrum of electronic systems, including video cameras set up to film the test, without damaging anything else.

That is the beauty of the HPM missile. Its microwave beam can penetrate bunkers where facilities are hidden without harming the humans inside. Even if a bunker is buried in a mountain, HPM penetrates the facility through its connections to power cables, communication lines, and antennas. HPM can zap any underground military facility and fry its electronics. When targeted at command and control centers, the missile could render any country's military inoperable. And one missile can hit multiple targets in succession. North Korea could attempt to shield its equipment, but U.S. officials doubt that would be effective against CHAMP.

Besides underground bunkers and command centers, HPM can disable fighter planes, tanks, ships, and missile systems. And it can wipe out facilities for developing and testing nuclear weapons.

Even more amazing, the missile renders inoperable any radar that might detect it as it flies to and from a target. Thus, a country cannot take out CHAMP before it strikes. Nor does an adversary have any way of knowing why its facilities have suddenly gone dead.

Until the announcement of the successful test, the project had been classified top secret. When it was announced, only a few trade publications picked up the story. Beyond a few mentions since then, the media have ignored the story. Instead, they have focused on how impossible it is to deal with the North Korea threat.

Unlike an electromagnetic pulse (EMP) created by detonating a nuclear weapon in the atmosphere, because it is targeted HPM leaves intact civilian facilities needed to sustain life. Unlike any other existing countermeasure like a cyberattack, CHAMP permanently destroys electronic equipment.

America's national laboratories operated by the Department of Energy have been working on these capabilities for decades. Equally impressive, one of those laboratories, Sandia National Laboratories, has been developing robots the size of insects that could assassinate the North Korean leader with deadly toxins. These robotic weapons using nanotechnology employed in surgical operations in hospitals are being developed secretly with funding by the Defense Advanced Research Projects Agency.

To be sure, back in 1976, President Ford banned political assassinations with an executive order. But given the threats we face today, that order is obsolete. It was predicated on the assumption that other world leaders are rational and would refrain from attempting an assassination of the U.S. president unless the United States tried to assassinate them. But we are dealing today with terrorist organizations and world leaders like the North Korean dictator who are not rational and do not care if they are killed.

With the stroke of a pen, President Trump could reverse Ford's executive order. Armed with robotlike weapons using nanotechnology, the CIA could wipe out Kim Jong-un without risking American lives.

While President Obama preached "strategic patience" in dealing with North Korea, Trump made it clear he would not stand by while the North Korean leader threatens the survival of America. As Trump constantly reminded the public, his predecessors should have taken care of the threat long ago. When handing over the reins of government to Trump, Obama told him that North Korea was the biggest challenge the new president would face. By that time, the threat was much greater than it had been under Bush.

Because of sequestration budget cuts, the CHAMP missiles did not become operational under the Obama administration. But after I emailed McMaster my op-ed about CHAMP, he thanked me for letting him know about the capability and ordered a briefing. As a result, the Pentagon is now funding the program. According to Mary Lou Robinson, the chief of the High Power Microwave Division of the Air Force Research Lab at Kirtland Air Force Base, the missiles will be operational and ready to take out any target by the time this book comes out.

Despite Trump's false claim that "Obama had my 'wires tapped' in Trump Tower just before the victory," Trump is tough on maintaining surveillance capabilities. Trump pushed aggressively for permanent reauthorization of the Foreign Intelligence Surveillance Act (FISA), including Section 702, which allows a federal court to approve and supervise the collection of information on foreign persons in foreign countries who happen to use American communications services and Internet technology. As one example of its effectiveness, intelligence collected under Section 702 helped prevent al-Qaeda's Najibullah Zazi from conducting a suicide bombing in the New York City subway system in 2009.

Trump's national security team launched a full-bore sales pitch to lawmakers and reporters about the value of the Section

702 surveillance powers. Top officials held an all-Senate briefing with lawmakers on the topic, following up on a field trip NSA had hosted for House members. Senior lawyers and intelligence officials from five national security agencies gathered to brief reporters on the privacy-enhancing tweaks the government has made to Section 702 surveillance efforts over the years.

The administration also pushed companies like Apple to enable the FBI with court orders to obtain access to encrypted mobile devices. The FBI confiscated the phone of the gunman who opened fire at a Texas church, killing twenty-six people and shooting crying babies at point-blank range. But the Bureau announced that it could not access the phone's inner workings as part of the ongoing investigation.

Wray said the Bureau was unable to gain access to the content of 7,775 devices in fiscal 2017—more than half of all the smartphones it tried to crack in that time period—despite having a warrant from a judge.

Wray called it a major public safety issue. The consequences could be "deadly," Attorney General Sessions noted.

For all the claims from the extreme left and the extreme right that the government is "spying on innocent Americans," a breathless term used freely by the media and critics to imply improper intent, no one has been able to credibly cite a case of the government actually engaging in an abuse of surveillance powers. Instead, critics have pointed to the *potential* for abuse. In the same way, a police officer or FBI agent could potentially abuse his position by using his or her weapon unlawfully. Is that a reason to disarm all police officers and FBI agents?

The NSA surveillance program is layered with oversight conducted by Congress, the Foreign Intelligence Surveillance Act (FISA) Court, the Justice Department, and the NSA inspector general. If an abuse were to occur, the proper course would be to prosecute those responsible—not dismantle a program that provides the FBI with leads that have allowed the Bureau to keep us safe from a foreign terrorist attack since 9/11.

As if they had discovered another Watergate scandal, the same media critics who pounced on the intelligence community after 9/11 for failing to connect the dots are the ones exposing and denouncing as an invasion of privacy the program that connects those intelligence dots. Instead of demonizing those who are trying to make us safe, raising hypothetical concerns, and endlessly criticizing programs that work, critics in the media and Congress should be hailing the efforts of the intelligence community to prevent another attack.

At national holidays, we recognize the military for preserving our freedoms. Yet no one mentions the equally important efforts of FBI agents, CIA officers, and NSA employees who work around the clock, sometimes at risk to their lives, to detect and roll up plots.

That's an American success story.

20

VICTIM MENTALITY

While Trump virtually wiped out ISIS and took a more aggressive stance toward threats abroad, he imposed a range of measures to enhance public safety in the United States.

President Obama rarely missed an opportunity to denounce the police's actions, usually erroneously, when a white police officer arrested or killed a black suspect. For instance, Obama said Trayvon Martin, the black teenager shot to death in Florida, "could have been me thirty-five years ago" and said Cambridge police acted "stupidly" when a white police officer arrested a black Harvard professor who was being obstreperous during an investigation of a report of a possible break-in. Obama later admitted he knew nothing about the case.

Weeks after police officer Darren Wilson shot and killed Michael Brown in Ferguson, Missouri, Obama said the shooting death of a black teen by a white police officer exposed the racial divide in the American justice system that "stains the heart of black children." Speaking at the annual Congressional Black Caucus Foundation dinner in Washington, Obama said the death of Brown "awakened our nation" to a reality that black citizens already understood.

In fact, through exhaustive interviews with witnesses, cross-checking their statements with previous statements to authorities and the media, ballistics examinations, DNA tests, and the findings of three autopsies, the Justice Department concluded that Wilson believed Brown matched a description of a suspect in the theft of cigarillos from a convenience store. When Wilson tried to question Brown, the teenager attacked him in his patrol car and tried to take his gun, then charged him outside the police vehicle, according to multiple witnesses. And the claim that Brown put his hands in the air and pleaded "don't shoot" was simply a lie.

As Obama repeatedly denounced police shootings as racist, executions of police officers by black men suddenly became common. For a criminal inclined to murder a police officer, what more excuse is needed than the president of the United States denouncing police shootings as racially motivated? As a result, police hesitated to act proactively to attack crime in the inner cities, fearful that if they had to use their weapon, they would be targeted by Black Lives Matter. Rioting after police shootings of black men became commonplace. And while gun sales saw a sharp increase under Obama, they dropped precipitously after Trump's election, according to FBI statistics, gun shop owners, and corporate reports of gun manufacturers.

Instead of inflaming race relations by making pronouncements about killings of blacks, Trump let local authorities sort out whether police officers who shot suspects had acted improperly and should be prosecuted. While bad cops walk the street and should be severely punished, if you have participated in "shoot, don't shoot" deadly force video scenarios, as I did at the FBI Academy in Quantico, Virginia, you know how nearly impossible it is to accurately decide in a split-second whether your life or another person's life is in danger. Given the minuscule number of bad police, Obama's crusade against the police was akin to denouncing all Muslims as terrorists.

It's difficult to imagine how searing racism in America once was. When I was editor of the Clark University paper in Worcester, Massachusetts, in 1963, I called twenty-three landlords who had placed classified ads for rental apartments in the Clark area and asked if the unit was still available. When told it was, I said, "By the way, my roommate is a Negro. Is that a problem?" Ten of the twenty-six—or 38 percent—said it would be. When I was a *Washington Post* reporter in 1984, I revealed that Lena Ferguson had been denied membership in the Daughters of the American Revolution (DAR) because she is black. DAR president general Sarah M. King acknowledged to me that being black can be a reason for an applicant's rejection by a local chapter, along with "divorce, spite, neighbors' dislike." The story resulted in Ferguson's acceptance as a member and selection as an officer by the local chapter. The DAR agreed to bar discrimination and take affirmative steps to recruit blacks with the necessary lineage.

But while racism still exists—as does anti-Semitism—the truth is that besides colleges that give preference to blacks in admitting students, many companies and organizations today seek to hire blacks and promote them over similarly qualified whites because they think it's the right thing to do or will enhance their public image.

While a Democrat and a liberal on most issues, in his book *Enough: The Phony Leaders, Dead-End Movements, and Culture of Failure That Are Undermining Black America—and What We Can Do About It*, Fox News host Juan Williams attacks the victim mentality that Democrats and black leaders like Al Sharpton and Jesse Jackson perpetrate on the black community today.

"This is a time when, unfortunately, there are too many black leaders who focus on grievance," Williams says. "The only time you see these guys on TV is when they say somebody has been racist or the police department has done something wrong. All they are doing is complain, and it leads young people to a victim mentality, where they don't think they can succeed in America. They don't think they have a chance. They hear from their leaders that if you're black or Hispanic, you don't have a chance."

Williams told me that the Democratic Party "has not delivered in terms of protecting the poor minorities in the country, on basic items, like education for your children, safety in our streets, making sure that you have the opportunity to have an economic foothold on the ladder of upward mobility."

In contrast to the victim mentality, Condoleezza Rice grew up in segregated Birmingham, Alabama, where blacks had to eat separately from whites and use different bathrooms and water fountains. Rice vividly remembered going into a store when she was seven with her mother Angelina. Rice spotted a dress she liked, and her mother asked the saleswoman if her daughter could try it on. The woman took the dress from Rice and motioned to a storage room.

"She'll have to try it on there," the woman said.

"My daughter will try on this dress in a dressing room or I'm not spending my money here," Condoleezza's mother told her.

Hoping to make a commission, the sales clerk furtively showed them the way to a dressing room.

"My parents," Rice told the *Washington Post*, "were very strategic. I was going to be so well prepared, and I was going to do all of these things that were revered in white society so well, so that I would be armored somehow from racism. I would be able to confront white society on its own terms." Rice, who became George W. Bush's national security adviser and secretary of state, lived in a place where restaurants wouldn't serve her a hamburger, she said, "But my parents were telling me I could be president."

Instead of handouts, Trump's remedy for impoverished blacks is growing the economy with tax cuts and deregulation to produce more jobs. The Republican alternative is simply, "Give a man a fish and you feed him for a day. Teach him how to fish and you feed him for a lifetime."

Often, Trump achieved results simply by virtue of his public exhortations. By making illegal immigration an issue, Trump discouraged illegal border crossings from Mexico, cutting the rate by 76 percent and diminishing the drug trade. By threatening to withhold federal funds from sanctuary cities that refuse to cooperate with the government to deport illegal immigrants who have committed crimes, Trump discouraged sanctuaries and made it less likely that illegal immigrants with a record of felonies would commit more crimes in the United States.

Since San Francisco is a sanctuary city, authorities there ignored a request from Immigration and Customs Enforcement

(ICE) that its agents receive notification before releasing from jail Jose Ines Garcia Zarate, an illegal alien with seven felony convictions who had been deported back to Mexico five times. If the authorities had complied with ICE's request, ICE would have picked him up and would have deported him as an illegal immigrant. Instead, he was free to stand along a San Francisco pier and fire a weapon, killing Kate Steinle, thirty-two. The bullet ricocheted off the ground about a hundred feet away before hitting her in the back. She screamed for her father, Jim, as she collapsed to the ground. He tried to save her by performing CPR until help arrived, but it was too late. Kate Steinle died in the hospital hours later.

Garcia Zarate claimed the shooting was an accident, and he was acquitted of murder and involuntary manslaughter. While those who favor sanctuary cities maintain that they aid law enforcement because illegal immigrants are more apt to report crimes if they do not fear being deported, the fact is that illegal immigrants also want to be safe. Kate Steinle and many like her would be alive today if sanctuary cities did not shield felons from immigration laws.

For years, the violent street gang MS-13 has been gaining strength. Mainly Salvadoran immigrants or people of Salvadoran descent, MS-13 members primarily target Hispanic communities. The gangs make money through extortion, prostitution, human trafficking, and drug trafficking. They use machetes to hack to death rivals. To instill fear and enhance their power, they engage in gang rape and cut their victims to pieces.

Instead of relying on local authorities to build cases to wipe them out, Trump used ICE to arrest and deport them as illegal aliens. Calling MS-13 members "animals," Trump said in a speech to law enforcement officers on Long Island, "We're going to destroy MS-13." Under Trump, arrests by ICE of MS-13 members increased on an annual basis by 83 percent.

Behind the initiatives was Priebus, who was in the White House typically from 6 a.m. to midnight seven days a week overseeing the process for drafting executive orders, bringing in CEOs and members of Congress, and arranging Trump's public appearances.

"Reince was engaged in policy more than anything," Steve Bannon says. "He does not have an ideological bent. There was not one big policy that he wasn't in the middle of. I thought Reince was fantastic."

It wasn't his way to attack colleagues through anonymous leaks to the press or to tout his own accomplishments. So Priebus's role in the success of the Trump White House never came out.

21

TAKING A KNEE

For many Trump supporters, the president's comments about the violence in Charlottesville were the last straw, making it difficult to continue to support him. Over several days, Trump seemed to seesaw back and forth about the violence.

It began with his comment from his golf club in Bedminster, New Jersey, when he said, "We condemn in the strongest possible terms this egregious display of hatred, bigotry, and violence on many sides." He repeated, "On many sides."

Moments after he gave this statement, an ABC News reporter shouted a question, asking if Trump wants the support of white nationalist groups, many of whom say they support him, and whether he feels he has denounced them strongly enough. Trump did not answer nor take any other questions from reporters.

Shortly after the president gave his statement, a White House official on background said: "The president was condemning ha-tred, bigotry, and violence from all sources and all sides. There was violence between protesters and counterprotesters today."

The following morning, a White House spokesperson who would not be publicly identified released a statement about Trump's comments.

"The president said very strongly in his statement yesterday that he condemns all forms of violence, bigotry, and hatred, and of course that includes white supremacists, KKK, neo-Nazi, and all extremist groups. He called for national unity and bringing all Americans together."

The next day at roughly 12:40 p.m., Trump made a televised statement at the White House. "Racism is evil," he said. "And those who cause violence in its name are criminals and thugs, including the KKK, neo-Nazis, white supremacists, and other hate groups that are repugnant to everything we hold dear as Americans."

The following day, during a press conference at Trump Tower in Manhattan, Trump lashed out at criticism of his initial state-ment. Asked about his immediate response, Trump quickly went on to blame both sides of protesters for the conflict, add-ing that there were "very fine people" in both the group of white supremacists and white nationalists as well as among the coun-terprotesters.

"I think there is blame on both sides. You look at both sides. I think there is blame on both sides," Trump insisted. "You had some very bad people in that group. You also had some very fine people on both sides," he added.

Finally, during a campaign rally in Phoenix, Arizona, Trump spent about twenty minutes going over his various statements about Charlottesville, omitting some of the most divisive comments and repeatedly criticizing the media for the portrayal of his statements, including how he said that there were "very fine" people on both sides of the violent rally.

"I said everything. I hit them with neo-Nazi. I hit them with everything. I got the white supremacists, the neo-Nazi. I got them all in there. Let's see. KKK, we have KKK. I got them all," Trump said.

Like many of Trump's more controversial comments, what he said was literally true: Given that some of the demonstrators were not Nazis and were simply against tearing down a Confederate statue, there were indeed decent people on both sides, as Trump said. Moreover, as a general proposition, both the extreme left and the extreme right engage in violence. But what Trump failed to see was the broader impression he conveyed.

"If you cross the street when there's a red light, and you get hit by a car, the first thing that people who run to the emergency room to see you don't generally say is, 'Well, it's kind of your fault.' They say, 'How are you? I hope you're okay.'" a Trump aide said. "And I think what happened was the president came out and said, 'Well, you know, they kind of were to blame,' meaning both sides shared responsibility for whatever happened. Okay, that may be true, but that's not exactly what people want to hear at that time. It just was not the right moment to have that explained."

Following Trump's remarks, twenty-one charities, including the International Red Cross Ball that Trump and his wife had attended for years, pulled out of holding fund-raisers at Mar-a-Lago. However, other groups immediately jumped into the breach. Mar-a-Lago's roster for the new season was packed with events, ranging from charities holding their first-ever fund-raisers there to private parties hosted by club members, including a seven-hundred-guest wedding. Billionaires were begging to join the club, but only a limited number of memberships open up each year.

But Trump again sabotaged his own agenda when, in an Oval Office meeting with legislators, he was pushing for an immigration system based on merit. As part of a bipartisan immigration deal, the issue of special protections for immigrants from Haiti, El Salvador, and African countries came up.

"Why are we having all these people from sh——hole countries come here?" Trump allegedly said, according to some who were present. Others in the meeting heard "sh——house," allowing some participants in the meeting, like Homeland Security Secretary Kirstjen Nielsen, to say she did not recall the president "using that exact phrase."

Trump then suggested that the United States instead bring in more people from countries such as Norway. He also suggested he would be open to more immigrants from Asian countries because he felt that immigrants from those countries would contribute to the United States economically. Trump went on to single out Haiti, saying, "Why do we need more Haitians?"

The next day, after attending a White House ceremony to honor Martin Luther King Jr., Isaac Newton Farris Jr., the civil rights leader's nephew, told CNN, "I don't think President Trump is a racist in the traditional sense as we know in this country. I think President Trump is racially ignorant and racially uninformed. But I don't think he is a racist in the traditional sense."

Trump's thoughtless comment brings to mind Lyndon Johnson. A champion of African-Americans, Johnson marshaled support from southern Democrats for his groundbreaking civil rights legislation. But his hypocrisy extended to regularly referring to blacks as "niggers." On *Air Force One*, Johnson was discussing his proposed civil rights bill with two governors. Explaining why it was so important to him, Johnson said it was simple: "I'll have them niggers voting Democratic for 200 years," Robert M. MacMillan, an *Air Force One* steward, told me.

Bannon told me he urged Trump on in the middle of the Charlottesville controversy, but within a week of that, he was gone. Bannon had never enjoyed working in the White House. He saw it as similar to his days in the Navy. A nondrinker, he had no use for White House parties or other perks that go with the job. As soon as Bannon arrived at the White House on Inauguration Day, he realized that he would not be long for the job. He felt that Trump had treated him as a peer during the presidential campaign, but he often complained to friends that when he joined the White House, "all of a sudden I was just a staffer."

Trump, meanwhile, complained publicly and privately that Bannon was taking too much credit for his help on the campaign. Trump told aides he was "annoyed" by *Time* magazine's cover story that included a photo of Bannon.

Focusing on Bannon's influence in the White House, the cover story asked, "Is Steve Bannon the Second Most Powerful Man in the World?"

"That doesn't just happen," Trump told a visitor, a phrase he frequently uses to express anger about subordinates who put their interests ahead of his.

Bannon's portrayal as Trump's puppet master by *Saturday Night Live* further infuriated a boss sharply attuned to his media image and allergic to sharing the stage, especially with someone said to be controlling him.

Soon after the *Time* cover was published, Trump, encouraged by Jared Kushner, humiliated Bannon by stripping him of his position on the National Security Council, cutting him out of key meetings, and declining to voice his faith in him. Trump pointedly told the *Wall Street Journal* that Bannon was just "a guy who works for me." He later added that he was his own strategist.

Trump had also been upset about Bannon's participation in a book by Bloomberg News reporter Joshua Green, *Devil's Bargain*. In particular, the jacket displaying a shared photo billing between Trump and his chief strategist did not sit well.

With John Kelly as chief of staff, when his job security was more precarious than ever, Bannon further imperiled his own standing by giving an interview to the liberal *American Prospect* magazine, in which he sniped by name at his enemies within the White House, including Gary Cohn, the National Economic Council director. He also publicly contradicted the administration's stance on North Korea, saying there was no military solution to the regime's race to develop missiles that could hit the U.S. mainland with nuclear weapons. That infuriated Kelly, who was outraged by the lack of discretion that Bannon displayed in the interview.

When Kelly arranged for his resignation, Bannon was ready to go and head Breitbart News again as executive chairman. After being dismissed from his White House job, Bannon self-importantly called it the end of an era—for the country, not just his career.

"The Trump presidency that we fought for, and won, is over," he said.

As with other former aides, Trump continued to call him. Bannon told Charlie Rose on CBS's *60 Minutes* that firing James Comey as FBI director was the biggest mistake in "modern political history." If Comey had not been fired, former FBI director

Robert Mueller would not have been appointed special counsel and would not be leading his investigation into Russian meddling in the 2016 election, Bannon said.

After the September 10, 2017, show, Trump called Bannon, who was in Asia, and congratulated him.

"He starts off by saying, 'You're such a piece of work,'" Bannon says. "We just start talking about Charlie Rose, and he starts talking about all the guys attacking him. He was on a roll."

As for Bannon's criticism of him for firing Comey, Trump did not mention it, Bannon says. "I told that to the president to his face on many occasions," Bannon says.

However, after Michael Wolff's book quoted Bannon calling Don Jr.'s meeting with a Russian lawyer during the campaign "treasonous," Trump denounced him, saying, "When Bannon was fired, he not only lost his job, he lost his mind." Soon, Bannon was gone from Breitbart. In his book *Fire and Fury*, Wolff claims he interviewed Trump, but Communications Director Hope Hicks told me Trump spoke to Wolff "about something unrelated in February [2017], and Michael is characterizing it as an interview for the book."

Even though Wolff writes for liberal publications such as *Vanity Fair*, Bannon pushed Wolff's book project, and the White House went along. Contrary to his claims, Wolff was not allowed to roam freely in the West Wing but operated like any other reporter with a White House hard pass.

Wolff's book claims that Bannon saw Trump's comments about the Charlottesville violence as a sign that he is mentally unfit for office and could be removed under the provisions of the Twenty-Fifth Amendment. But I was interviewing Bannon for this book in the middle of the Charlottesville controversy.

Our interview took place in Bannon's temporary office in the Eisenhower Executive Office when the White House was being renovated.

Contrary to Wolff's portrayal, Bannon was gleeful about the president's comments. He told me he spoke with Trump twice by phone as the backlash over his comments erupted and had urged him on. He said he told Trump that if he retracted or modified anything he had said, the press would only attack him for not being vehement enough and saying too little, too late. Thus, instead of being horrified by Trump's comments, he told me he was congratulating him.

Wolff's book is riddled with false claims, many obviously so: that Melania did not want Trump to run for president or to win, that he did not want to win and assured her he would not win, that he looked like a ghost when he did win, that she cried when he won and when he was inaugurated, that Trump and Melania have separate bedrooms, that he wanted a lock on his bedroom but the Secret Service objected, that Trump spends little time with Melania and barely knows Barron, that he goes to McDonald's because he fears he will be poisoned and eats McDonald's hamburgers in bed, that his memory is so impaired that he failed to recognize a succession of old friends at Mar-a-Lago, that he doesn't read, that he did not know who former House Speaker John Boehner was, and that a hundred percent of his staff—including Ivanka and Jared—question his intelligence and fitness for office.

But after a three-hour physical exam, Dr. Ronny Jackson, the White House doctor, pronounced Trump at seventy-one mentally and physically fit for office, having achieved a perfect score on the cognitive test. Dr. Jackson said Trump agreed to work on plans to improve his diet and to introduce physical exercise to his routine. Wolff actually conducted many of his White House interviews without recording or taking notes. The fact that most of the mainstream media took such a book seriously is a testament to how far journalistic standards have sunk.

If Trump undercut his own support with ambiguous remarks about the violence in Charlottesville, he more than made up for it by condemning professional football players who make tens of millions of dollars a year and yet cannot bring themselves to honor the country by standing for the national anthem.

The flap began when San Francisco 49ers quarterback Colin Kaepernick started protesting by taking a knee—football terminology for when the quarterback puts a knee to the ground to signal the end of a play—instead of standing while the national anthem was being played before the start of games. Kaepernick saw his gesture as a way to point to what he viewed as the oppression of people of color in the United States. During practice sessions, the quarterback wore socks that depicted policemen as cartoon pigs.

Kaepernick was first noticed sitting down during the singing of "The Star-Spangled Banner" at the 49er's third preseason game in August 2016. In a postgame interview, he explained his position, saying, "I am not going to stand up to show pride in a flag for a country that oppresses black people and people of color. To me, this is bigger than football, and it would be selfish on my part to look the other way. There are bodies in the street and people getting paid leave and getting away with murder," referring to allegations of improper shooting of black men by police officers. Never mind that according to a *Washington Post* analysis, police fatally shot twice as many whites as blacks in 2017. For good measure, Kaepernick threw in references to slavery.

Kaepernick's protest set off a wave of similar demonstrations by professional athletes, most of them black, and a national debate about the very nature of America. Meanwhile, the football player opted out of his contract after he played poorly for two seasons. He then complained he was being discriminated against because no one wanted to hire him.

In September 2017, Trump sent out multiple tweets saying that National Football League players should be either fired or suspended if they fail to stand for the national anthem. In response, many NFL owners and players came together to protest Trump's position. The protest movement morphed into a condemnation of Trump. The players knelt, locked arms, or even remained in the locker room as the anthem was played. Trump fueled the controversy by praising National Association for Stock Car Auto Racing (NASCAR) drivers who stood for the anthem.

The California chapter of the NAACP supported Kaepernick's protest and called for the removal of "The Star-Spangled Banner" as the national anthem on the grounds it is racist. The chapter's beef was with the third stanza, which is rarely sung, because it mentions slaves: "Their blood has wash'd out their foul footstep's pollution. No refuge could save the hireling and slave from the terror of flight or the gloom of the grave." Based on that tortured reasoning, Congress should adopt a new national anthem that is not "another song that disenfranchises part of the American population," said California NAACP president Alice Huffman.

No other president would have called out a black man over his disrespect for a symbol of America. When no team wanted to hire Kaepernick, TV pundits claimed his First Amendment rights were being violated, forgetting that as employees themselves, they would be fired on the spot for kneeling on air while the national anthem was being played or to demonstrate support for any cause.

Trump's new chief of staff John Kelly waded into the national anthem controversy, telling other aides he fully supported the president's position that NFL players should be suspended or fired if they refuse to stand for the national anthem.

"Every American should take the three minutes or so that it takes for the national anthem to play to stand up, remove their hat, put their hand over their heart, and think about the men and women that have been named, sacrificing their lives, so that song can be played in the stadium," Kelly said in a statement released by the White House.

Meanwhile, attendance at games slumped, and NFL TV audiences declined by 9 percent over the previous season because most fans watch the games for entertainment, not to see disrespect for a symbol of America. During the same period, television viewership of National Basketball Association games increased by 15 percent.

The media saw Trump's moves as a cynical way to appeal to white working-class supporters. While it had that effect, the fact is that Trump has always been deeply patriotic and respectful of the symbols that define America. Indeed, if you want to know what Donald Trump is all about, drive past his Mar-a-Lago home and club on South Ocean Boulevard in Palm Beach.

Fluttering over the landscape is a massive American flag visible in all directions. When Trump had it erected in 2006, the flag was closer to the street and mounted on a much taller flag pole. Then the town of Palm Beach claimed the flag's height exceeded zoning regulations and began fining Trump $1,250 a day unless he removed it.

Trump sued for twenty-five million dollars, claiming his First Amendment rights were being violated. In 2007, Trump and the town settled. Trump agreed to mount the flag on a shorter flagpole. Instead of paying the fine that by then totaled $120,000, Trump agreed to donate $100,000 to Iraq War veterans' charities or the local VA hospital.

As he is glad to tell you, Trump usually wins in the end. He moved the flag to ground that he had his workers elevate, so now it towers over the landscape as much as before.

Tony Senecal, Trump's former butler at Mar-a-Lago, attributes the Mar-a-Lago spat to Trump's patriotism. "You know Donald Trump was born on Flag Day, and I swear it's in his blood," Senecal says, referring to Trump's June 14, 1946, birth. "He really is red, white, and blue."

22

HAIR SPRAY

When Trump became president, he gave up flying on his Boeing 757-200, which he bought for a hundred million dollars in 2011. That plane boasts twenty-four-karat gold-plated seat belts and bathroom fittings, mohair couches, creamy calfskin seats, two bedrooms with gold silk sheets and pillows embroidered with the Trump family crest, and powerful Rolls-Royce turbofan engines. A one-hour flight costs $10,800 for fuel and maintenance.

As president, Trump traded up to *Air Force One*, which seats seventy people, compared with forty-three on what Trump called *Trump Force One*. Known by the Secret Service code name Angel, *Air Force One* got its name when Dwight D. Eisenhower was president. Prior to that, the aircraft used by Franklin D. Roosevelt and Harry S. Truman had been known by Air Force designations. Because a flight controller mistook the president's plane for a commercial one, the pilot suggested calling the plane the president was using *Air Force One*.

The current presidential plane is a Boeing 747-200B bubble top jumbo jet acquired in 1990 when George H. W. Bush was president. It has a range of 7,825 miles and a maximum cruising altitude of 45,100 feet. It cruises at 600 miles per hour but can achieve speeds of 701 miles per hour. In addition to two pilots, a navigator, and a flight engineer, the 231-foot-long plane has eighty-seven telephones.

While the average 747 has 485,000 feet of electrical wire, the presidential plane has 1.2 million feet, all shielded from the electromagnetic pulse that would be emitted during a nuclear blast. Near the front of the six-story-high plane, the president has an executive suite with a stateroom, dressing room, and bathroom with shower. The president also has a private office near the stateroom and a combination dining room and conference room. Toward the back are areas for the staff, Secret Service, guests, and the press. The cost of hourly operation is $142,380, not including flight crew salaries.

Under Federal Aviation Administration regulations, *Air Force One* takes precedence over all other aircraft. When approaching an airport, it bumps other planes that preceded it into the air space. Before it lands, Secret Service agents on the ground check the runway for explosives or objects such as stray tires. Generally, other aircraft may not land on the same runway for fifteen or twenty minutes before *Air Force One* lands.

Before buying his Boeing 757-200 from Microsoft cofounder Paul Allen, Trump owned a Boeing 727-100. Like the newer plane, it had gold-plated fixtures, including gold-plated seat belts. Trump's pilot, Mike Donovan, had been an Eastern Airlines pilot for twenty-seven years. He flew the plane for Trump for fifteen years as his director of flight operations and chief pilot, piloting fifteen hundred round-trip flights with Trump. Each round trip between New York and Palm Beach cost $40,000 for fuel and maintenance.

A jovial redhead, Donovan considered Trump a good boss, someone who issued clear instructions, was considerate, and never tried to push him to fly hours beyond the maximum allowed by FAA regulations.

"Trump wanted to make sure that we were running a legal and safe operation," Donovan tells me.

One morning, Donovan was flying Trump to Chicago, along with Ivanka; Michael Cohen, the Trump Organization's executive vice president and special counsel; and Larry Glick, Trump's executive vice president for development. Handing over control to his copilot, Donovan went back into the cabin to greet his passengers. At that point, Cohen came out of the lavatory looking ashen.

"What's the matter, Mike?" Donovan asked.

Cohen showed his hands, palms up. They were blue. Cohen explained that he was sitting on a gold silk couch and opened his fountain pen. The ink splattered all over his hands and spread all over the couch.

"I could tell right away that the boss was very, very unhappy, very upset," Donovan says. "He asked what I could do about it now. And I said there's really nothing I could do. By that time, Michael Cohen thought he had lost his job."

They continued to Midway International Airport. When the passengers had left the plane, Donovan asked a ramp attendant if he had any solution. The man took a look at the mess.

"Do you have any hair spray?" the attendant asked.

"We got all kinds of hair spray," Donovan said.

Donovan went into Trump's bedroom and snagged a can of Mink, Trump's favorite. He also uses Aqua Net.

The ramp attendant sprayed the entire can of hair spray on the couch, telling Donovan to check it in an hour after it had set.

"About an hour later, we came back up, and sure enough, the ink was gone," Donovan says.

When Trump returned to the plane, he was surprised not to see the giant ink blot.

"What happened?" he asked.

Donovan explained how Trump's hair spray made the ink disappear.

"If that's what it does to the couch, what is it doing to my hair?" Trump said.

Trump usually did not want to spend money on a flight attendant or fancy meals. He would often eat a deli sandwich on the plane. On the flight to Mar-a-Lago as part of my research for my book *The Season*, Trump kept walking back to the 727's galley for another hard pretzel. Then he broke out the Pringles. He seemed to need constant refueling.

Now on *Air Force One*, Trump munches on Starburst candies—strawberry, cherry, orange, or lemon chewy candies made by Mars. He may also eat a Hershey's milk chocolate bar, no almonds.

Until Trump's father, Fred, became too frail to travel, Trump included both his parents as well as his siblings on weekend trips to Mar-a-Lago. When Fred could no longer travel, "Once everybody was on the airplane, they'd bring his father out, and he'd come up into the airplane, and they'd sit there for twenty five minutes or so just to include everybody," Donovan says. "It meant so much to his father and his mother."

Trump displays black-and-white photos of both parents on the table behind his desk chair in the Oval Office.

As with *Air Force One*, Mar-a-Lago, and the White House it-self, Trump uses his golf courses to help forge personal relation-ships and woo those he needs to his side. Trump owns almost two dozen golf courses all over the world, from Bali in Indone-sia to Turnberry in Scotland. Each has an expansive pool sur-rounded by lush landscaping. When in the New York area, he stays at the golf club in Bedminster, New Jersey, rather than the one in Westchester, New York, because Melania prefers the accommodations at Bedminster, located on six hundred acres forty minutes from Manhattan.

Depending on where they are located, insiders say, "I'm going to Trump," meaning the closest one of his golf clubs or hotels, such as Trump International Hotel in Washington.

Contrary to the caricatures, Trump routinely promotes blacks and Hispanics at his clubs. Trump promoted Kenneth Baloyi, an African-American waiter at Mar-a-Lago, to somme-lier, then to food and beverage director at Mar-a-Lago, then to director of membership and marketing at Trump National Golf Club Westchester in Briarcliff Manor, New York.

It was at the previous incarnation of that golf club that Trump met Dan Scavino, who became the head of Trump's so-cial media operation during the campaign and now directs it at the White House. Scavino was in high school and took a job cleaning golf clubs at what was then Briar Hall Country Club, which Trump bought at foreclosure and turned into his West-chester golf club. Trump pulled into the parking lot in a stretch limousine, and Scavino, age sixteen, was chosen to be the mo-gul's caddy.

Wait until the kids at school hear about this on Monday, Sca-vino thought to himself.

"I was star-struck," he told *Westchester* magazine. "I remember his first gratuity. It was two bills—two hundred-dollar bills. I said, 'I am never spending this money.' I still have both bills."

In 2004, Scavino started working as assistant manager at Trump National Golf Club. He was promoted to executive vice president and general manager in 2008.

During work hours, Trump will dictate tweets for Scavino or other staffers to transcribe and send from the president's account, Trump's way of bypassing the mainstream media. Scavino occasionally politely raises objections to Trump's tweets, and Trump listens to him. But when Trump retreats to his private quarters for the evening, for better or worse, it's just Trump and his phone.

Even though Senator Rand Paul kept voting against bills Trump was pushing, until Paul sustained broken ribs after a vicious attack by a neighbor, Trump repeatedly played golf with the junior senator from Kentucky. Eventually, Paul supported Trump's health-care bill.

During one presidential primary debate, Trump called Paul a "spoiled brat." He also went after his physical appearance at a debate when he said: "I never attacked him on his look and believe me there's plenty of subject matter there."

But Trump drove the golf cart as the two played at Trump National Golf Club, his eight-hundred-acre club at Lowes Island in Potomac Falls, Virginia. Paul's senior aide Sergio Gor came with them, and Trump sometimes invited Mike Mulvaney, director of the Office of Management and Budget. Including the motorcade between the White House and the club, breakfast and lunch at the club, and eighteen holes of golf, the day usually lasted eight to nine hours.

"The president never loses, didn't you know?" Paul quipped

to reporters when asked after golfing with him how the president had done. "The president and his partner beat myself and my partner by three holes. He's a little better golfer than I am, admittedly, but we had a good time."

Paul brought copies of *The Art of the Deal* with him to a meeting with the House Freedom Caucus and urged members to brush up on Trump's tactics. "The worst thing you can possibly do in a deal is seem desperate to make it," Trump wrote. "That makes the other guy smell blood, and then you're dead." The Republican senator also brought a poster with a quote from a chapter on how to "use your leverage."

Playing golf with Paul is "a strategy, because Trump knows that eventually, it's going to pay off," Priebus says. "People keep telling him, well, don't waste your time. I think his negotiation is very long term. People always say he's just transactional. He is transactional, but he also thinks long term."

As a golfer, Trump has a two or three handicap, meaning he is in the top echelon of club golfers, says Trump's friend Gary Giulietti, who belongs to both Mar-a-Lago and Trump International Golf Course in West Palm Beach. On the golf course, "He's a tiger. He wants to win. He wants to win on the golf course. He wants to win in business. He wants to win for the country. I've never met anybody like him. He's about as tough a competitor as there is no matter what."

The golf cart paths at the Westchester club had just been repaved when Trump noticed track marks on the new pavement from a snow removal machine.

"Trump went crazy on the club manager," Giulietti recalls. "A few hours later, he is with the guy, putting his arm around him, telling him how much he appreciates his effort."

"I hope you understand that what I was trying to do is educate you, because now that I have to repave, I can't just repave this little piece," Trump told him. "I've got to make it all match, all for an innocent mistake."

Giulietti then saw Trump give the manager two one-hundred-dollar bills.

23

THE RED BUTTON

Trump wakes up at 5 a.m. and sleeps only four hours a night. Before entering the White House, he slept even less. A cleanliness freak, the president likes to take a long shower of fifteen minutes. Then he sprays his famous hair.

"What's the difference between a wet raccoon and Donald J. Trump's hair?" Trump asked during his Comedy Central roast in 2011. "A wet raccoon doesn't have seven billion f—ing dollars in the bank."

"I do not wear a toupee," he told supporters at a campaign rally, pulling a woman from the audience to prove it by having her touch his very real, not-a-toupee hair. At another rally, he complained that hair spray is not what it used to be because of concerns that it affects the ozone layer.

Over breakfast, Trump will start reading the papers. At 6 a.m., he begins watching the news. He watches Fox News, CNN, and MSNBC. Then he switches to ABC, NBC, and CBS.

Trump reads the *New York Times, Washington Post,* and *Wall Street Journal* cover to cover. Trump also reads op-eds in the *Washington Times* and looks at the *New York Post* and the *Financial Times.*

"He reads magazines as they come in, particularly if it's about him," Bannon says. "He's a voracious consumer of the cable news channels. He just watches those nonstop. He watches all the morning shows."

Trump does not use a computer or go online, but staffers will print him out articles that appear on Breitbart News and the Daily Caller. Melania also gives him articles, sometimes with handwritten notes with her comments or pointing out particular sections that he should read. Trump will walk around with a box of press clippings he plans to peruse.

Aides who wanted to discredit Bannon internally would give Trump articles from Breitbart to make the president mad at him, suggesting he is not the president's friend. Bannon would deny he had anything to do with the articles critical of the president or of White House aides and say he did not control Breitbart.

By 10 a.m., Trump is in the Oval Office. Trump himself selected new Oval Office wallpaper from York Wallcoverings in Pennsylvania, where executives first thought the order was a prank. The print was a baroque floral damask pattern with tones of white, light taupe, and gold, Trump's favorite color. It had been supplied to previous administrations but was discontinued in 2014. Yet the White House insisted on having it delivered the same day it was ordered. It was to be part of a White House renovation plan that included a new heating and air-conditioning system, repainting, and replacement of all the carpeting.

The company halted other work and assigned twenty employees to the job. They had to mix all the inks by hand. But ninety-six rolls of the wallpaper arrived at the White House on time.

In case an intruder is able to penetrate the White House, the Secret Service provides secret alarms in the Oval Office and the White House residence. The Secret Service's Technical Security Division (TSD) also installs devices at White House entrances to detect radiation and explosives. Populated with real-life Qs, James Bond's fictional gadget master, TSD sweeps the White House and hotel rooms for electronic bugs. While electronic bugs have never been found in the White House, they are occasionally found in hotel rooms where they had been planted to pick up conversations of previous guests.

TSD samples the air and water in the White House for contaminants, radioactivity, and deadly bacteria. It keeps the air in the White House at high pressure to expel possible contaminants. It provides agents with special hoods called expedient hoods to be placed over the president's head in the event of a chemical attack. Each year, TSD screens nearly a million pieces of mail sent to the White House for pathogens and other biological threats. In conjunction with Los Alamos National Laboratory or Sandia National Laboratories, it runs top-secret risk assessments to find any holes in physical or cyber security measures.

In case an assassin manages to penetrate all the security while trying to see the president, TSD has installed panic buttons and alarms in the Oval Office and the residence part of the White House. They can be used if there is a medical emergency or physical threat. Many of the alarm triggers are small presidential seals that sit on tables or desks and are activated if knocked over.

The panic alarms bring Secret Service agents running, guns drawn. Besides agents and uniformed officers stationed around the Oval Office, agents deploy from W-16, a staging room used by the Secret Service under the Oval Office.

The White House has emergency escape routes, including a tunnel ten feet wide and seven feet high. It extends from a sub-basement of the White House under the east wing to the basement of the Treasury Department adjacent to the White House grounds.

After 9/11, the Defense Department began drawing up plans for a secret bunker under the North Lawn. At least five stories deep, the bunker, which was completed near the end of President Obama's tenure, can house the staff of the entire West Wing indefinitely in the event of a weapons of mass destruction attack. After Trump became president, top staffers toured the bunker, whose existence is classified. While it was being built, the General Services Administration, which provides federal office space, issued bogus claims that the construction on the North Lawn was to relocate utility lines.

In protecting the White House, the Secret Service's Uniformed Division employs what it calls canine units. In all, the agency has seventy-five of the dogs. Mainly Belgian Malinois, most of the dogs are cross-trained to sniff out explosives and attack an intruder. While they resemble German shepherds, the breed is believed to be higher energy and more agile. The dogs are prey-driven, and ball play is their reward after they locate their "prey."

While waiting to check cleared vehicles that arrive at the White House's southwest gate, the dogs stand on a white concrete pad that is refrigerated in summer so their paws don't get hot. Each dog eagerly checks out about a hundred cars a day.

When Trump arrives at the Oval Office each morning, he usually starts off by discussing with his staff the latest news reports and how to convey the White House message. Occasionally, he tries to guess the source of critical items or leaks, but most of the time he assumes the material is made up with no actual sources.

"When he comes in in the morning, he knows every article, good, bad, and indifferent," Priebus says.

By 10:30 a.m., Trump is receiving an intelligence report from the CIA. He reads his copy of the President's Daily Brief (PDB), the top-secret digest of the latest intelligence. He interrupts the briefers with questions and demands brevity. He likes to pore over visuals—maps, charts, pictures, and videos, as well as "killer graphics," as CIA director Mike Pompeo has phrased it. Besides Pompeo, McMaster, John F. Kelly, and Pence usually attend. Depending on the topic of the day, other administration principals join, including Defense Secretary James "Mad Dog" Mattis. The briefings last thirty to forty-five minutes.

"He always asks hard questions, which I think is the sign of a good intelligence consumer," Pompeo says. "He'll challenge analytic lines that we'll present, which is again completely appropriate. It is frequently the case that we'll find that we need to go back and do more work to develop something, to round something out."

"There was never a lack of detailed questioning from the president," Priebus says. "In fact, he loves getting the intelligence leads. That was something that people out there would be proud of, the way he deliberates on serious military conflicts. People have this assumption that he shoots from the hip with Twitter and all that. When it comes to using the military, it would give everyone a lot of comfort if they saw how he acts privately when it comes to the use of the military. He is actually slower and more deliberate than the generals around him. Everyone thinks that the generals are the big moderating force for the president. The truth is the president is methodical and slow to the trigger."

When it came to unleashing missiles on Syria, for example, "The president was very deliberative, very thoughtful, had no problem slowing things down and saying we're going to talk again tomorrow," Priebus says. "In situations like that, I think both Republicans and Democrats would be proud to know the kind of leadership he displays."

Nor, when it came to increasing the number of troops in Afghanistan, was Trump in a hurry, Priebus says. "He didn't care if they wanted to drag him down in the Situation Room ten times. He cares a lot about using the military wisely, and he just doesn't like the idea of just throwing troops around the Middle East."

Whether under Priebus or Kelly, Trump functions as his own chief of staff. He does not like to feel overmanaged. His reaction to being restricted is to open the floodgates and allow more people access, not less.

Trump usually leaves the office by 6:30 p.m. and almost always has dinner plans. John McEntee, his personal aide or body man, tries to keep him on schedule, and he is rarely late. McEntee, twenty-six years old, was a signal caller on the University of Connecticut's football team, then went to work for Fox News as a production assistant. He volunteered for the Trump campaign and became trip director.

In contrast to Trump, Secret Service agents on Bill Clinton's detail referred to "Clinton Standard Time," meaning Clinton was always one to two hours late.

"Bill Clinton was never on time," former agent Jeff Crane says. "He didn't care how late he was or whether it strained our resources."

If Clinton was inconsiderate, Hillary is a shrew. Hillary pretends to be a compassionate woman who cares about the "little people" and is a champion of the middle class. The reality is that behind the scenes, she is abusive to those same people.

As detailed in my book *The First Family Detail*, Hillary is so nasty to Secret Service agents who would lay down their lives for her that being assigned to her detail is considered a form of punishment and the worst assignment in the Secret Service.

"We were basically told, the Clintons don't want to see you, they don't want to hear you, get out of the way," says a former Secret Service agent of the Clintons' White House years. "If Hillary was walking down a hall, you were supposed to hide behind drapes used as partitions. Supervisors would tell us, 'Listen, stand behind this curtain. They're coming,' or 'Just stand out of the way, don't be seen.'"

Agents say Hillary's nastiness and contempt for them, and disdain for law enforcement and the military in general, has continued, both when she was secretary of state and now that she is protected as a former first lady, earning her the distinction of being considered the Secret Service's most detested protectee.

"Hillary would cuss at Secret Service drivers for going over bumps," former agent Crane says.

FBI agents assigned by Independent Counsel Ken Starr to investigate the death of Vince Foster found that Hillary Clinton triggered her friend's suicide, humiliating the already depressed deputy White House counsel in front of his colleagues at a

White House meeting. She called him a small town hick lawyer who would never make it in the big time and who had failed the Clintons. Based on interviews with aides present at the meeting and with Foster's family members and friends, the FBI found that his mood plummeted after Hillary's attack, leading to his suicide a week later.

In contrast to the image he wanted to project, Biden was so thoughtless that he would swim naked in the swimming pools at the vice president's residence and at his home in Wilmington, offending female Secret Service agents. They signed up to take a bullet for the president or vice president—not to see Joe Biden naked.

Trump never swims at Mar-a-Lago, but he is vigorous and gets some exercise by playing golf. He has always gone for six strips of bacon at breakfast or sausages with three eggs. He likes hamburgers without the bun and steak well done, often eaten with ketchup. He rarely eats vegetables. And he has rich desserts with two scoops of ice cream. When campaigning, he went for Kentucky Fried Chicken, Domino's Pizza, or burgers from Wendy's or McDonald's.

Now that he is president, the Secret Service has put a stop to Trump's impromptu visits to fast-food outlets. When the president is eating out, Secret Service agents run background checks on employees and supervise the food preparation. Whether in Washington, Palm Beach, or New York, Trump almost never dines at an establishment he does not own. Why promote other businesses?

At Mar-a-Lago, Trump orders either the dry aged prime strip steak that club manager Bernd Lembcke orders from Bush Brothers Provision Co. in West Palm Beach or the meatloaf that, per Trump's order, is always on the menu and is said to be made from his mother's recipe.

With his preference for steak well done, Trump emulates Ronald Reagan. Besides steak, Reagan liked hamburger soup—made with ground beef, tomatoes, and carrots—roast beef hash, beef and kidney pie, and osso buco. Nancy Reagan liked paella à la Valenciana, salmon mousse, and chicken pot pie. For dessert, the Reagans both liked apple brown betty, prune whip, fruit with Cointreau, and plum pudding.

Trump does not drink alcohol. Melania sometimes drinks a glass of red wine at dinner, but Trump drinks a Diet Coke or occasionally a virgin piña colada mixed for him at the bar overlooking the main pool at Mar-a-Lago. In the Oval Office, when Trump presses a red button on a box on his desk, a butler arrives with a Diet Coke. He then may order other items as well, such as Lay's potato chips, classic style, which he eats during the day as a snack.

Trump has attributed his decision to abstain from drinking to seeing his brother Fred Jr. struggle with alcoholism. His brother, who died in 1981 at the age of forty-three, was the second oldest of Trump's siblings. Maryanne Trump Barry is the oldest. After Freddy came Elizabeth, Donald, and Robert. Fred Jr. worked briefly for his father in the family real estate business but left to become a pilot. He married and had two children.

Drinking became a problem for Freddy when he was in his twenties. He gave up flying because he knew his drinking could lead to disaster. He divorced and tried his hand at commercial fishing in Florida, but he failed at that. By the late 1970s, he was living with his parents and working as a maintenance worker for his father.

Donald was in college when he met Freddy for dinner in a Queens apartment complex built by their father. Also at the dinner were Freddy's best friend and the friend's girlfriend,

Annamaria Schifano. Freddy had a gift for imitating W. C. Fields, according to a *New York Times* report. As he joked around, his younger brother grew impatient. "Grow up, get serious, and make something of yourself in the family business, Donald scolded," according to the *New York Times'* story.

"Donald put Freddy down quite a bit," Schifano told the paper. "There was a lot of combustion." However, Trump later asked Freddy to be best man at his first marriage in 1977 to Ivana Zelnickova, a Czech model who became an accomplished business woman restoring and managing Trump's landmark Plaza Hotel.

According to the *Times*, "Trump said he had learned by watching his brother how bad choices could drag down even those who seemed destined to rise. Seeing his brother's agony fighting his alcoholism led him to avoid ever trying alcohol or cigarettes, he said."

As president, Trump personalized his antidrug message at the White House when he declared the opioid crisis a public health emergency and announced an education program and other measures to combat the crisis. To fight the epidemic that had led to sixty-four thousand overdose deaths a year, the president said the government would produce "really tough, really big, really great advertising" aimed at persuading Americans not to start using opioids in the first place. Campaigns aimed at smoking are a model. In 1955, 45 percent of American adults said they smoked cigarettes. Today, the rate is 15 percent.

Speaking about the opioid crisis at the White House, Trump remembered his brother as a "great guy, best looking guy," with a personality "much better than mine." But "he had a problem, he had a problem with alcohol. I learned because of Fred."

When his brother urged him not to smoke or drink, Trump

said he listened to him. "And to this day, I've never had a drink, and I have no longing for it. I have no interest in it. To this day, I've never had a cigarette." Trump said, "If we can teach young people and people generally not to start, it's really, really easy not to take [drugs]."

As they were growing up, Trump constantly drilled the same message into his kids.

"No tattoos, no piercings outside of the ears, there were a lot of rules," Ivanka Trump said of her life growing up. "But I think more than everything he really tried to lead us by example. He was a disciplinarian, but I could get around it often," she laughed in a *Fox & Friends* interview. "Once in a while I'd find my way through."

While his daughter Tiffany lived in California with her mother, Marla Maples, Trump made it a point to fly to California regularly to visit her.

No matter how important the meeting he was conducting, Trump always made it a practice to take his children's phone calls. At the age of ten, Ivanka would call her father collect from a pay phone at school every day during recess. He picked up the phone every time. Unusual with men, he kisses his sons on the cheek when he sees them. And he made sure all the children understood the value of a dollar.

"I think at the end of each of our lives, if we can be judged by nothing else, if you choose one way to be judged, I'm sure we would all prefer that to be how we impacted the next generation, our progeny," Kellyanne Conway notes. And no matter how people line up politically, almost everyone recognizes that Trump has raised five outstanding children. "They are moral, generous, kind, and loving people," Conway says. "On that, Donald Trump is five for five."

24

INTERVIEW WITH
THE PRESIDENT

The air was chilly outside Mar-a-Lago on the night before the New Year's Eve party that would usher in 2018. Instead of dining on the terrace as they usually do, Trump and Melania were having dinner inside the living room at a large round table in front of the fireplace.

Compared with the previous New Year's Eve after Trump had been elected, security was enhanced. A thicket of bushes at the edge of the front lawn had been thinned to allow Secret Service agents to see through. Clad in black battle-dress uniform, the Secret Service's counterassault teams armed with semi-automatic Stoner SR-16 rifles, SIG Sauer P229 pistols, flash bang grenades for diversionary tactics, and smoke grenades were deployed in the parking lot leading to the Beach Club's pool on the ocean. Lasers detected intruders at night. Secret Service agents seemed to be everywhere.

Pam and I were dining with our friends Gary and Mary Ellen Giulietti in the dining room called the tea room that adjoins the Mar-a-Lago living room. Jared and Ivanka were eating alone near us. Just after 10:30 p.m., we stopped at the president's table. Trump greeted us and immediately tore into Steve Bannon, saying Bannon had little to do with his success.

I asked for an interview, which I had been teeing up for some months. Trump agreed to do it the next day but was not saying when. Sitting next to him, Melania lent her support for the interview by suggesting that he call over John McEntee, his personal aide, to set a time.

Later, as we were talking with McEntee, the president came over and said, "Let's do it now." We went to a corner of the Venetian palace living room. Two stories high, the living room provides a view of the ocean to the east and the Intracoastal Waterway to the west. The ceiling is gilded in gold leaf.

At the time, major companies had begun announcing bonuses of $1,000, pay raises, or increased contributions to 401(k) plans because a tax reduction had been passed. Within a few weeks, the number would grow to 250 companies giving bonuses to over three million employees who would receive the bonuses along with cuts in withholding for their personal income taxes.

In the only interview for a book Trump said he has given or will give as president, I asked him why he thinks Democrats and the mainstream media don't understand why such measures as the tax cut help the middle class and create jobs.

"The Democrats understand it, they just hate that we were able to get it approved because they know ultimately it is the kiss of death for them," Trump said. "They opposed it. And anybody that ran against it and refused to sign these massive tax cuts for the middle class, helping to create jobs, is going to have, I think, some very difficult times."

Asked why they ignore the progress the Trump administration has made, he said, "Well, they have their thing. They're obstructionists, and we'll see how it all works out. I think we're going to do very well. I think we're going to have a big surprise in '18. It's just kicking in and is much bigger than anyone ever anticipated. It's going to be one of the great bills in terms of jobs, in terms of economic development, and in terms of the middle class."

Less than a week after we talked at Mar-a-Lago, the Dow hit 25,000 for the first time ever, advancing by 1,000 points in twenty-three days, the shortest span between 1,000-point gains in the history of the Dow. Since Trump's election, the Dow had achieved a record close eighty-nine times.

I asked Trump why he believes working-class people understand him more than other groups.

"I think because ultimately that's the people I care about," Trump said. "I care about all people, but I care very much for the people I call the forgotten men and women. They have been forgotten, and they're not going to be forgotten again."

"What do you think people should know about you that they don't understand?" I asked.

"I think they're starting to understand me pretty well," Trump said. "I get things done. There's no president that has come close to doing what I've done in the first twelve months. Not even close. The cutting of regulations, the signing of legislation, the numbers of judicial appointments. We have a record. Federal judges, the appointment of Justice Gorsuch, so many things. We're taking care of the vets. It's really culminating and all coming together like a beautiful ribbon on top of a present with the tax cuts."

If he had not been elected, "ISIS would still be flourishing," Trump said. "I fixed that by being strong with the military and letting them fight like they're supposed to fight. Not calling the White House every day and saying do you think we can attack and getting the okay four weeks later. Excuse me. Those people are gone. We fought good."

Trump cited job growth numbers achieved despite disruptions caused by devastating hurricanes since he became president.

"How much of the animosity is all about jealousy toward you?" I asked.

"I don't want to say jealousy," Trump said. "But it's an extreme hate, and I think it clouds their minds."

Trump talked about what he likes to call the fake news media and how it never gives him credit for building a great company. But when it came to my question about the tips of hundred-dollar bills he hands out to janitors and workmen, Trump punted.

"What tips?" he said. "For who? Where?" he asked. When I pressed him, he finally acknowledged, "I just like taking care of people. I love those people. I take care of the people. They take care of me, I take care of them."

Asked for an example of advice Melania has given that he adopted, Trump said that when he told her he was thinking of running, Melania responded by saying, "You know, if you run, you will win."

"Well, I don't know that," he answered.

"If you run, you will win," she repeated. "So, are you prepared to give up four or eight years of your life for that?"

"Well, I'm not sure that I would win, but maybe," he said to her.

"She doesn't want you to tweet so much, right?" Pam asked.

"Without social media, I might not be here," Trump said. "Because the news is so biased and so dishonest and so fake that without social media, I would have no way of fighting. I have way over a hundred million people when you add them all up. And I'm able to fight back because of social media. If I didn't have that, there'd be no way I could fight back the dishonesty of CNN and the dishonesty of ABC or CBS or NBC."

Trump cited the *New York Times* story that began with the lede, "Donald J. Trump had barely met Rowanne Brewer Lane when he asked her to change out of her clothes." As described in chapter 8 of this book, the story represented the opposite of what happened between Trump and Brewer Lane at Mar-a-Lago. It buried in the sixteenth paragraph the fact that the model began dating Trump. The day after the story appeared, Trump said he saw Brewer Lane on Fox News's *Fox & Friends* saying the story was a lie and that Trump was a perfect gentleman.

"I said I want a retraction of the story," Trump said. "They wouldn't do it."

Given that the entire Russia collusion story is bogus, I asked Trump why he gets agitated about the investigation by Special Counsel Robert Mueller.

"It's not a question of agitation, because I like the truth," Trump said. "It gives an excuse for the Democrats who lost the election. They came up with Russia. It's the Russia hoax, and it was nothing other than an excuse for the Democrats losing the election. And now it's turning to all of the dishonesty on the other side. The only collusion is the collusion with the Democrats on Russia."

Trump asked if I like and respect the former FBI director.

I told Trump that Mueller is a man of integrity who turned around the FBI to make it more prevention oriented.

"I hope he's going to be fair," Trump said. "Say hello to him." A month later, Trump offered to be interviewed by Mueller under oath.

Contrary to the claims in Michael Wolff's book, Trump was as sharp as ever, totally on top of his game. When I brought up Norma Foerderer's characterization of the two Donald Trumps, he said, "What a woman, huh? You hate to say they don't make them that way, but very few people are like Norma."

The next night was New Year's Eve, and on the roadside on the way to Mar-a-Lago, the emergency lights on the police cars alternately flashed like diamonds, rubies, and sapphires. In a parking lot across from the club, Lamborghinis, Rolls-Royces, and Bentleys had to run a gauntlet of security checks with bomb-sniffing dogs. Given the go-ahead, the cars drove onto the estate, passed the Trump helicopter, and stopped at the foot of the red carpet that had been unfurled across the back lawn. Leaving their cars to the waiting valets, the guests went through metal detectors, the women invariably setting them off with some jewelry, and then strolled along the red carpet to be photographed at the main pool.

Among the guests were Treasury Secretary Steven Mnuchin and his Scottish actress wife, Louise Linton, who has appeared in films such as *Cabin Fever* and in minor TV roles in *CSI: NY* and *Cold Case*. Also at the party was former baseball-star-turned-commentator Keith Hernandez. Aside from Fox News anchor Lou Dobbs, Pam and I were the only journalists present.

On the lawn around the pool were bars and hors d'oeuvres

stations with caviar on blini, oysters on the half shell, stone crab claws, and sushi and sashimi as well as hot items like risotto with seafood and steamed lobster on skewers. Trump champagne, coconut shrimp, and pigs in a blanket with an artful dab of mustard were among the passed offerings. Dressed in shimmering gowns of gold lamé or silver chain mail, the women did their best to maneuver to the caviar station, given that their stiletto heels sank into the turf.

At 8 p.m., the 750 guests made their way to the ballroom, where Party on the Moon was performing. The menu included Trump iceberg lettuce wedge, Maine lobster ravioli, and sliced tenderloin and seared sea bass with taro root purée, morel mushrooms, and Burgundy *au jus*. Dessert was baked Alaska.

Overhead, the chandeliers flickered in time with the music, and a lighting sculpture of stalactites glowed and pulsated over the dance floor. As when Trump was first elected, he and Melania and the rest of the Trump family did not dance. A phalanx of Secret Service agents surrounded the long head table. The agents faced out into the room and collapsed the formation as necessary to let someone in, such as the golf pro who had shot a round with Trump that afternoon. Another group of agents lined the wall between the head table and the door. The agents all wore white shirts, their suit jackets open, their hands held free in front of their chests, just in case they had to reach for their SIG Sauer 229 pistols. One agent kept his hand firmly on the handle of his weapon.

Young scion Barron, dressed in black tie, left around 10:30 p.m. with two agents flanking him.

Just before midnight, the lead singer of the upbeat, high-energy Party on the Moon introduced Trump, noting that they had been coming to play this gig for years and choking up when he said that this was the first time with Trump as president. Trump took the mic to speak to the cheering partygoers. He was relaxed, in his element. Introducing Melania as an incredible inspiration, Trump told the crowd that people at rallies hold up signs reading, "We love our first lady! We love our first lady!"

"Jobs are pouring back into the country," Trump said as the televised countdown from Times Square began. "And there's more to come."

25

BRAVADO

By the end of his first year in office, Trump could point to a spectacular rise in the stock market. Consumer confidence, manufacturing activity, and employment were at historic highs. New U.S. home sales saw their largest increase in more than twenty-five years, illegal border crossings from Mexico had plunged, and Trump had placed an outstanding conservative appeals court judge on the Supreme Court.

The number of Americans receiving unemployment benefits fell to the lowest level in forty-four years. Unemployment among African Americans and Hispanics plummeted to the lowest level in the forty-five years records have been kept. Small business optimism soared to the highest level in thirty-four years. Retail holiday sales scored its biggest increase since 2011.

Moreover, ISIS was almost totally defeated and driven out of Iraq and Raqqa, the group's de facto Syrian capital. While President Obama claimed that ISIS was not an existential threat, FBI agents and CIA officers believe ISIS was attempting to develop weapons of mass destruction that could wipe out millions of Americans and bring the country to its knees. Indeed, ISIS used chemical weapons in Syria and Iraq.

By threatening Syria with consequences if it used chemical weapons and then following through with a missile strike when it did, Trump demonstrated to the world what he told me in June 2006 about what he would do if he were president: "No country would ever dare push the United States around because they would suffer the wrath." In contrast, Obama drew a red line on Syria's use of chemical weapons and then backed down.

As a result of Trump initiatives, Arab countries were working together to stop financing terrorists and promoting radical Islamic ideology. Both China and Russia had taken the unprecedented action of voting at the United Nations to impose sanctions on North Korea. Because of pressure he exerted on China, Trump got Chinese president Xi Jinping to order Chinese banks to cease conducting business with North Korean entities.

By denouncing the police whenever a racial controversy erupted, Obama singlehandedly made police a target of executions, perhaps his most clear-cut legacy, along with a sluggish economy, the rise of ISIS, and a doubling of the national debt to twenty trillion dollars. In contrast, Trump never missed an opportunity to praise the police and the military.

Trump's fiery rhetoric, which horrified those in the media, and his bobbing and weaving on issues like North Korea or Russia, magnified his power. Besides the possibility of a direct nuclear hit or other WMD attack, Trump had to face the new threats of a cyberattack on the country's infrastructure or annihilation with an electromagnetic pulse (EMP) attack.

A single nuclear bomb exploded over the United States would generate an electromagnetic pulse that would destroy the chips that are at the heart of every electronic device. While military and intelligence networks may be shielded against EMP, most of the rest of the country's technological infrastructure is not.

An EMP attack would wipe out personal computers and the Internet. Cars would not start, gasoline pumps would not work, and airplanes could not take off. Heating systems and air-conditioning would shut down, supermarkets would have to close, telephones would go dead, tap water would stop, and radio and television sets would not turn on. Banks would close their doors, and ATMs would stop functioning. Credit cards would become useless, and emergency services and hospital operating rooms would close. Financial records, including stock portfolios and retirement plans, would vanish. In the ensuing chaos, most Americans would die from starvation, and the country would be taken back to the fourteenth century.

To be sure, Trump has his quirks, but they do not compare with the recklessness of John F. Kennedy, the criminal cover-up known as Watergate that Richard Nixon engaged in, the bizarre behavior of Lyndon Johnson, or the repugnant conduct of Bill Clinton. In years past, the media would not report on the private lives of presidents and what they were really like. Today, the media continue to filter the news. Because of the liberal bias of the mainstream media, many of Trump's achievements are either underplayed or not reported at all.

"The press is so stupid, they don't get it," says Trump's friend Gary Giulietti. "They think he has some ulterior motive for what he does. There never is. Trump sees the end game and works toward that end by making a deal. That's what he has done all his life. He's trying to befriend you, gets you to like him, tees it up.

He's going to give you the carrot and a big stick and then he's going to start giving you more carrots and less stick. He's brilliant like that."

To a sizable portion of the country sick of political correctness, a sluggish economy, and a passive foreign policy, Trump was exactly what the doctor ordered.

The fact that the so-called working class is enraptured by Trump goes back to the fact that plumbers, carpenters, truck drivers, and small business owners have to achieve practical results to survive: If a carpenter does not drive a nail correctly into a strut, he will be fired. On the other hand, a Harvard professor can spout theories without any accountability.

Those who are judged by practical results understand that Trump, like them, is all about results, as he demonstrated when he totally rebuilt Wollman Rink in New York City's Central Park in four months—after the city had worked on the ice rink fruitlessly for six years and spent twelve million dollars for nothing. After he took it over, Trump finished the rink in two and a half years and opened it ahead of schedule at a cost $750,000 below his own projected three-million-dollar budget.

"Donald is a total genius, he really is," his longtime top aide, Norma Foerderer, told me. "Here he was, this young man working out of a limo, he came to New York, and he saw this old building, the Commodore Hotel, and he decided that this could be a good hotel. And it was—for the homeless. And so he, by sheer tenacity and vision, got the Hyatt people in Chicago to support him, and they worked with him and funded it. And he built the Grand Hyatt hotel, and it began the renaissance of Forty-Second Street."

"We are guided by outcomes, not ideology," Trump declared in his maiden speech to the United Nations General Assembly.

When I asked Trump in June 2006 what his Secret Service code name would be if he were elected president, he said, "Get It Done."

Beyond the results, like Ronald Reagan, Trump has charisma and a showman's sense of humor and flare.

"Trump speaks in a vernacular that does not sound like a politician," Bannon says. "He speaks like a human being. He connects. Trump is totally authentic because it's coming from his heart and his own being. That being is what connects to the working-class and the middle-class people, and it's very powerful."

"One of the things that Trump is supersmart about is he focuses in on a narrative like no one I have seen in politics, whether it's about the rise in the stock market or the issue of football players taking a knee," Priebus says. "He is focused on perception. Reality is important, but he understands that in some cases perception is more important."

In the 2008 presidential election, the press hoodwinked Americans into thinking Barack Obama was the messiah. The press never reported that Obama had no significant achievements. As a community organizer, his only success was removing some of the asbestos from one Chicago apartment project. That did not take place until a year after he had left Chicago to attend Harvard Law School.

In a revealing passage in his memoir *Dreams from My Father*, Obama wrote, "When classmates in college asked me just what it was that a community organizer did, I couldn't answer them directly." Instead, he said, "I'd pronounce on the need for change. Change in the White House, where Reagan and his minions were carrying on their dirty deeds. Change in the Congress, compliant and corrupt. Change in the mood of the country, manic and self-absorbed. Change won't come from the top, I would say. Change will come from a mobilized grass roots."

Nor did the press report until it was too late in the primary process during his first run for president that Obama had spent twenty years listening to the anti-white, anti-America, anti-Israel hate speech of his self-described friend and mentor, the Reverend Jeremiah Wright Jr. In one of his sermons, Wright blamed America for starting the AIDS virus to kill off blacks, training professional killers, importing drugs, and creating a racist society that would never elect a black man as president. Through his church Wright gave an award for lifetime achievement to Louis Farrakhan, who has repeatedly made hate-filled statements targeting Jews, whites, America, and gays. If Trump had attended such services and not walked out, the media would have crucified him.

In contrast to Obama, just as they did with Reagan, the media portray Trump as a fool and a danger to humanity. The anti-Trump hysteria reached such proportions that a Potomac, Maryland, couple said they would forgo taking vacations because they did not want to contribute to Trump's economy. *CQ*'s Keith Olbermann said on ABC's *The View* that Trump has done more to harm America than Osama bin Laden and ISIS combined. Patrisse Cullors, a cofounder of Black Lives Matter, said she believes Trump is "literally" trying to "kill our communities" on a scale comparable to Adolf Hitler. Not to be outdone, *Newsweek* compared Trump with mass murderer Charles Manson.

But like Trump, Reagan achieved solid results, growing the economy by cutting taxes and confronting the Evil Empire, leading to the demise of the Soviet Union. The annualized increase in the gross national product of 3.5 percent during Reagan's two terms in office showed that the Gipper knew what he was doing.

By the third quarter of 2017, Trump was closing in on that growth rate at 3.2 percent. Trump had eliminated twenty-two regulations for every new one created. With business no longer being painted as the villain by the White House, the National Association of Manufacturers released its Manufacturers' Outlook Survey showing the highest level of optimism in twenty years. Small business owners' optimism reached a ten-year high. The index of consumer confidence hit a seventeen-year high.

Trump worked tirelessly to get a historic $1.5 trillion tax cut for individuals and businesses through the House and Senate, even calling members of Congress at three a.m. from Asia to solicit their support. The bill narrowly passed with only Republican votes, giving Trump the first major legislative achievement of his presidency. The most sweeping tax overhaul in three decades, the tax cut was expected to stimulate the economy, attract more businesses to the United States, incentivize companies to bring back profits stashed overseas, and put more money in people's pockets. Significantly, the bill also did away with the penalty imposed by Obamacare for not buying health insurance, jeopardizing the future of Obama's signature legislative achievement.

Democrats and the mainstream media desperately looked for any corner of the tax plan that would raise taxes. In fact, the plan cuts taxes for 80 percent of Americans. Only 5 percent of Americans would see a tax increase of more than ten dollars, according to the non-partisan Tax Policy Center. But the biggest charade was the claim made by Democrats and the mainstream media that "Republicans delivered the biggest gains to the wealthy," as the *Washington Post* said in the second paragraph of its lead story. That's because as it is, the top 20 percent of Americans who file a tax return pay 95 percent of all income taxes. If you make more money, a cut in the tax rate will save you more dollars than if you make less or pay no taxes at all. If the *Post* had cited that fact in its story, its claim in a news article that the wealthy would benefit more than others would have been exposed as liberal propaganda.

Citing the tax cuts, companies ranging from AT&T and Comcast to Walmart, FedEx, Wells Fargo, Bank of America, American Airlines, and Southwest Airlines announced bonuses for employees of $1,000, pay hikes, new hiring, and billions of dollars in new spending on infrastructure. Betraying their elitism, Democrats and liberal media outlets that claim to champion the middle class derided the $1,000 bonuses as a "PR stunt" (Maryland senator Chris Van Hollen) that throw "pennies" at workers (*Vanity Fair*) and are "crumbs" that are "pathetic" (Nancy Pelosi).

The cherry on top came a month after the tax bill was passed. Apple Inc., the world's most valuable publicly traded company, said it would take advantage of the tax bill's provisions by bringing back to the United States nearly all of the $252 billion in cash that it held abroad and said it would directly contribute $350 billion to the U.S. economy over the next five years. That includes $30 billion in capital spending, including a new domestic campus, generating 20,000 jobs. And Apple said that following the new tax law's provisions, it will pay $38 billion in taxes on the money it returns to the United States. Liberal icon Tim Cook, the CEO of Apple, announced as well that the company will issue stock bonuses of $2,500 to each of its 84,000 employees.

On the morning of Trump's election victory, Paul Krugman of the *New York Times* predicted that the stock market would crash that day and "never" recover. Indeed, Krugman wrote that with Trump in the White House, ". . . we are very probably looking at a global recession, with no end in sight." The same day that his story appeared, instead of collapsing, the Dow Jones Industrial

Average was up 256 points and surged to an all-time high shortly before the closing bell. A year after Trump was elected, the Dow was up 28 percent. The increase in the Dow a year after Trump was elected was the largest postelection bump since 1945.

Most remarkably, by the first anniversary of Trump's presidency, the Dow was up 40 percent since his election.

In most people's minds, that speaks for itself, but liberals and the mainstream media tried to undercut Trump's record of achievement by saying only wealthy people can invest in the stock market. But over the years, the Gallup poll has found that more than half of all Americans own stocks either directly or through stock market funds such as 401(k)s and individual retirement accounts (IRAs), along with pension funds. According to Crain's, the stock market boom could mean that New York City may be able to pump the $10 billion it contributes annually to pension funds for police, teachers, and other city employees into worthwhile projects like improving the subways.

Contrary to the scary image of Trump liberals like to portray, unlike Obama, Trump made sure that services like the national park system remained open during a three-day government shutdown that the Associated Press and other mainstream outlets blamed on the Democrats.

From mourning those who jumped to their deaths from the burning World Trade Center, the country had gone to creating politically correct "safe spaces" on college campuses, where the supposedly tolerant and compassionate left considered any praise of Donald Trump to be hate speech, and to a media world where any criticism of a person of color is slammed as racist. Thus, when Trump hit back at the black father of University of California at Los Angeles basketball player LiAngelo Ball for suggesting that Trump had had nothing to do with freeing his son from jail in China where he had been charged with shoplifting, Joe Scarborough said on MSNBC's *Morning Joe* that "of course, there's racist overtures here where the black man was not appreciative of what the white man did for him." Antipolice sentiment on college campuses became so vicious that Brooklyn College in New York advised New York City police officers to use bathrooms out of sight of students to avoid possibly offending them. Summarizing the sentiment, a student said the NYPD "made safe spaces not feel safe."

More than anything, Trump stood for restoring American values that consider men and women in the military and police officers to be heroes, Martin Luther King Jr. to be a patriot, and free speech to be among our most precious freedoms.

Unlike Michelle Obama, who said during her husband's campaign, "For the first time in my adult lifetime, I am really proud of my country," Melania Trump is proud to be a U.S. citizen and gives Trump wise advice that impresses his aides. Greeting the world's celebrities as Trump's wife, she was perfectly prepared to take on her new role as first lady.

After his firmness and defense buildup led to the collapse of the Soviet Union, many in the press—such as CBS's Lesley Stahl in a tribute to the late president—acknowledged that they had been wrong about Reagan. Indeed, in a 2011 Gallup poll, Americans rated Reagan as the greatest U.S. president, followed by John F. Kennedy, Abraham Lincoln, and Bill Clinton.

Whether on the right or the left, almost no journalist or pundit gave Trump any chance of winning the election. "I honestly believe that Trump would crash in the general election like so much blue ice from an Aeroflot jetliner," Jonah Goldberg of *National Review* and Fox News said. Dana Milbank wrote in his *Washington Post* column, "I'm so certain Trump won't win the nomination that I'll eat my words if he does. Literally: The day Trump clinches the nomination, I will eat the page on which this column is printed in Sunday's *Post*." "The chance of his winning [the] nomination and election is exactly zero," James Fallows wrote in the *Atlantic*.

Well, *almost* no journalist or pundit gave him any chance. Back on January 20, 2011, I wrote a column headlined "Don't Underestimate Trump for President." In a January 6, 2016, article, I predicted that he would win the presidency.

Like Reagan, Trump will eventually be seen as one of America's greatest presidents. Instead of leading from behind, the famous characterization of President Obama's approach by one of his aides, Trump led from strength. Instead of knocking America, as Obama did when he apologized for American "arrogance," Trump is a cheerleader for the United States, telling government and business leaders at Davos that "America is open for business and competitive once again." Trump did not build an empire worth billions of dollars by being an idiot, a nut, or a bigot.

Throughout history, unconventional thinkers like Copernicus have been laughed at, only to be proven right in the end: The earth does indeed revolve around the sun. If Trump's words often get him in trouble, he is simply following his own advice in *The Art of the Deal*: "The final key to the way I promote is bravado," he said. "I play to people's fantasies."

For those who want to succeed, "I would tell them to dream, and to have a vision and a goal," Norma Foerderer said. "Think about what you want to do, love it, and if you love it enough, you'll realize your dreams. That's what Donald's done."

Trump's actions, as opposed to some of his words, are indeed making America great again and changing the rules of the game.

ACKNOWLEDGMENTS

My wife, Pamela Kessler, is the love of my life and my partner in writing books. A former *Washington Post* reporter and the author of *Undercover Washington: Where Famous Spies Lived, Worked, and Loved*, Pam contributes vivid descriptions to my books, preedits them, and provides wise counsel throughout.

Whether interviewing Donald Trump on our way to Mar-a-Lago or visiting the FBI laboratory and firing range or the Secret Service training facility, Pam accompanies me. Her descriptions in this book and my previous books are the best writing in them. She has also come up with the titles to many of my books, including this one.

None of my twenty-one books would have been possible if Pam had not strongly supported my risky decision when we were both at the *Washington Post* to leave the paper to write books.

ACKNOWLEDGMENTS

My children, Rachel Kessler, an independent New York public relations consultant, and Greg Kessler, a New York artist, are a source of pride and support. My stepson, Mike Whitehead, a musician, is an endearing part of that team.

Robert Gottlieb, chairman of Trident Media, has been my agent since 1991. His counsel and support have been critical to my book publishing career.

This is my fourth book with Mary Reynics, executive editor of Crown. I am so lucky to be the recipient of her brilliant editing suggestions and astute publishing judgment. Tina Constable, senior vice president, and Campbell Wharton, associate publisher, round out a team unmatched in the book publishing world.

INDEX

ABOUT THE AUTHOR

RONALD KESSLER is the *New York Times* bestselling author of *The First Family Detail, The Secrets of the FBI, In the President's Secret Service,* and *The CIA at War.* A former *Wall Street Journal* and *Washington Post* investigative reporter, Kessler has won eighteen journalism awards, including two George Polk Awards: one for national reporting and one for community service. He was named a Washingtonian of the Year by *Washingtonian* magazine. Kessler lives in Potomac, Maryland, with his wife, author Pamela Kessler.